fushigi yûgi.

The Mysterious Play
VOL. 3: DISCIPLE

To rene... ease cor... & Art By
...ATASE

| Issue: 02 | | Issue Date... |

FUSHIGI YÛGI
THE MYSTERIOUS PLAY, VOL. 3: DISCIPLE
Gollancz Manga Edition

STORY AND ART BY YUU WATASE

English Adaptation/Yuji Oniki
Translation Assist./Kaori Kawakubo Inoue
Touch-Up & Lettering/Andy Ristaino
Design/Hidemi Sahara
Editor/William Flanagan and Elizabeth Kawasaki
UK Cover Adaptation/Sue Michniewicz

© 1992 Yuu WATASE/Shogakukan Inc.
First published by Shogakukan Inc. in Japan as "Fushigi Yugi"
English publication rights in United Kingdom arranged by Shogakukan Inc.
through VIZ Media, LLC, U.S.A and Tuttle-Mori Agency, Inc., Japan and Ed Victor Ltd., U.K.
New and adapted artwork and text © VIZ Media,LLC, 2004.
The FUSHIGI YÛGI logo is a trademark of VIZ Media, LLC. All rights reserved.
This edition published in Great Britain in 2005 by Gollancz Manga,
an imprint of the Orion Publishing Group, Orion House, 5 Upper St Martin's Lane,
London WC2H 9EA, and a licensee of VIZ Media LLC.

1 3 5 7 9 10 8 6 4 2

The right of Yuu Watase to be identified as the author of this work has been asserted by her in
accordance with the Copyright, Designs and Patents Act 1988.

A CIP catalogue record for this book is available from the British Library

ISBN 0 575 07748 4

Printed and bound at Mackays of Chatham, PLC

CONTENTS

STORY THUS FAR

Chipper junior high school girl Miaka is trying as hard as she can to get into Jonan High School like her mother wants her to. During a study session in the library, Miaka and her best friend, Yui, are physically drawn into the world of a strange book—*THE UNIVERSE OF THE FOUR GODS*. The handsome-but-greedy Tamahome rescues them before they are returned to the real world.

Following an argument with her mother, Miaka returns alone to the world of the book, and is offered the role of the lead character, the Priestess of Suzaku. After a few months of adventures, Miaka returns to the modern world once more, aided by Yui, but this time it's Yui who has disappeared! During her short time back home, Miaka realizes how much she has come to love Tamahome.

Returning a third time to ancient China, this time to find Yui, Miaka is told that in order to avert a war between Hong-Nan and its neighboring country, Qu-Dong, she must gather all seven celestial warriors of Suzaku. She knows about the handsome Tamahome, regal Hotohori and super-strong, cross-dressing Nuriko, but four of her warriors still remain undiscovered. Miaka sets out with Nuriko to find Tamahome again, but as soon as she is reunited with him, Miaka is abducted by a mysterious man in the shadows!

THE UNIVERSE OF THE FOUR GODS is based on ancient Chinese legend, but Japanese pronunciation of Chinese names differs slightly from their Chinese equivalents. Here is a short glossary of the Japanese pronunciation of the Chinese names in this graphic novel:

CHINESE	JAPANESE	PERSON OR PLACE	MEANING
Hong-Nan	Konan	Southern Kingdom	Crimson South
Qu-Dong	Kutô	Eastern Kingdom	Gathered East
Zhong-Rong	Chûei	Second son	Loyalty & Honor
Chun-Jing	Shunkei	Third son	Spring & Respect
Yu-Lun	Gyokuran	Eldest daughter	Jewel & Orchid
Jie-Lian	Yuiren	Youngest daughter	Connection & Lotus
Tai Yi-Jun	Tai Itsukun	An Oracle	Preeminent Person
Daichi-San	Daikyokuzan	A Mountain	Greatest Mountain
Lai Lai	Nyan Nyan	A Servant	Nanny

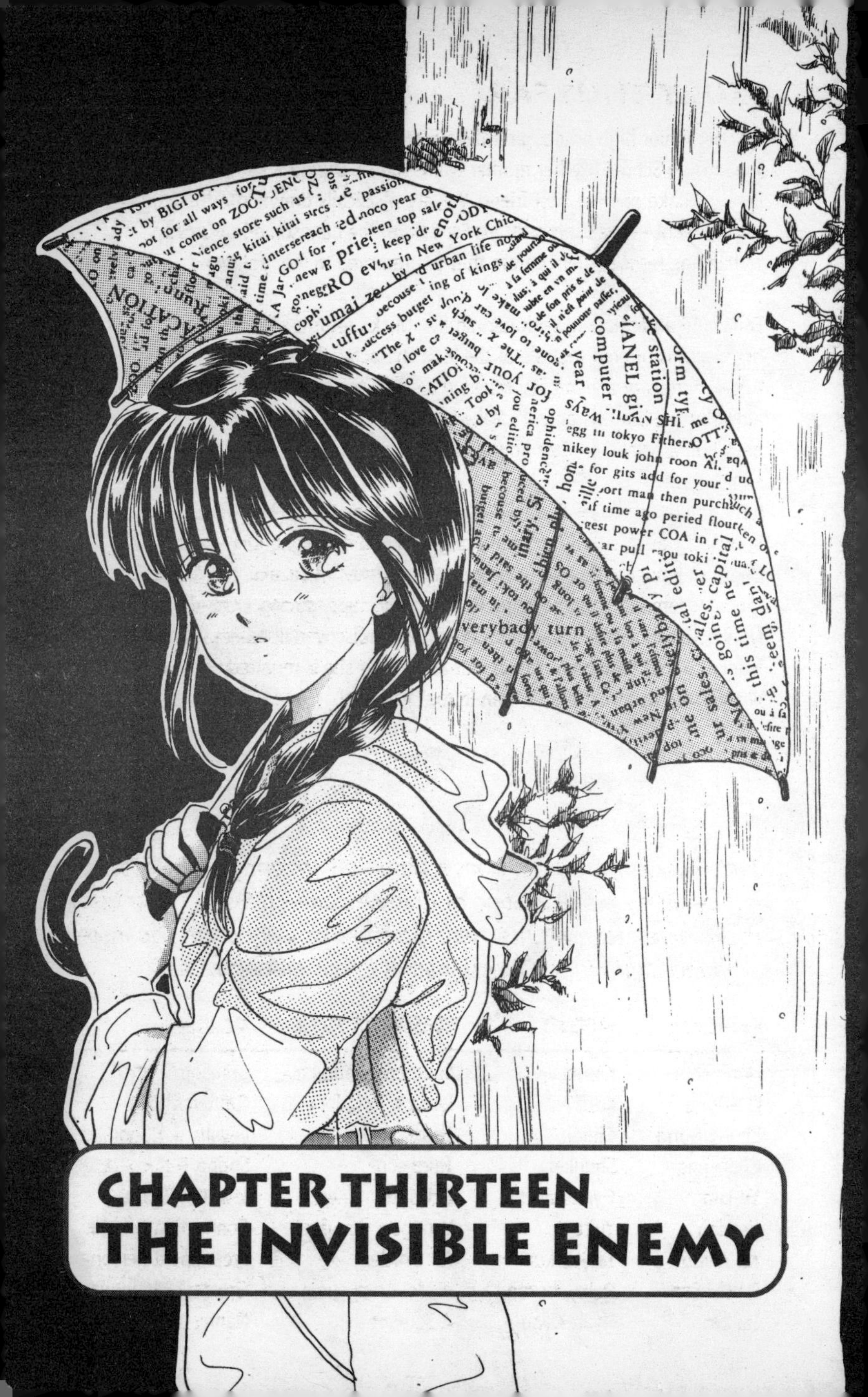

CHAPTER THIRTEEN
THE INVISIBLE ENEMY

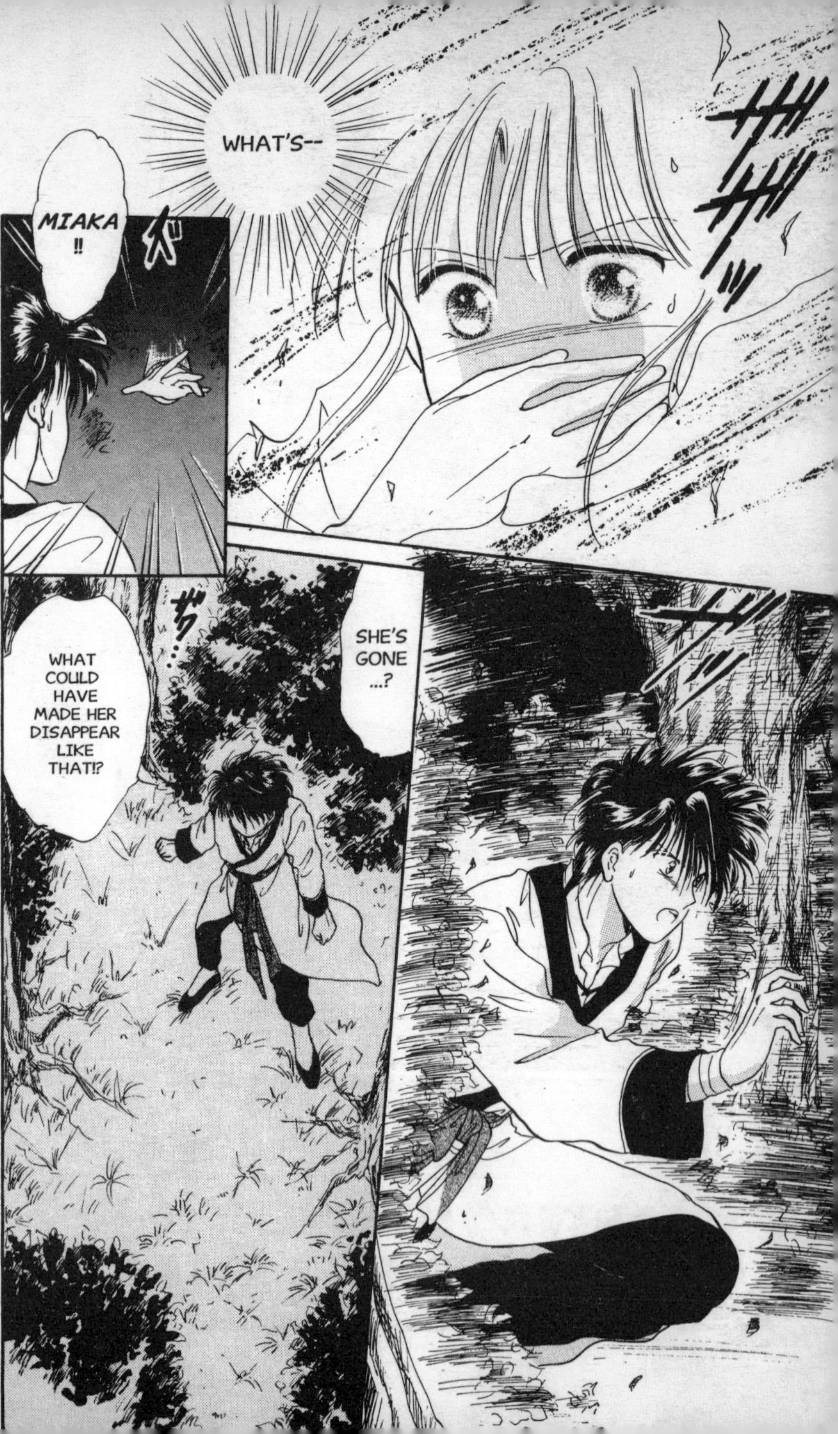
WHAT'S--
MIAKA!!
SHE'S GONE ...?
WHAT COULD HAVE MADE HER DISAPPEAR LIKE THAT!?

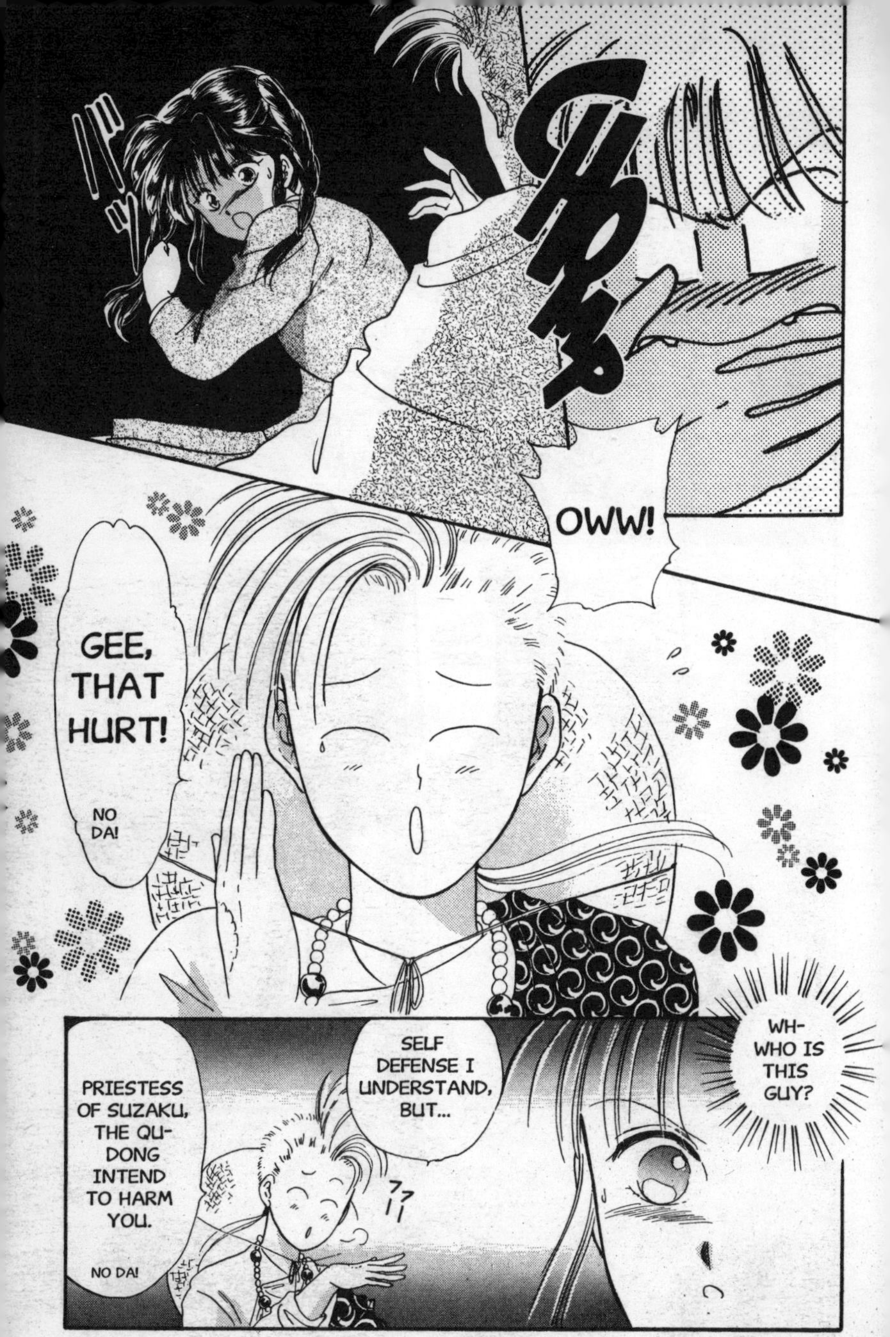
CHOMP
OWW!
GEE, THAT HURT!
NO DA!
WH- WHO IS THIS GUY?
SELF DEFENSE I UNDERSTAND, BUT...
PRIESTESS OF SUZAKU, THE QU-DONG INTEND TO HARM YOU.
NO DA!

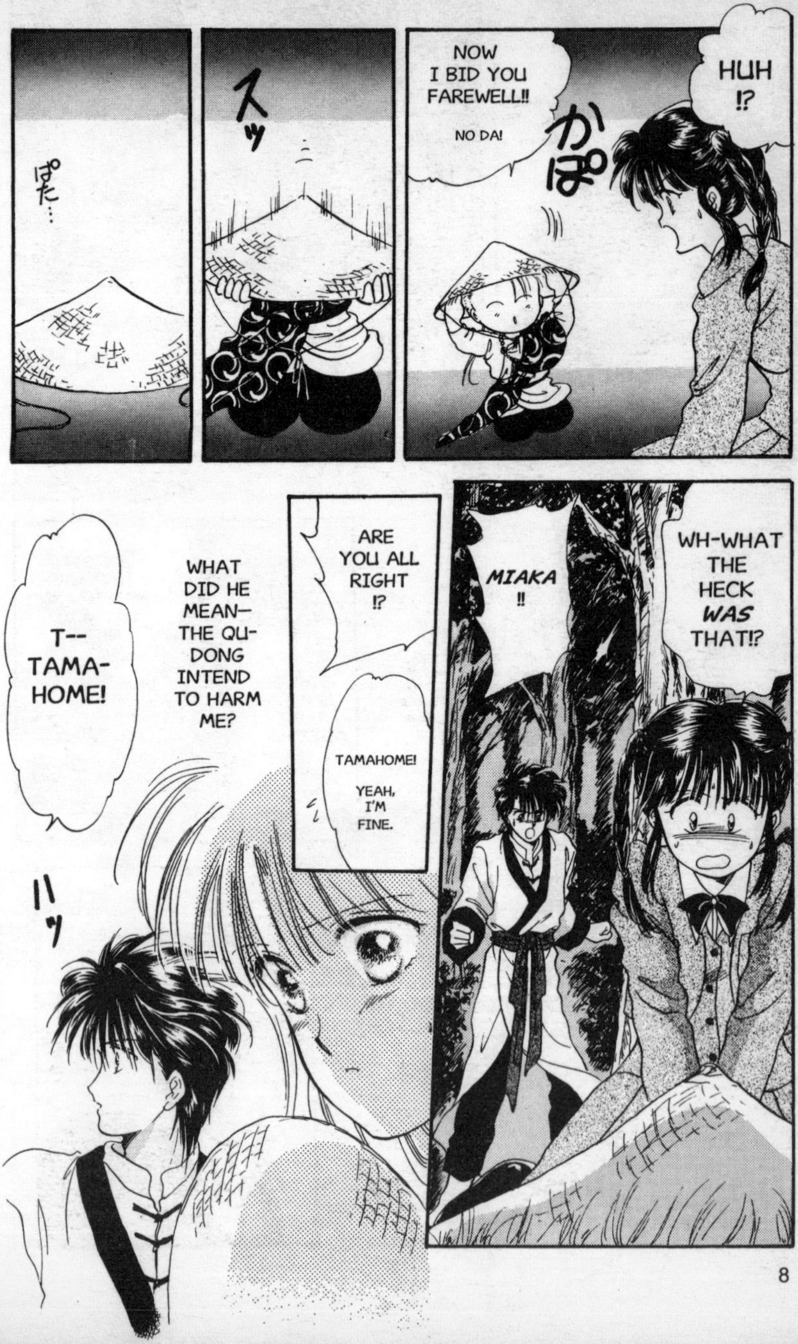
HUH !?
NOW I BID YOU FAREWELL!!
NO DA!
かぽ
スッ
ぱた…
WH-WHAT THE HECK WAS THAT!?
MIAKA !!
ARE YOU ALL RIGHT !?
TAMAHOME! YEAH, I'M FINE.
WHAT DID HE MEAN— THE QU-DONG INTEND TO HARM ME?
T-- TAMA-HOME!
ハッ

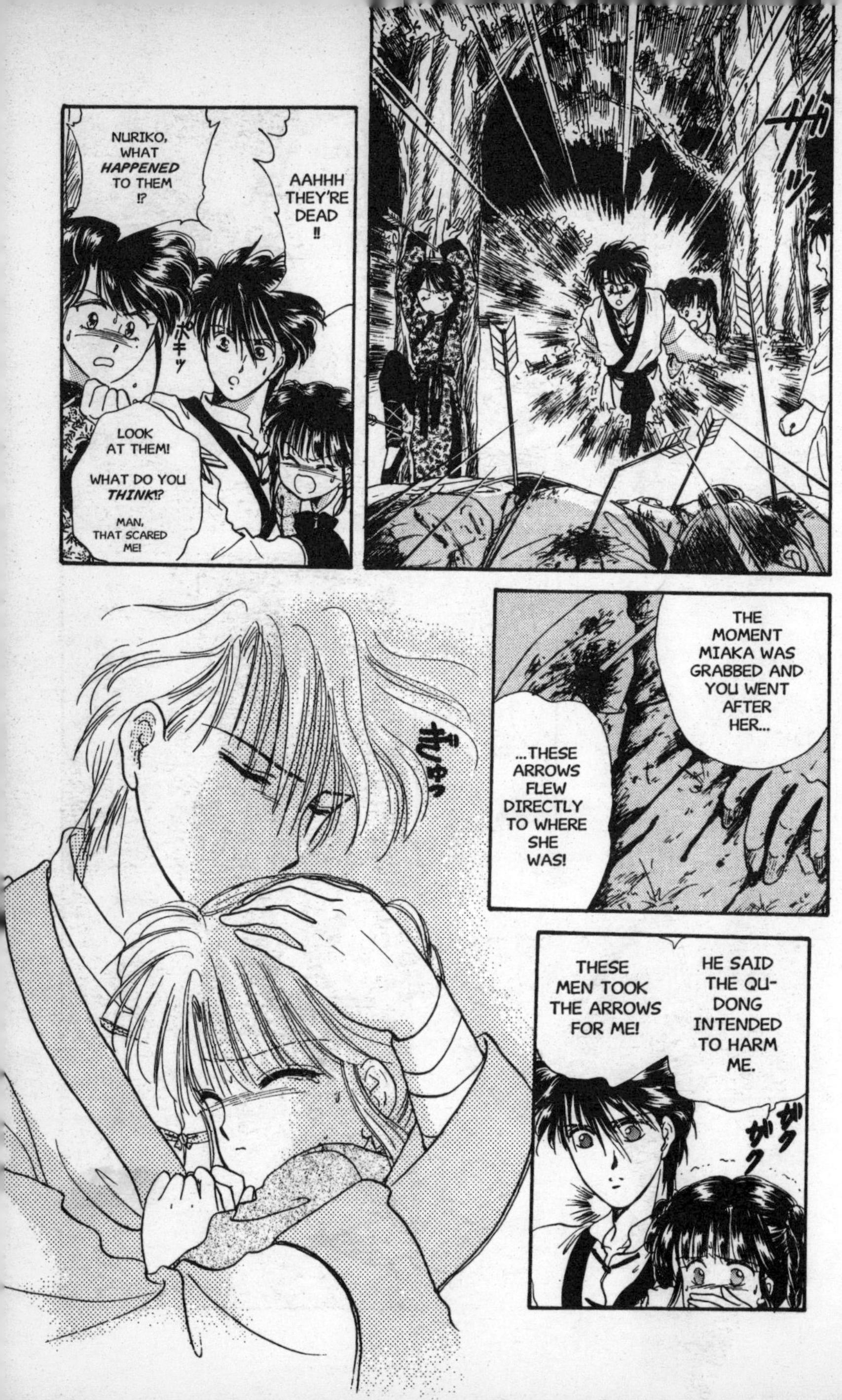
AAHHH THEY'RE DEAD!!
NURIKO, WHAT HAPPENED TO THEM!?
ポキッ
LOOK AT THEM! WHAT DO YOU THINK!?
MAN, THAT SCARED ME!
THE MOMENT MIAKA WAS GRABBED AND YOU WENT AFTER HER...
...THESE ARROWS FLEW DIRECTLY TO WHERE SHE WAS!
HE SAID THE QU-DONG INTENDED TO HARM ME.
THESE MEN TOOK THE ARROWS FOR ME!
ぎゅっ

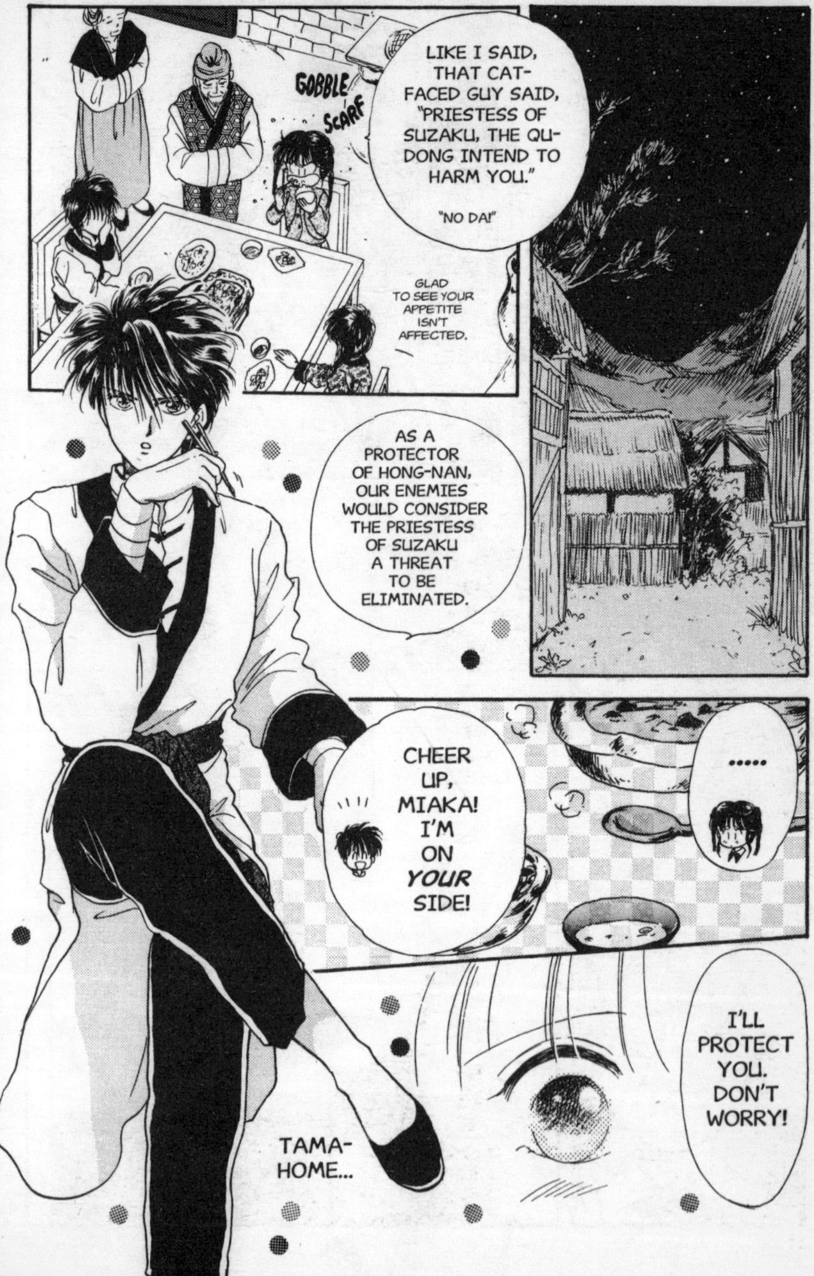

LIKE I SAID, THAT CAT-FACED GUY SAID, "PRIESTESS OF SUZAKU, THE QU-DONG INTEND TO HARM YOU."
"NO DA!"
GOBBLE
SCARF
GLAD TO SEE YOUR APPETITE ISN'T AFFECTED.
AS A PROTECTOR OF HONG-NAN, OUR ENEMIES WOULD CONSIDER THE PRIESTESS OF SUZAKU A THREAT TO BE ELIMINATED.
.....
CHEER UP, MIAKA! I'M ON *YOUR* SIDE!
I'LL PROTECT YOU. DON'T WORRY!
TAMA-HOME...

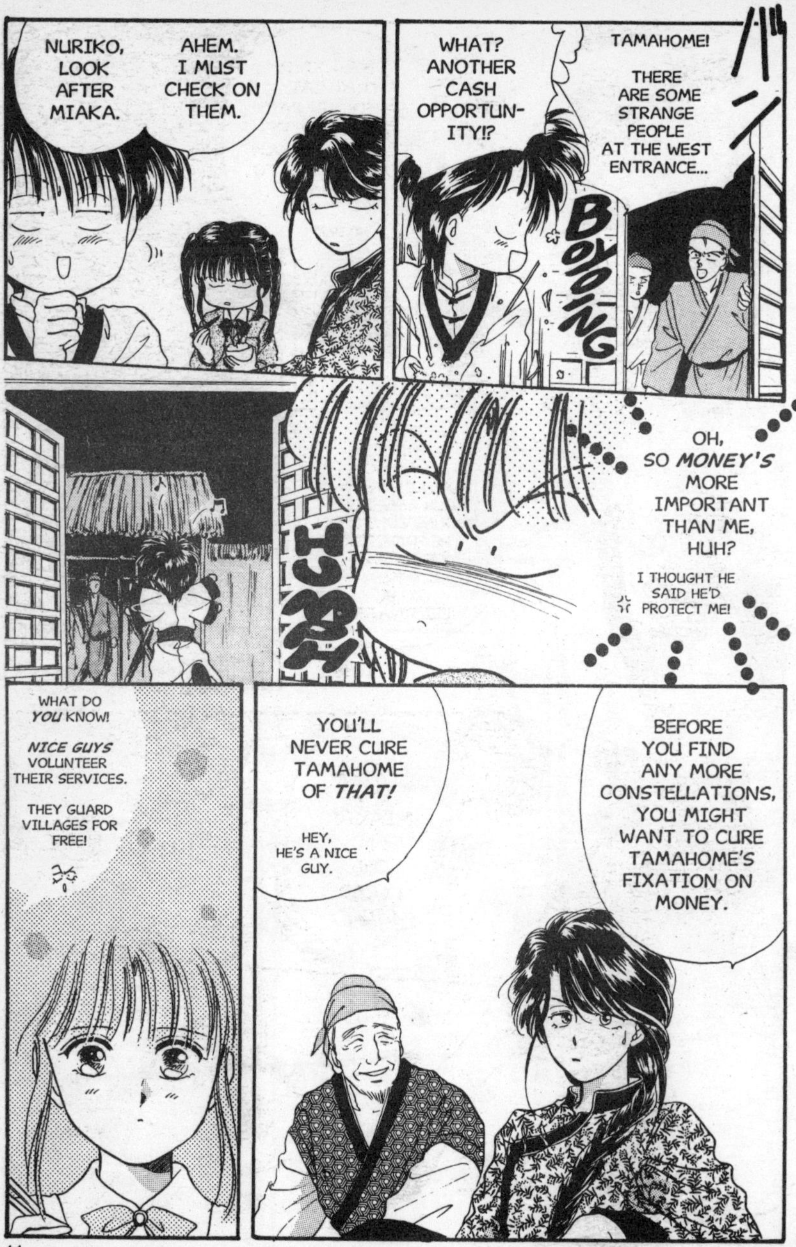

TAMAHOME!
THERE ARE SOME STRANGE PEOPLE AT THE WEST ENTRANCE...
WHAT? ANOTHER CASH OPPORTUN-ITY!?
BOYOING
AHEM. I MUST CHECK ON THEM.
NURIKO, LOOK AFTER MIAKA.
HUMPH
OH, SO MONEY'S MORE IMPORTANT THAN ME, HUH?
I THOUGHT HE SAID HE'D PROTECT ME!
BEFORE YOU FIND ANY MORE CONSTELLATIONS, YOU MIGHT WANT TO CURE TAMAHOME'S FIXATION ON MONEY.
YOU'LL NEVER CURE TAMAHOME OF THAT!
HEY, HE'S A NICE GUY.
WHAT DO YOU KNOW!
NICE GUYS VOLUNTEER THEIR SERVICES.
THEY GUARD VILLAGES FOR FREE!

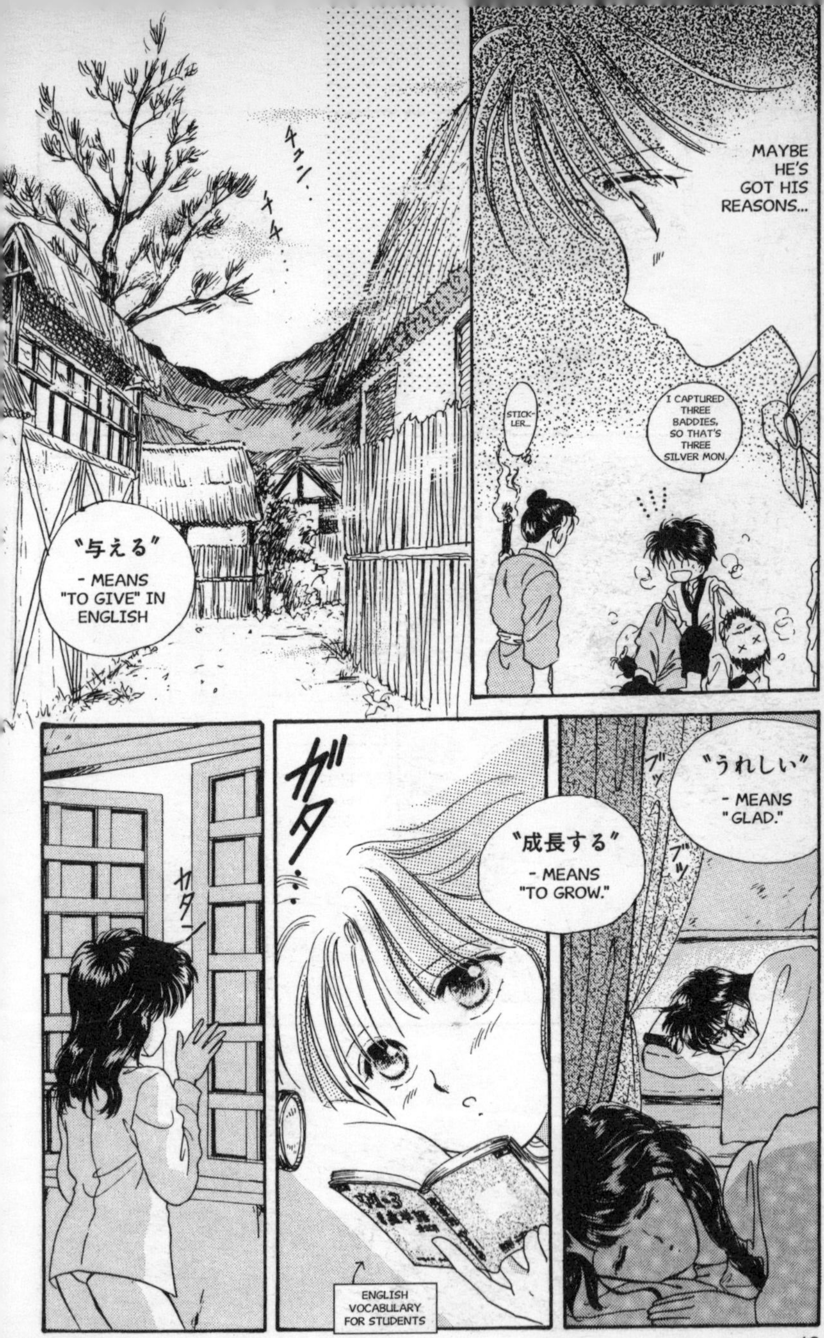
MAYBE HE'S GOT HIS REASONS...
I CAPTURED THREE BADDIES, SO THAT'S THREE SILVER MON.
STICK-LER...
"与える" - MEANS "TO GIVE" IN ENGLISH
"うれしい" - MEANS "GLAD."
"成長する" - MEANS "TO GROW."
ガタ
ENGLISH VOCABULARY FOR STUDENTS

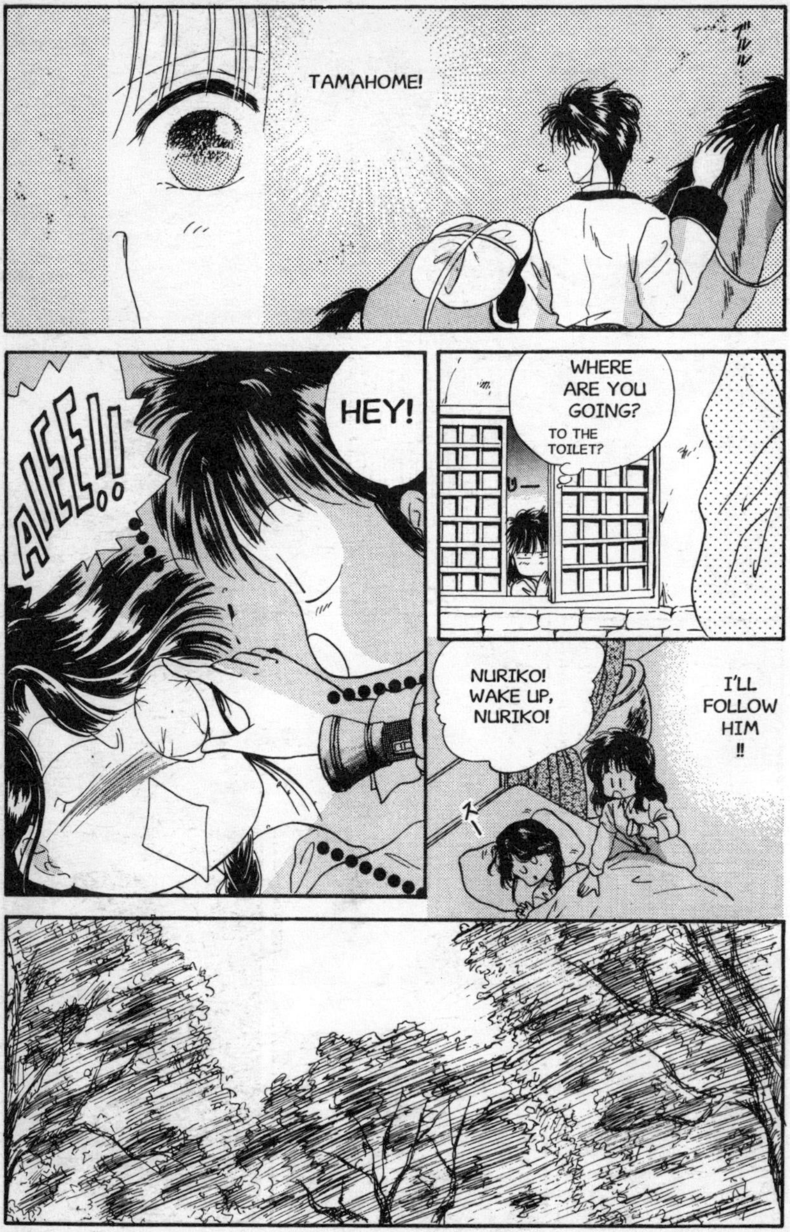
TAMAHOME!
WHERE ARE YOU GOING?
TO THE TOILET?
I'LL FOLLOW HIM!!
NURIKO! WAKE UP, NURIKO!
HEY!
AIEE!!

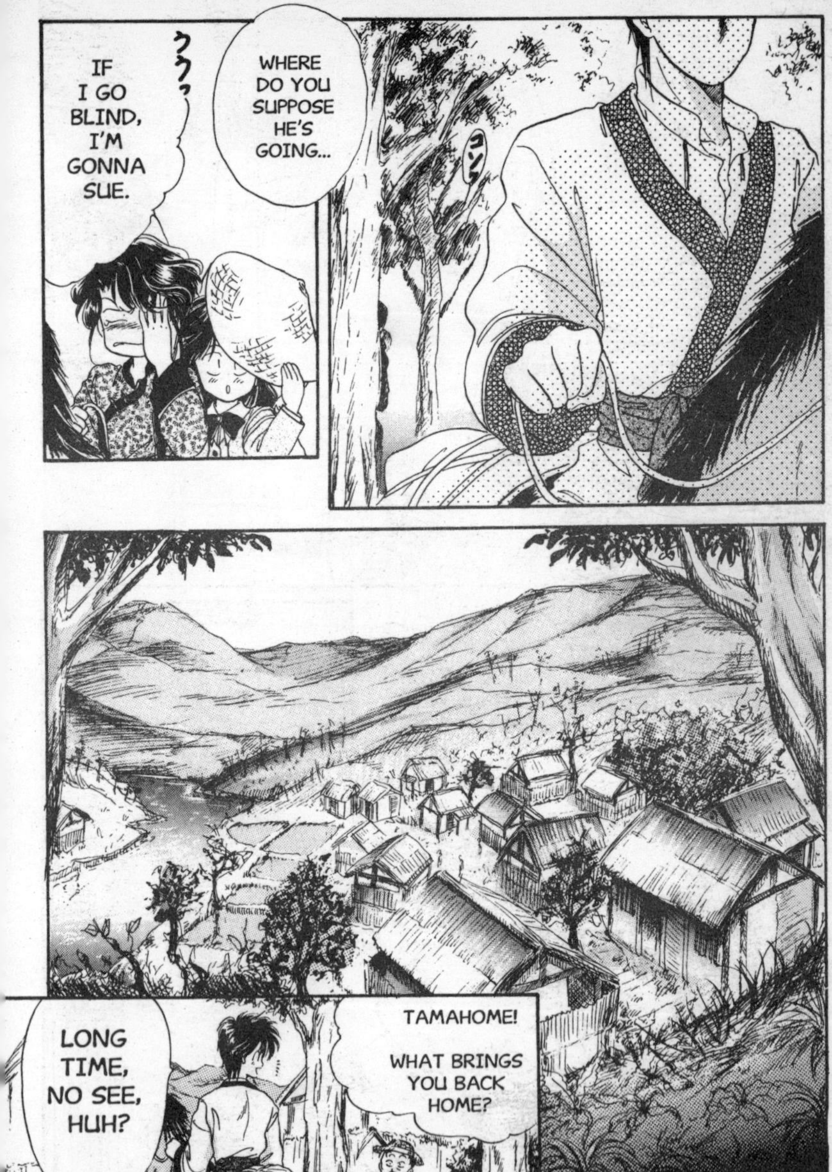
WHERE DO YOU SUPPOSE HE'S GOING...
IF I GO BLIND, I'M GONNA SUE.
TAMAHOME! WHAT BRINGS YOU BACK HOME?
LONG TIME, NO SEE, HUH?

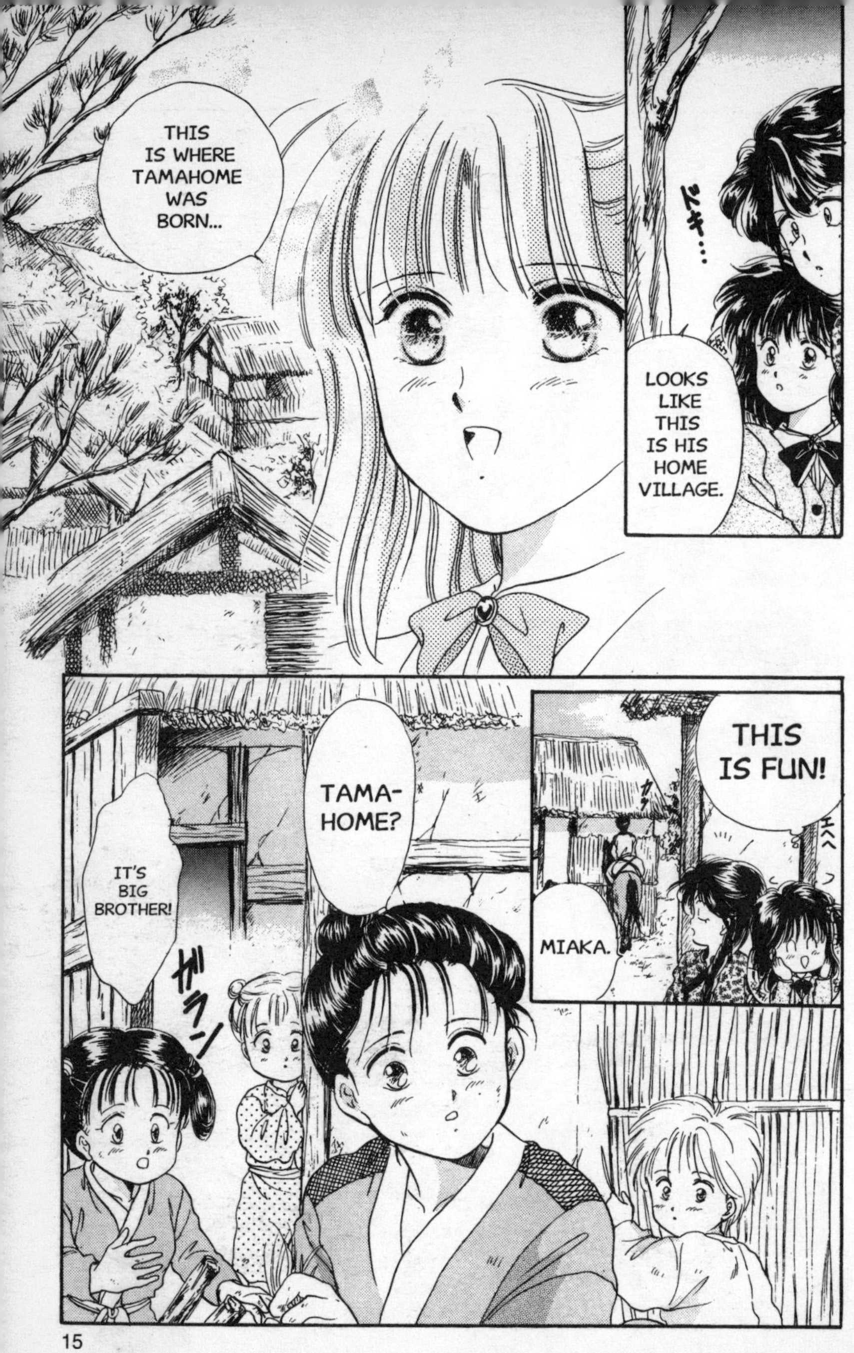
ドキ…
LOOKS LIKE THIS IS HIS HOME VILLAGE.
THIS IS WHERE TAMAHOME WAS BORN...
THIS IS FUN!
MIAKA.
TAMA-HOME?
IT'S BIG BROTHER!
ガラン

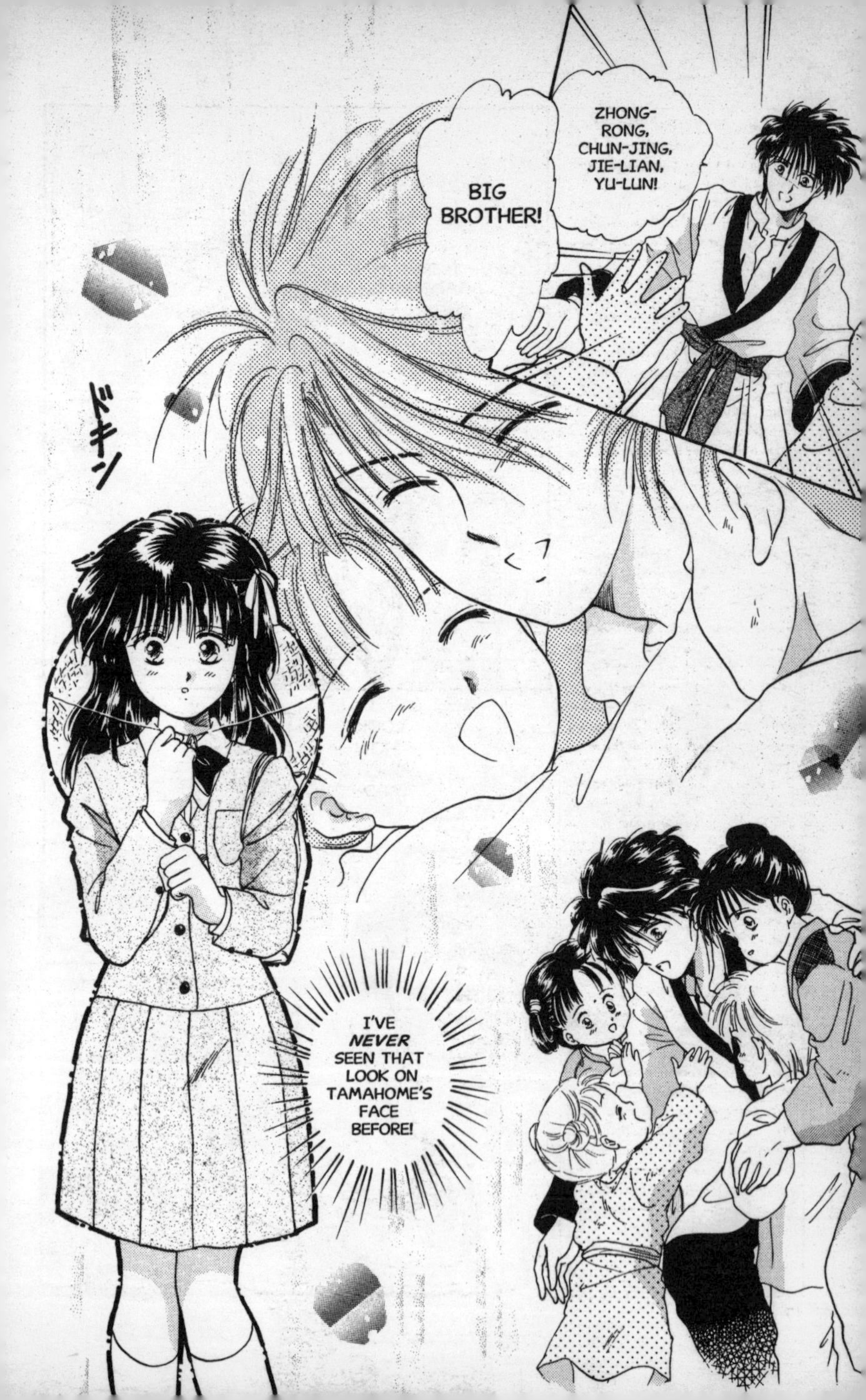
ZHONG-RONG, CHUN-JING, JIE-LIAN, YU-LUN!
BIG BROTHER!
ドキン
I'VE NEVER SEEN THAT LOOK ON TAMAHOME'S FACE BEFORE!

How are you all doing? This'll be the start of the third volume!! Time passes quickly. Right now, I'm drawing the last issue of the volume.
I thought at first, given this rapid pace, the story might be completed soon, but that ain't-a gonna happen. (Where'd the old-west sheriff come from?) If I don't watch myself, it could easily go into 10 volumes. That might not even be enough. Enjoy the ride!

I received many letters of encouragement after my whining in volume 2. I really wasn't begging for letters. Sorry to have worried you. I'm all right. I usually don't get depressed at all. Nobody could be depressed and still be a successful manga artist. Usually I draw with a grin on my face. But sometimes I frown when I concentrate.

I like my manga and my drawings! (You can't draw if you hate your own drawings!) When I said I couldn't face my own art, I was just exaggerating. When I see the first printing of my manga, I'm really happy, and I'm always asking for my editor to send me more copies. I was just complaining because my art hasn't fully matured. I'll keep on improving, waiting for that day when I'm perfect. Will it ever really come?
One thing I know for sure: more than anything else, I love drawing manga. Nobody could like drawing manga more than I do! But I'll bet other manga artists say the same thing.
Maybe my readership has gotten wider because I only hear, "I can't stand your manga," once in a very blue moon.

I: I said I like them--not that I'm any good at them! (:)

They can say it if they want. They're just criticizing my entire existence, that's all! I'm crushed!
Recently, several other manga-artist friends and I have come up with the proper response. "Then why don't you try drawing manga, huh!? You can't even draw, you loser!!" Actually this thought occurs to many a manga artist when his or her work is rejected by an editor. (Yeah!) And I've decided to say that to anyone with harsh criticism of my work!

Like I ever could! I'm just acting strong.

sniff

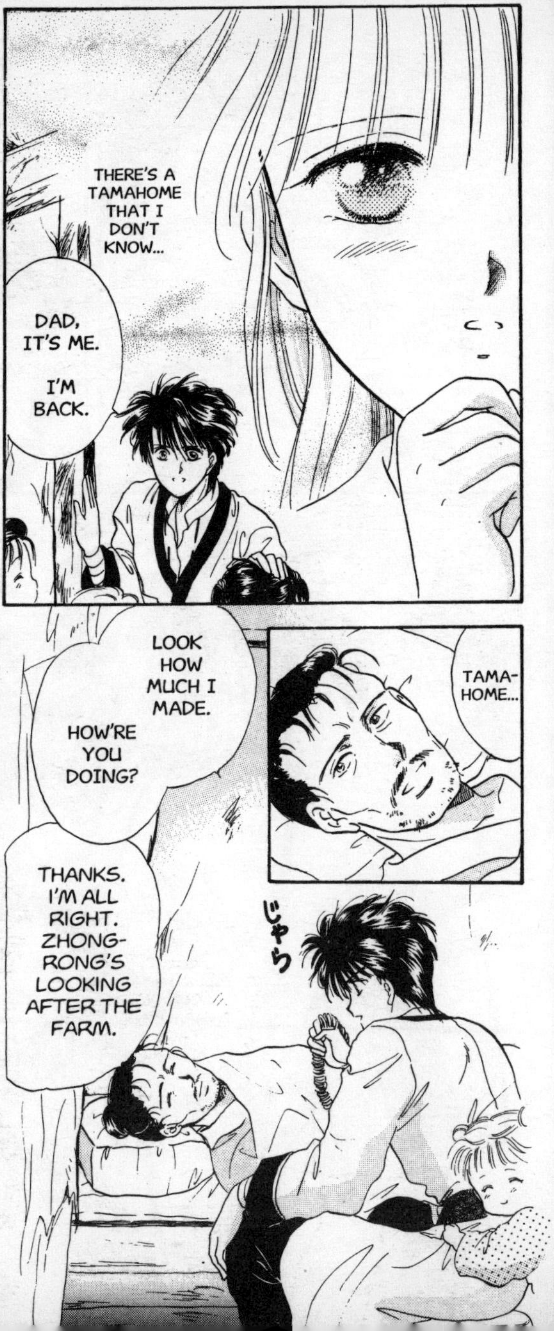

THERE'S A TAMAHOME THAT I DON'T KNOW...
DAD, IT'S ME.
I'M BACK.
TAMA-HOME...
LOOK HOW MUCH I MADE.
HOW'RE YOU DOING?
THANKS. I'M ALL RIGHT. ZHONG-RONG'S LOOKING AFTER THE FARM.
じゃら

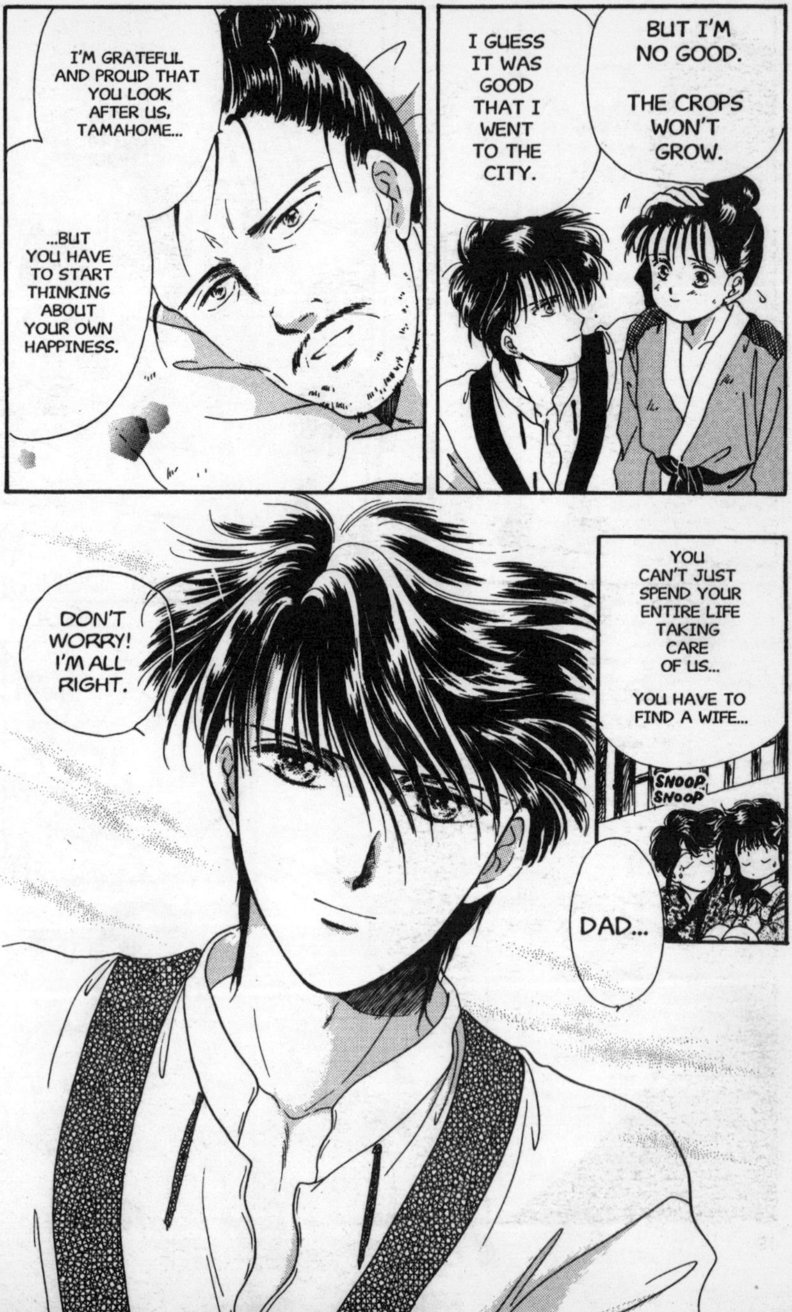
I'M GRATEFUL AND PROUD THAT YOU LOOK AFTER US, TAMAHOME...
...BUT YOU HAVE TO START THINKING ABOUT YOUR OWN HAPPINESS.
I GUESS IT WAS GOOD THAT I WENT TO THE CITY.
BUT I'M NO GOOD.
THE CROPS WON'T GROW.
YOU CAN'T JUST SPEND YOUR ENTIRE LIFE TAKING CARE OF US...
YOU HAVE TO FIND A WIFE...
SNOOP SNOOP
DAD...
DON'T WORRY! I'M ALL RIGHT.

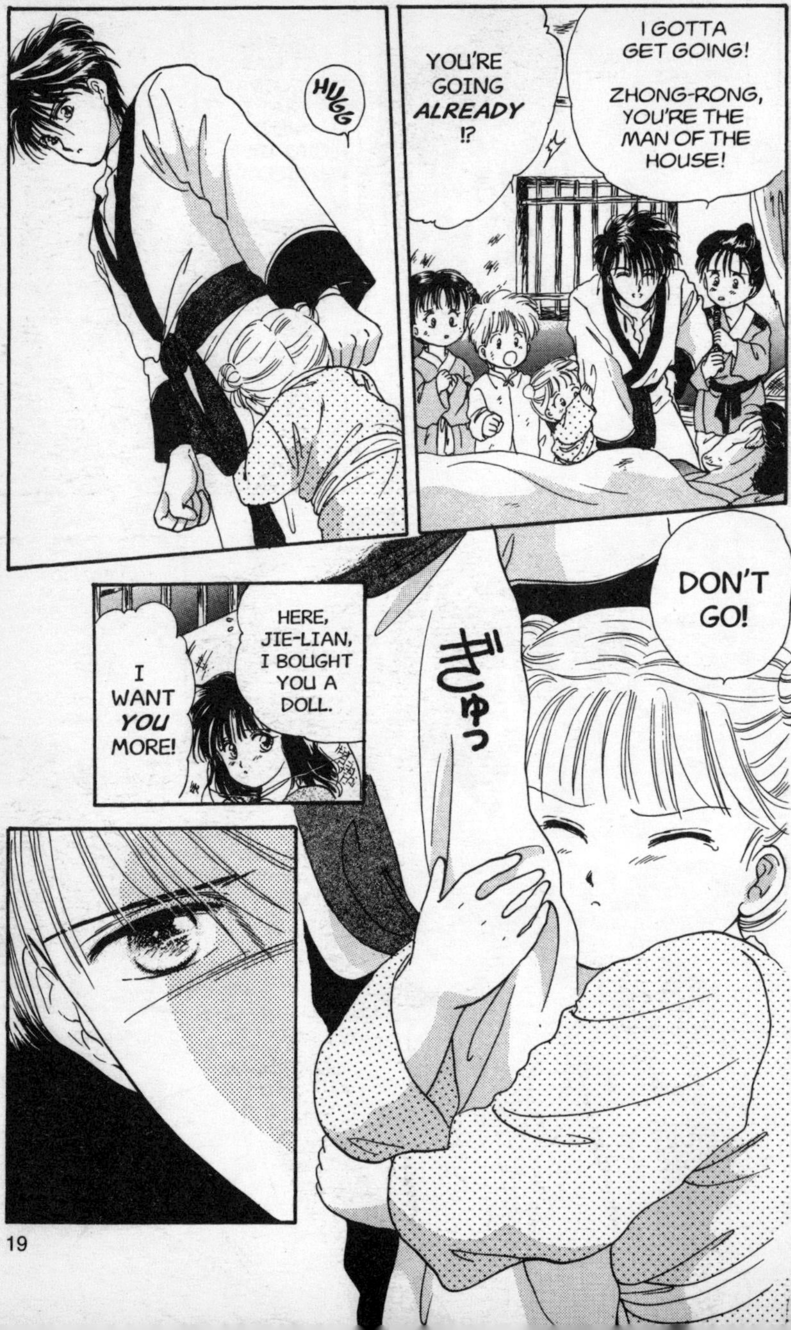
I GOTTA GET GOING!
ZHONG-RONG, YOU'RE THE MAN OF THE HOUSE!
YOU'RE GOING ALREADY !?
HUGG
DON'T GO!
ぎゅっ
HERE, JIE-LIAN, I BOUGHT YOU A DOLL.
I WANT YOU MORE!

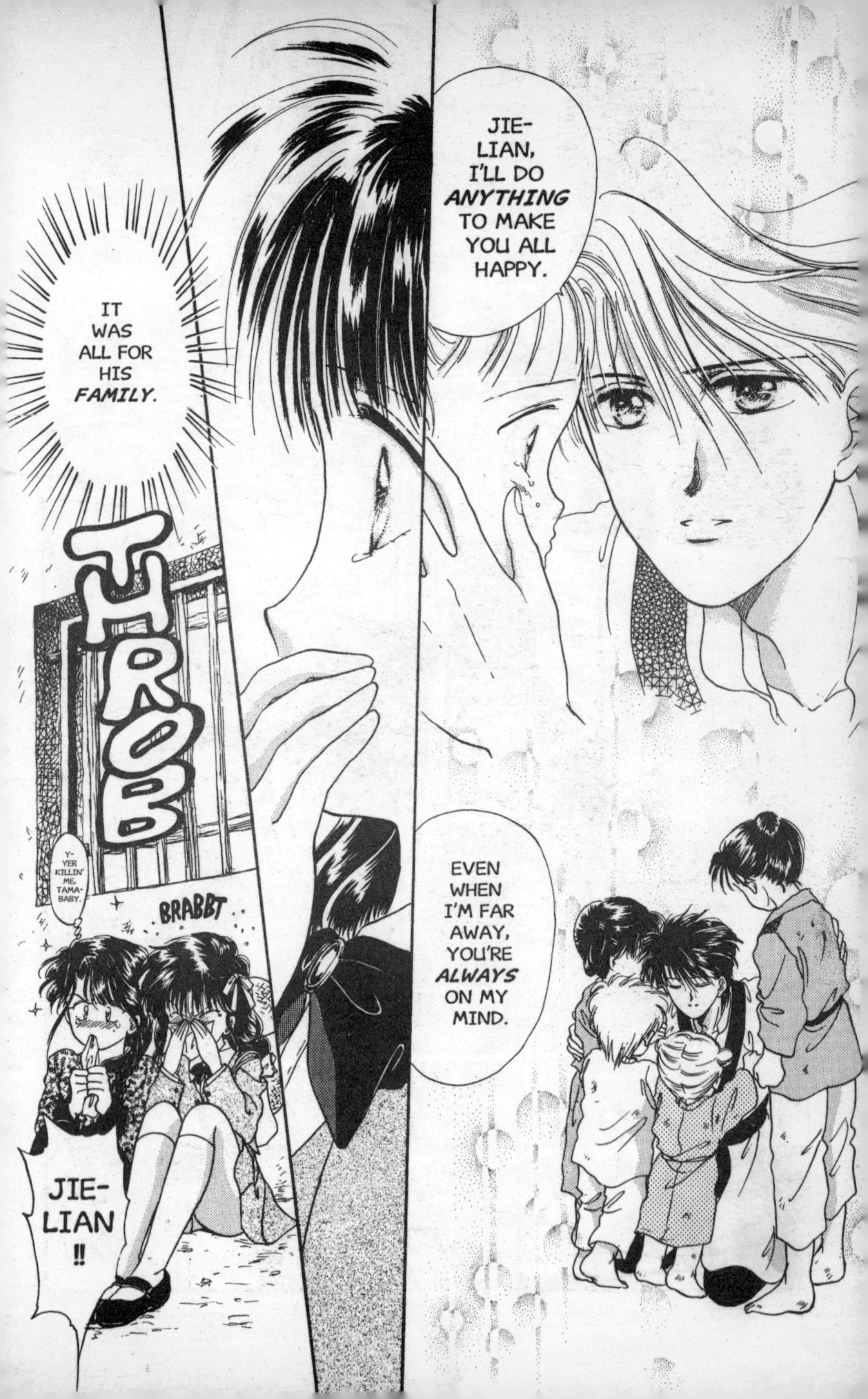
JIE-LIAN, I'LL DO *ANYTHING* TO MAKE YOU ALL HAPPY.
EVEN WHEN I'M FAR AWAY, YOU'RE *ALWAYS* ON MY MIND.
IT WAS ALL FOR HIS *FAMILY*.
THROB
Y-YER KILLIN' ME, TAMA-BABY.
BRABBT
JIE-LIAN!!

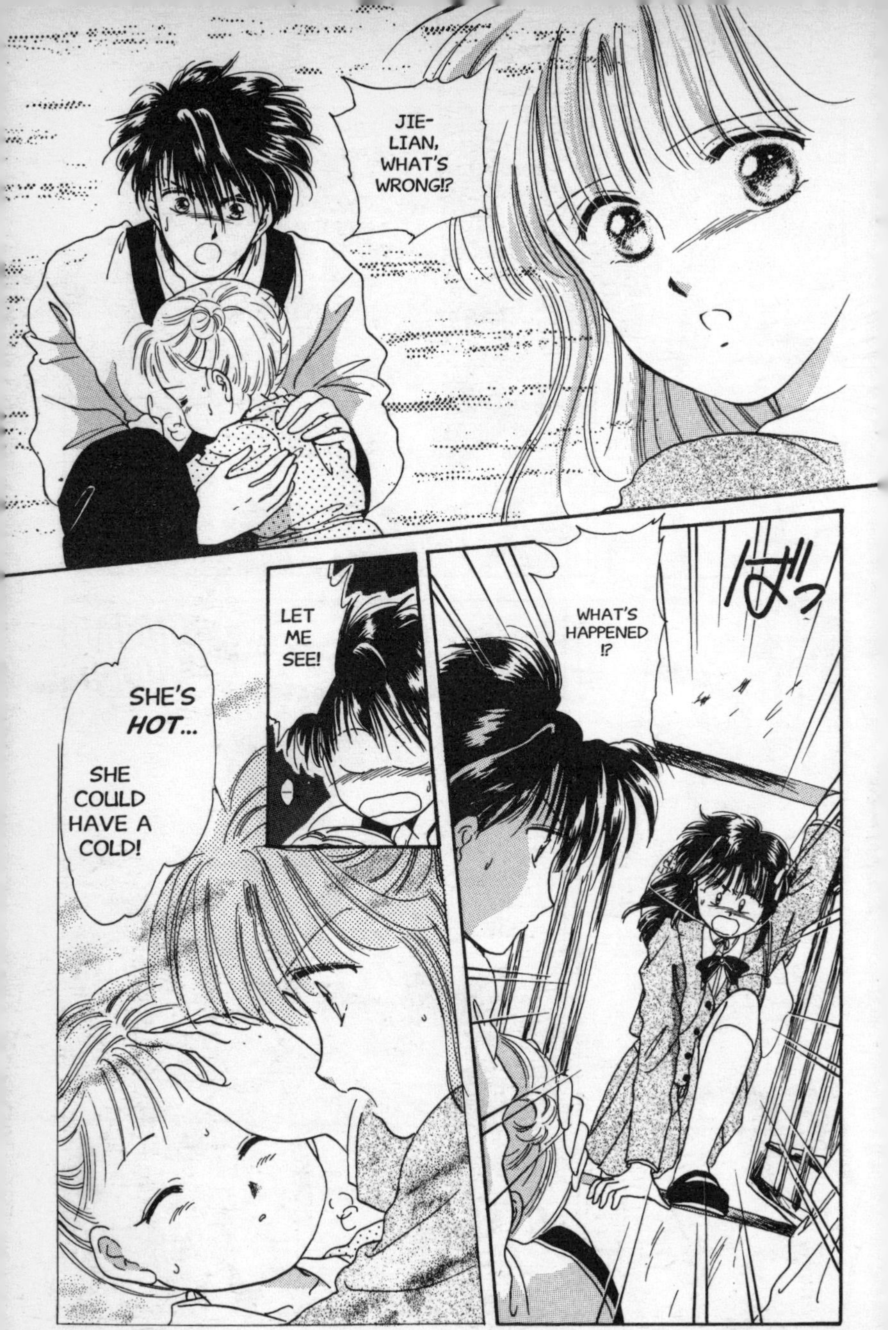
JIE-LIAN, WHAT'S WRONG!?
ぱっ
WHAT'S HAPPENED !?
LET ME SEE!
SHE'S *HOT*...
SHE COULD HAVE A COLD!

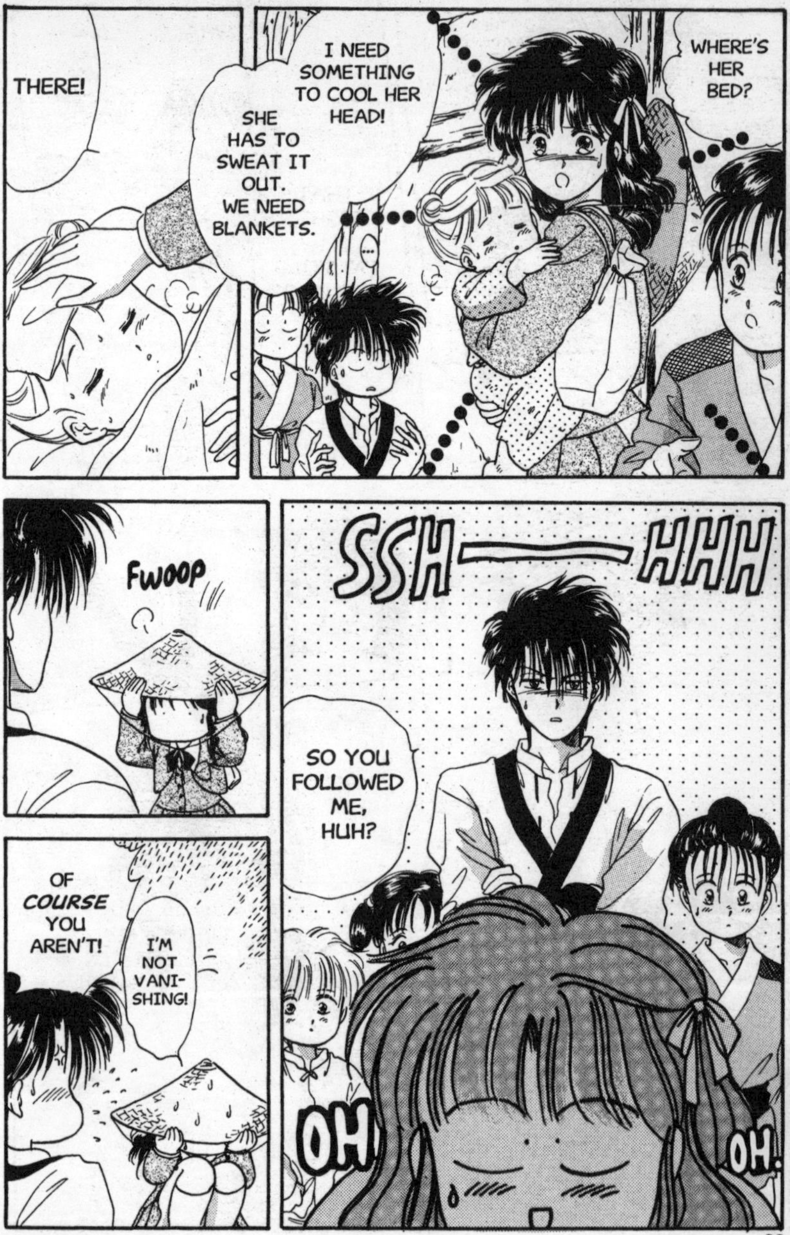
THERE!
I NEED SOMETHING TO COOL HER HEAD!
SHE HAS TO SWEAT IT OUT. WE NEED BLANKETS.
WHERE'S HER BED?
FWOOP
I'M NOT VANISHING!
OF *COURSE* YOU AREN'T!
SSH——HHH
SO YOU FOLLOWED ME, HUH?
OH
OH.

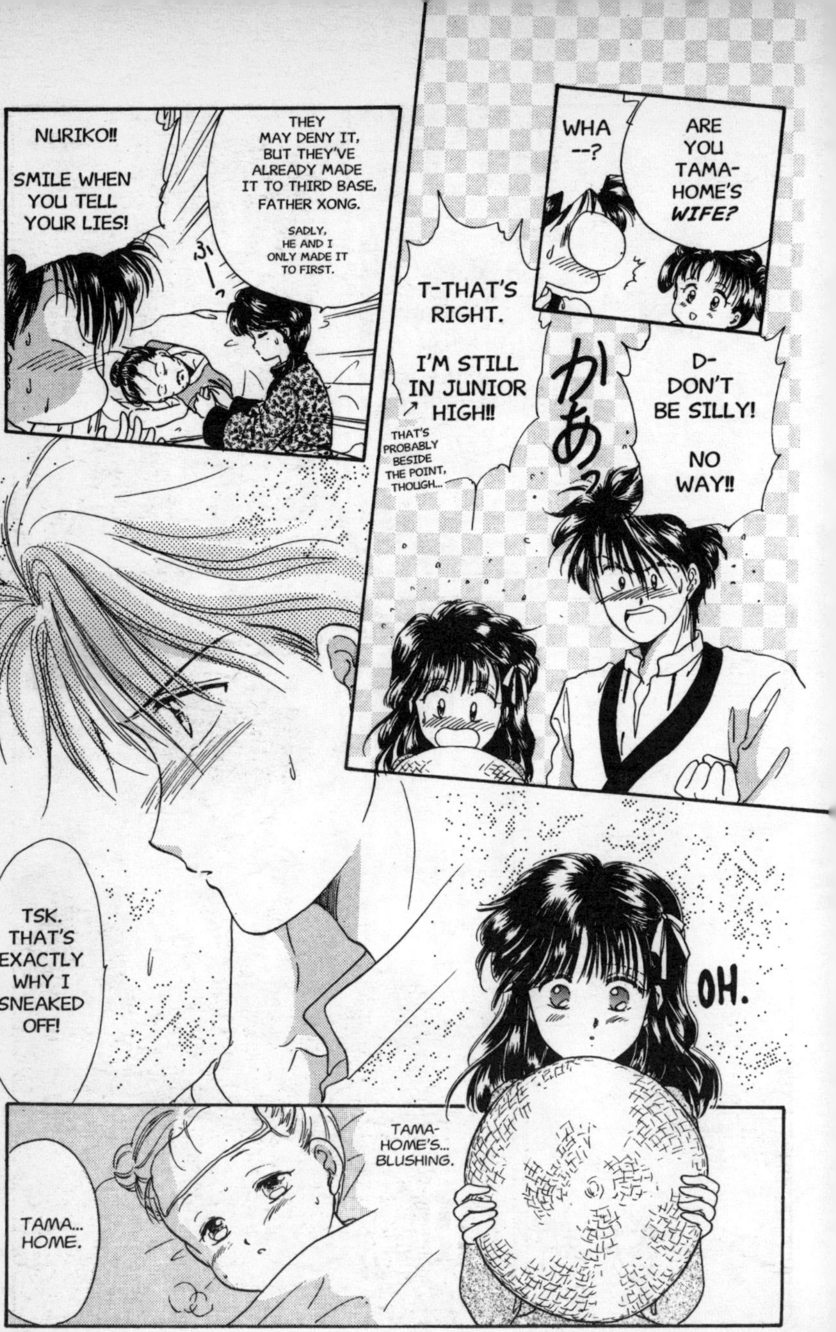

ARE YOU TAMA-HOME'S *WIFE?*
WHA --?
D-DON'T BE SILLY!
NO WAY!!
かあっ
T-THAT'S RIGHT.
I'M STILL IN JUNIOR HIGH!!
THAT'S PROBABLY BESIDE THE POINT, THOUGH...
THEY MAY DENY IT, BUT THEY'VE ALREADY MADE IT TO THIRD BASE, FATHER XONG.
SADLY, HE AND I ONLY MADE IT TO FIRST.
ふーっ
NURIKO!!
SMILE WHEN YOU TELL YOUR LIES!
OH.
TSK. THAT'S EXACTLY WHY I SNEAKED OFF!
TAMA-HOME'S... BLUSHING.
TAMA... HOME.

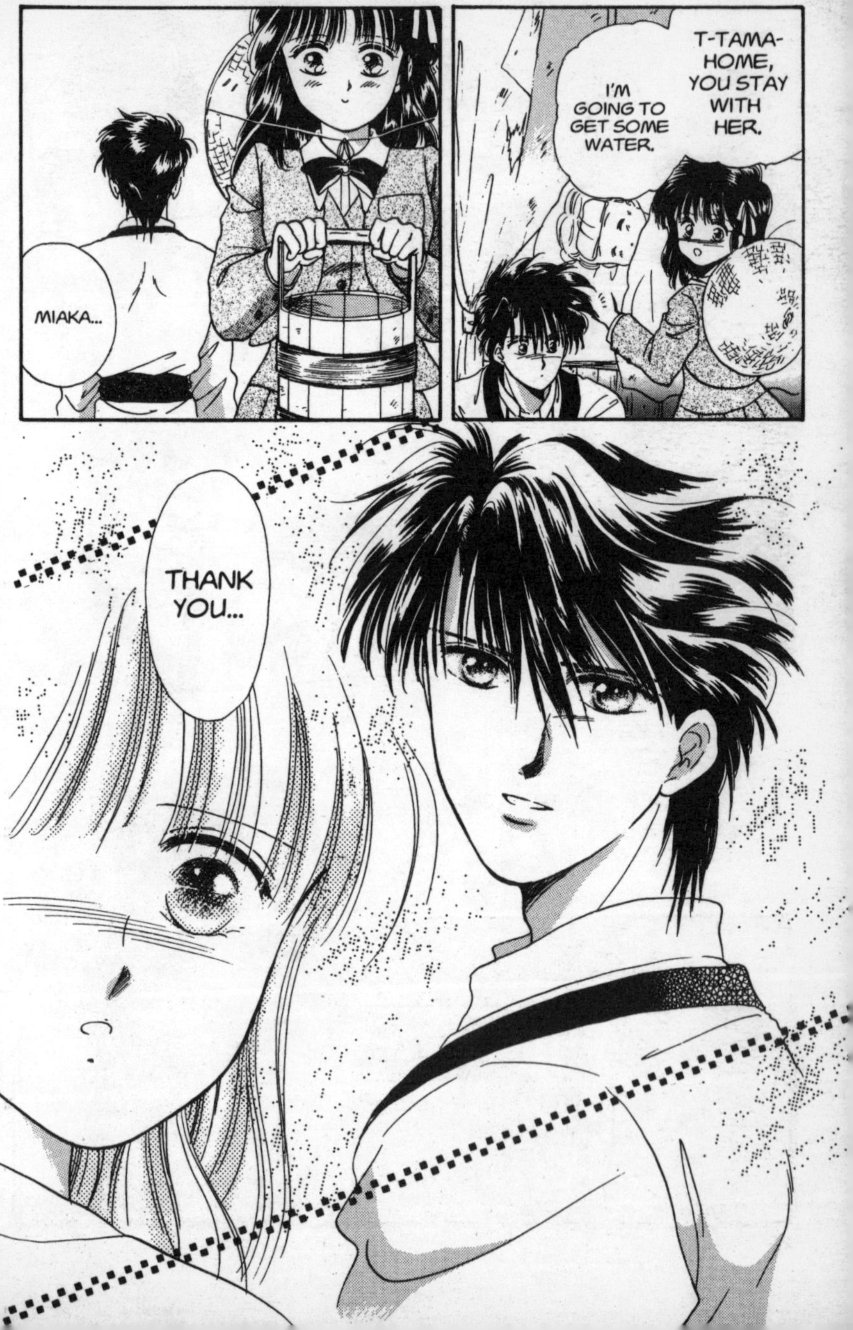
T-TAMA-HOME, YOU STAY WITH HER.
I'M GOING TO GET SOME WATER.
MIAKA...
THANK YOU...

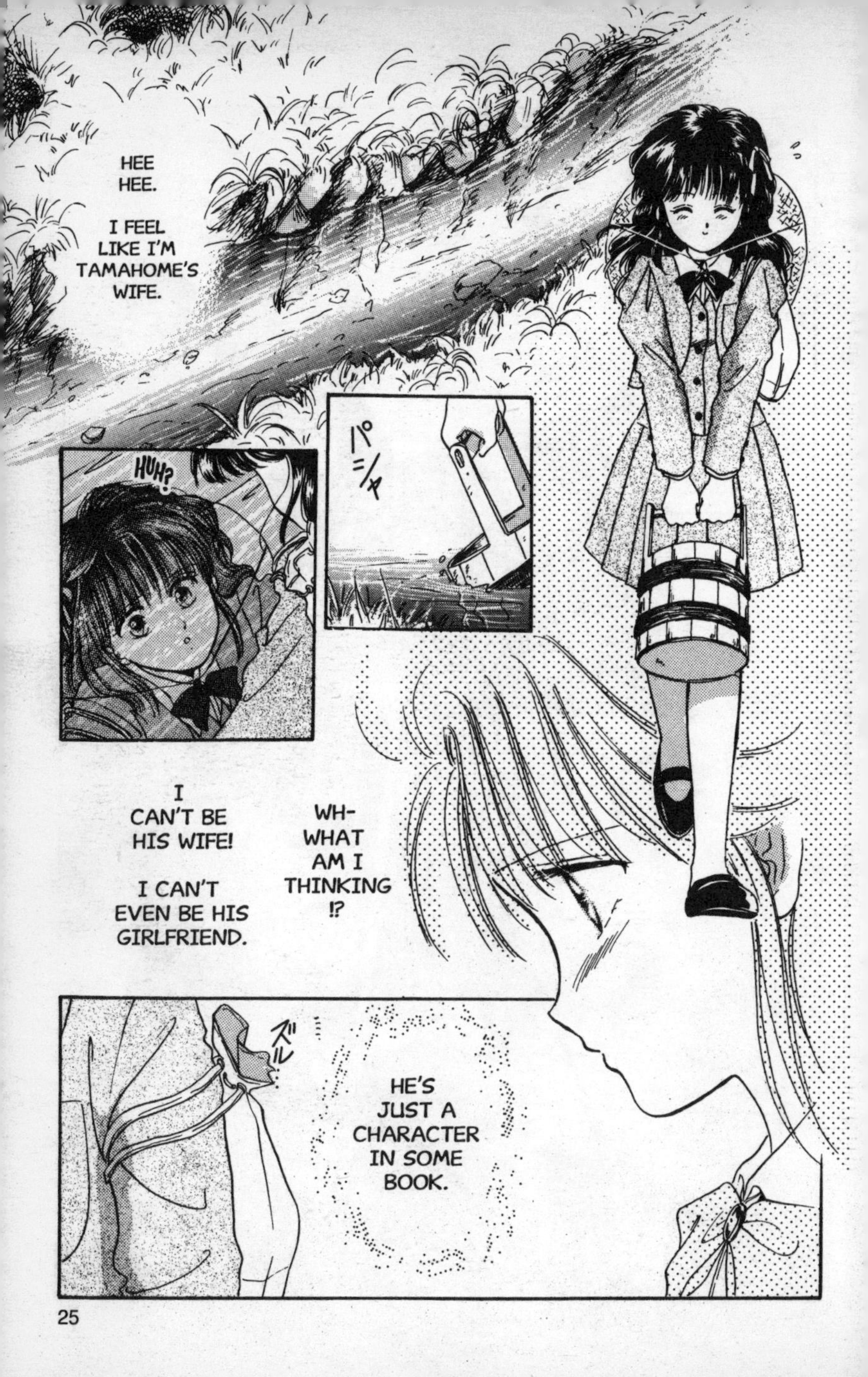
HEE HEE.
I FEEL LIKE I'M TAMAHOME'S WIFE.
パニャ
HUH?
WH-WHAT AM I THINKING!?
I CAN'T BE HIS WIFE!
I CAN'T EVEN BE HIS GIRLFRIEND.
ズル
HE'S JUST A CHARACTER IN SOME BOOK.

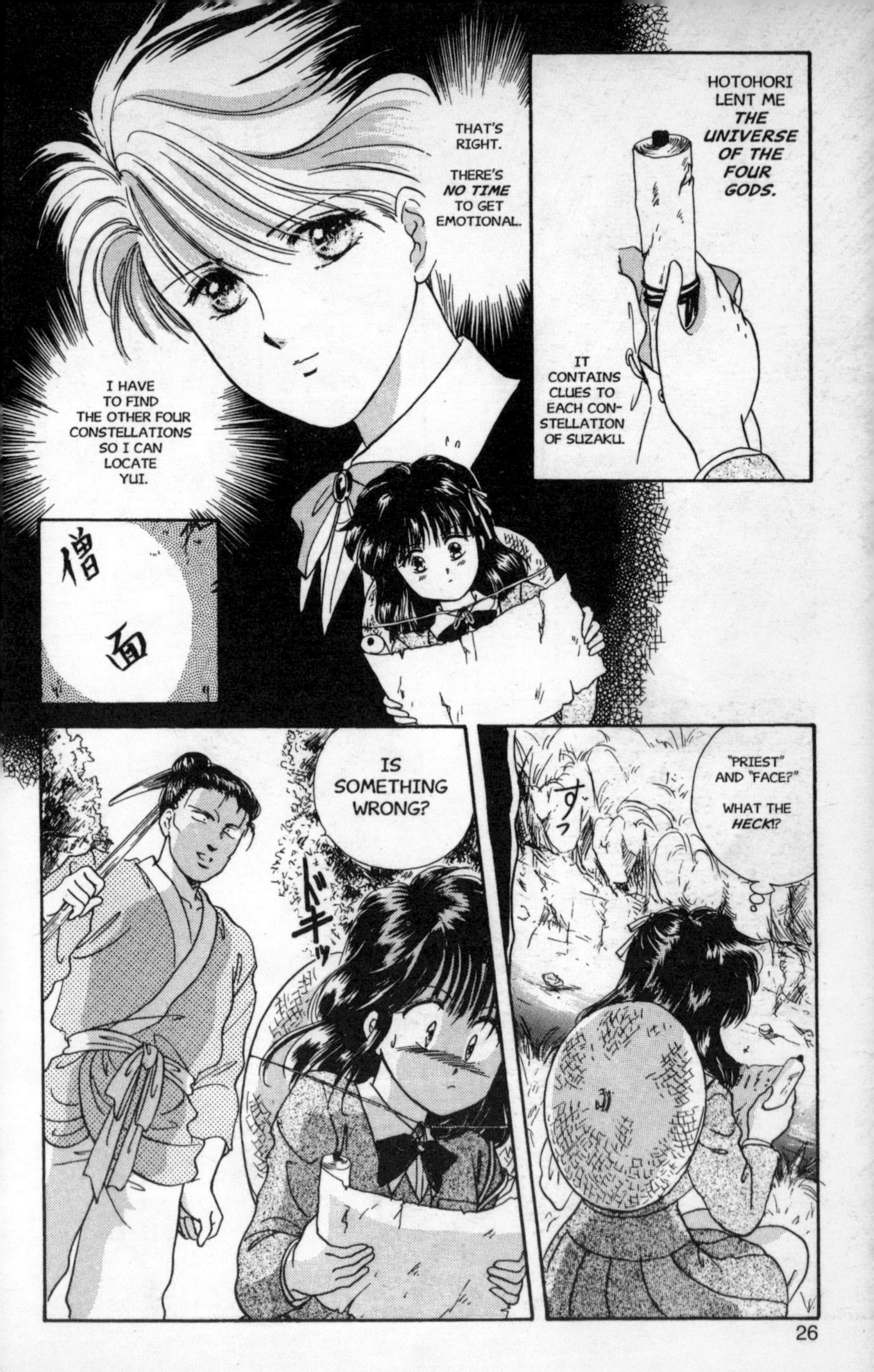
HOTOHORI LENT ME *THE UNIVERSE OF THE FOUR GODS.*
IT CONTAINS CLUES TO EACH CON-STELLATION OF SUZAKU.
THAT'S RIGHT.
THERE'S *NO TIME* TO GET EMOTIONAL.
I HAVE TO FIND THE OTHER FOUR CONSTELLATIONS SO I CAN LOCATE YUI.
僧
面
"PRIEST" AND "FACE?"
WHAT THE *HECK!?*
IS SOMETHING WRONG?
ドキッ

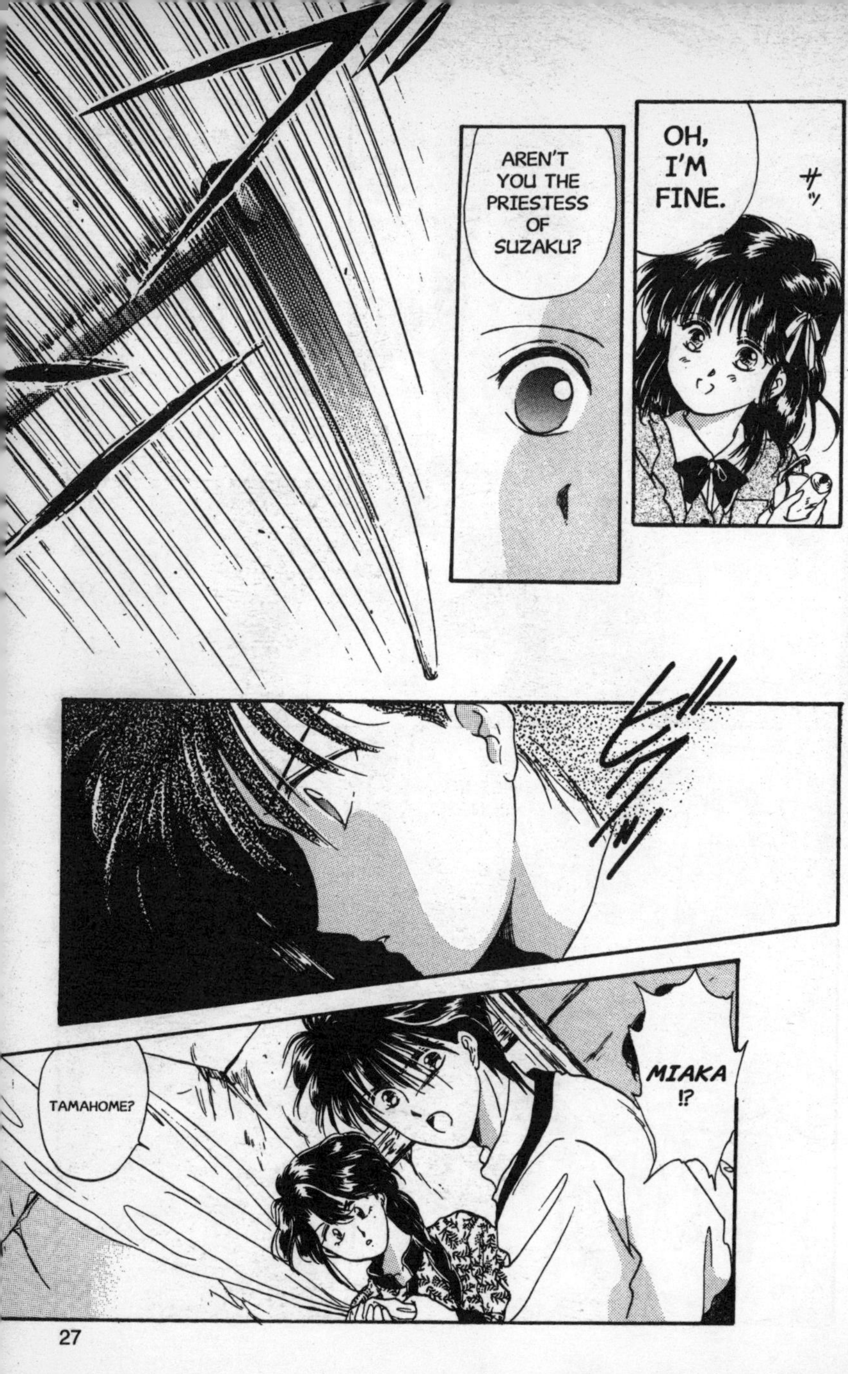

OH, I'M FINE.
サッ
AREN'T YOU THE PRIESTESS OF SUZAKU?
MIAKA !?
TAMAHOME?

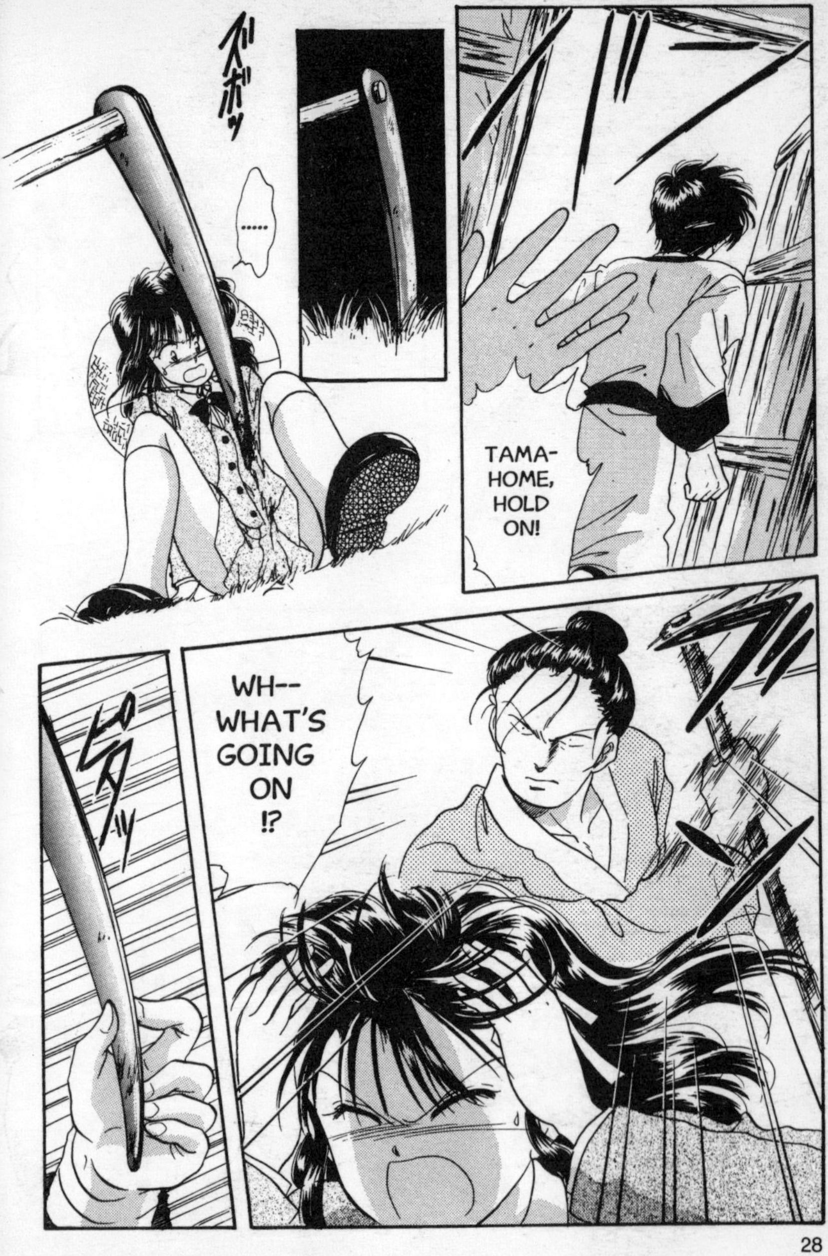
TAMA-HOME, HOLD ON!
ズボッ
......
WH-- WHAT'S GOING ON !?
ピタッ

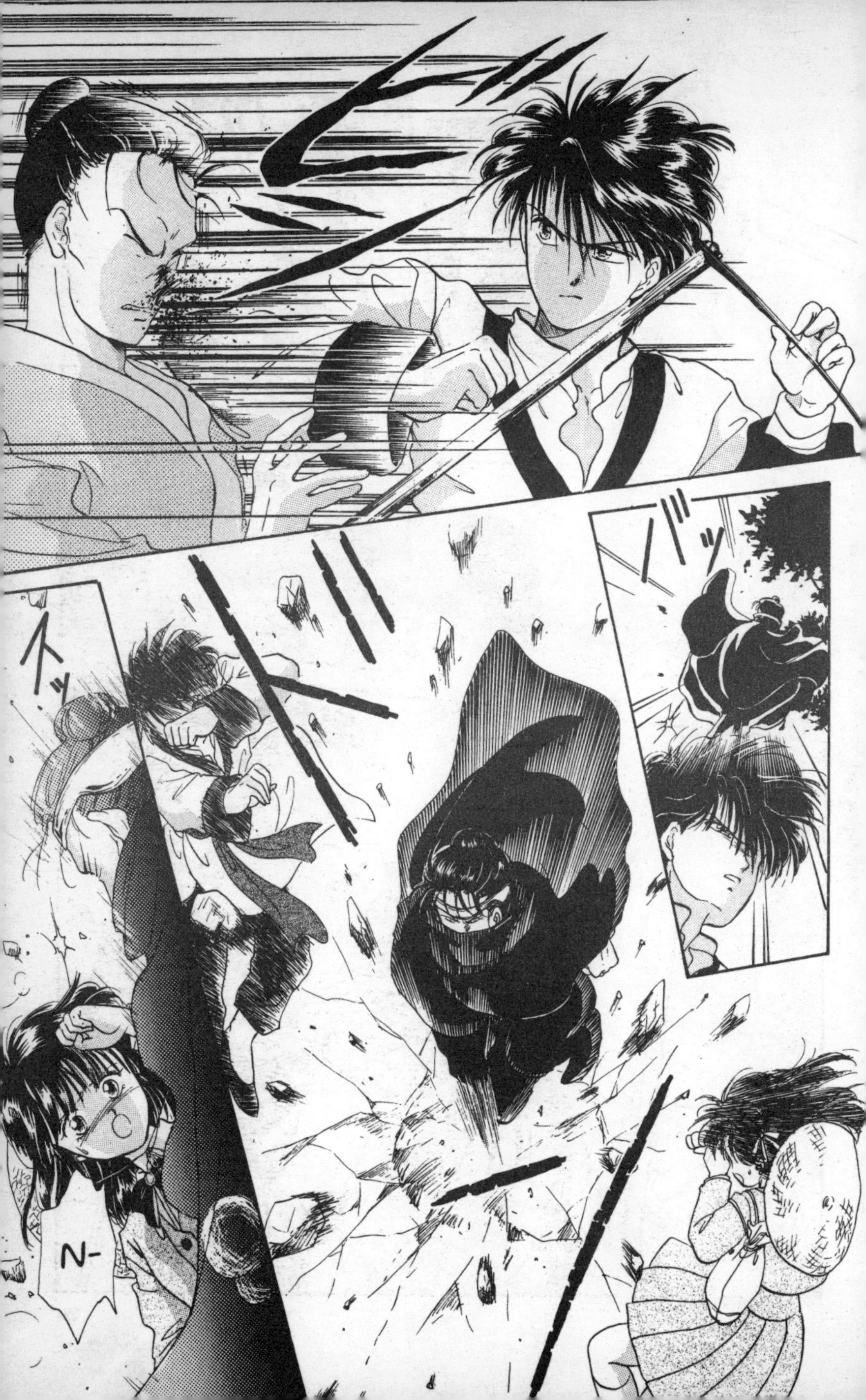
バッ
N-

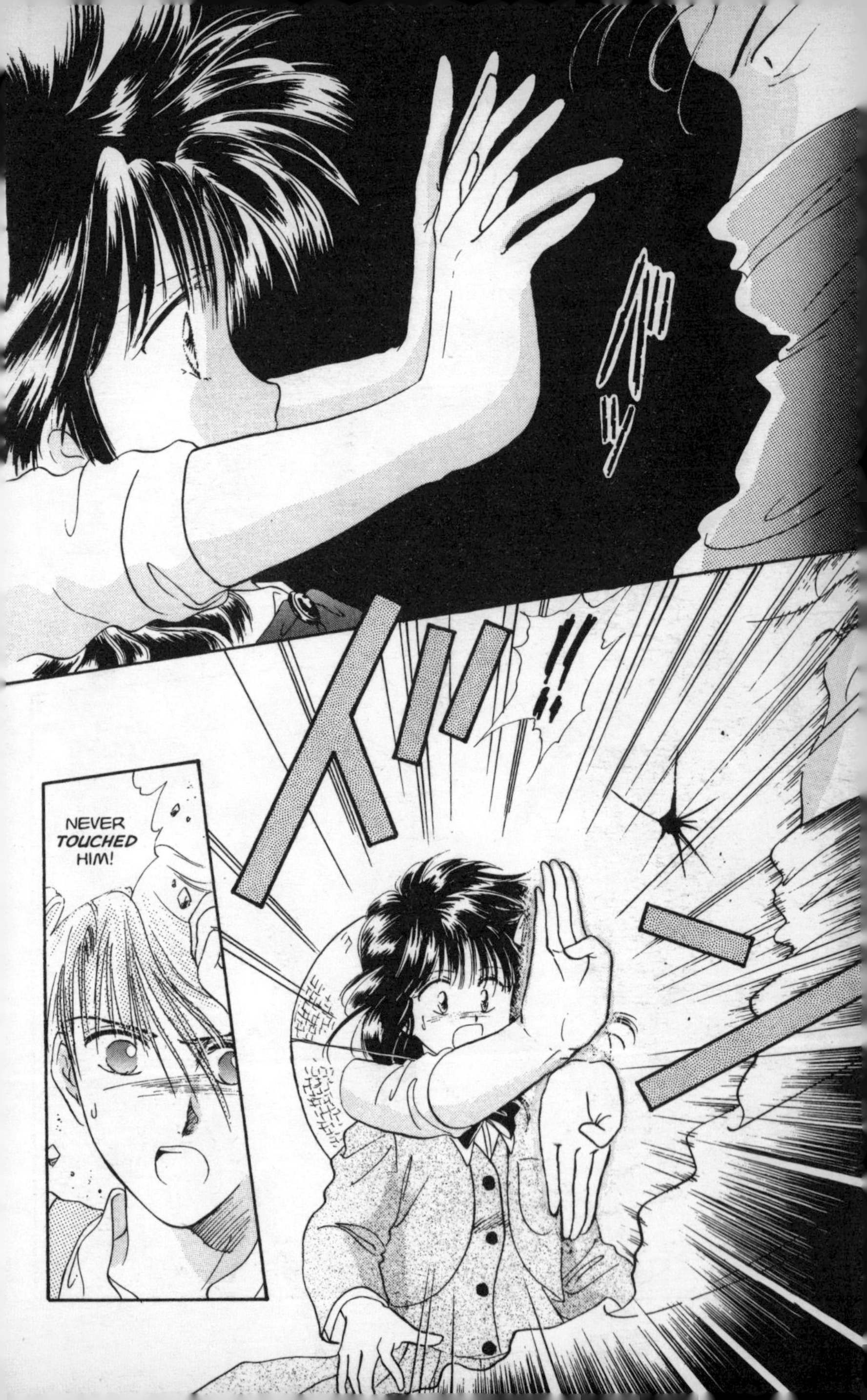
NEVER *TOUCHED* HIM!

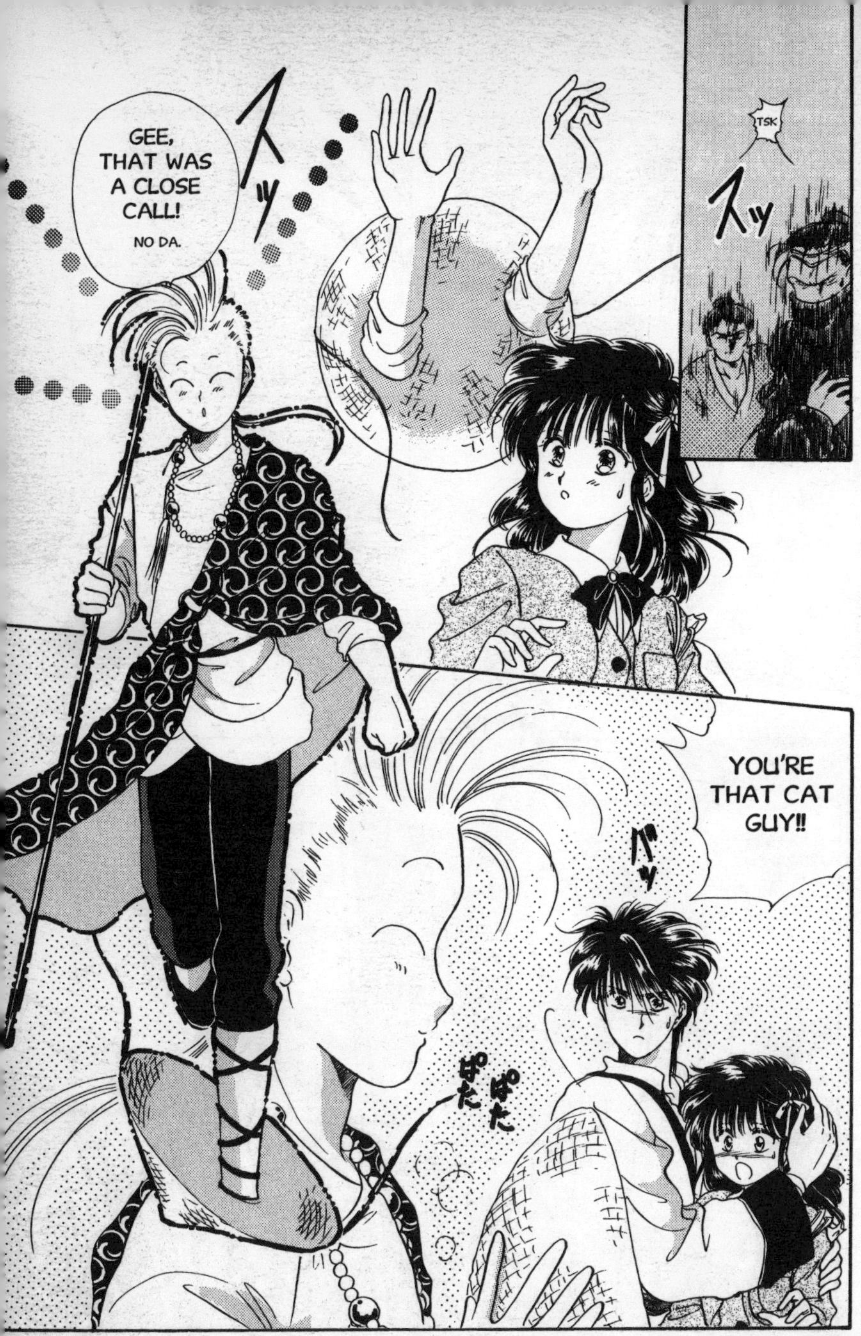
TSK
スッ
GEE, THAT WAS A CLOSE CALL!
NO DA.
スッ
YOU'RE THAT CAT GUY!!
バッ
ぱたぱた

32

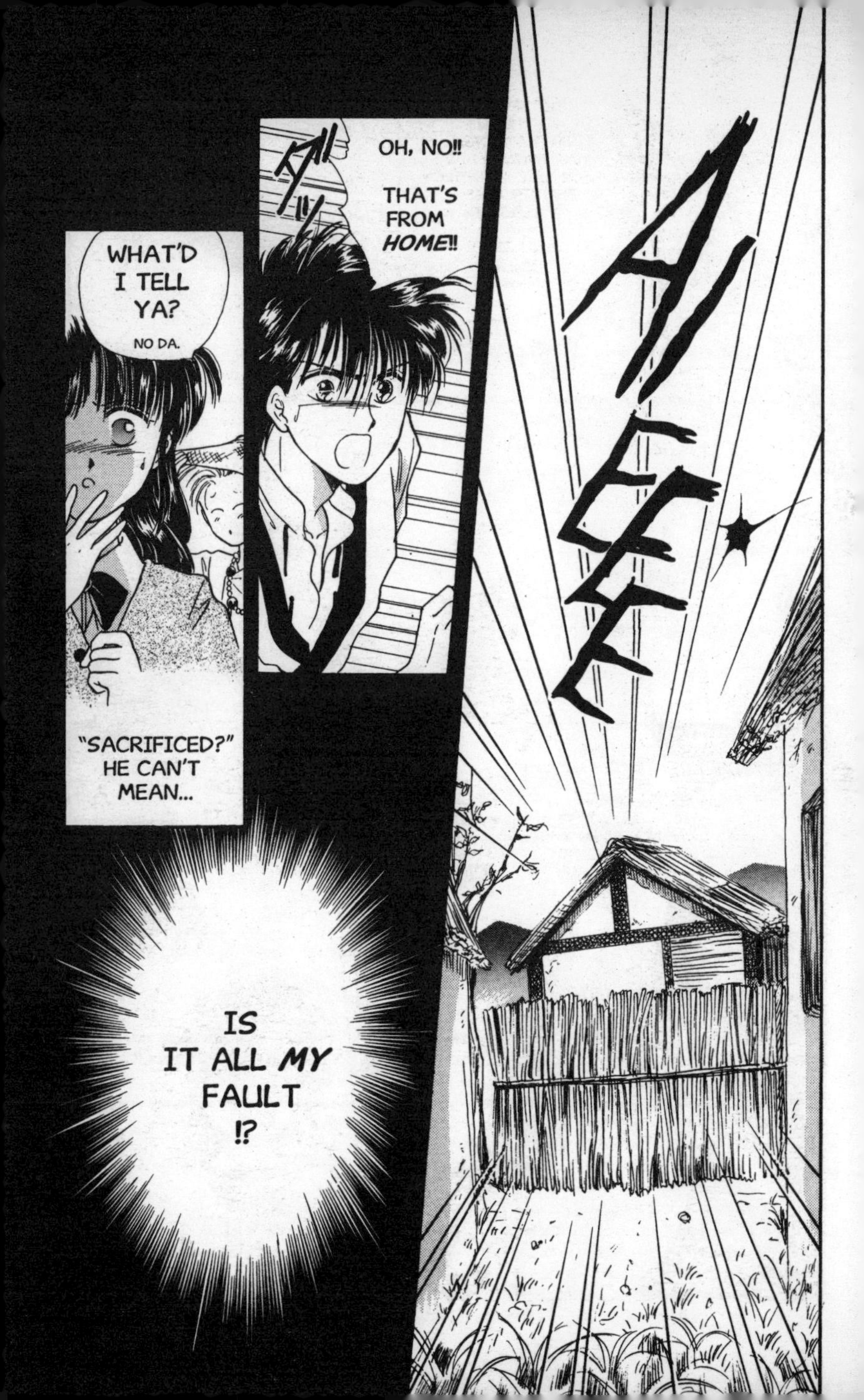
AIEEE
OH, NO!!
THAT'S FROM *HOME*!!
WHAT'D I TELL YA?
NO DA.
"SACRIFICED?" HE CAN'T MEAN...
IS IT ALL *MY* FAULT !?

TELL ME MORE ABOUT "THE UNIVERSE OF THE FOUR GODS"

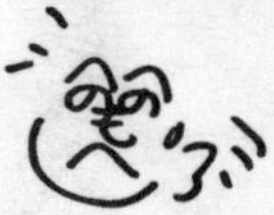

This is one of the questions I hear frequently. If you keep reading the story, you'll find out all about it. But for the impatient who still INSIST! I've decided to expose a few details.

I've never seen constellations attributed to the Four Gods, so I might be the first. (Usually they've been used as compass directions or for the identities of monsters. Other than that, their names have been used for invocations.) The anime OAV Maryū Senki used them as monsters. I think Suzaku was female, but this anime gets pretty heavily into erotic-grotesque so I can't recommend it... I'll describe the gods and their constellations. (That way you can find them in the night sky.)

We'll list the Four Gods according to ancient Chinese astrological names rather than geographical areas (which might appear later in the story) or compass directions.

EASTERN SEIRYU SEVEN CONSTELLATIONS (MAY-JULY) Suboshi (Virgo), Amiboshi (Virgo), Tomo (Libra), Soi (Scorpio), Nakago (Scorpio), Ashitare (Scorpio), Mi (Sagittarius)

WESTERN BYAKKO SEVEN CONSTELLATIONS (NOVEMBER-JANUARY) Tokaki (Andromeda), Tatara (Aries), Kokie (Aries), Subaru (Taurus), Amefuri (Taurus), Toroki (Orion), Karasuki (Orion)

SOUTHERN SUZAKU SEVEN CONSTELLATIONS (FEBRUARY-MAY) Chichiri (Gemini), Tamahome (Cancer), Nuriko (Hydra), Chiriko (Hydra), Tasuki (Crater), Mitsukake (Corvus)

NORTHERN GENBU SEVEN CONSTELLATIONS (AUGUST-NOVEMBER) Hikitsu (Sagittarius), Inami (Capricorn), Uruki (Aquarius), Urumiya (Aquarius), Hatsui (Pegasus), Namame (Pegasus)

Usually, when you see the character for Chichiri's name, you read it as "I," and when you see the character for Tamahome's name, you see it as "ki," etc. So most of the tables list the constellation names with the Chinese pronunciations for each of the characters. There are very few which list the Japanese phonetic reading such as "Tamahome," but in the Buddhist Philosophy Encyclopedia I have, the character was listed as "Tamahome." (You'll only find this book at a large bookstore. It costs a whopping ¥80,000!)
The rest I looked up in the constellation tables in the appendices of a Japanese/Chinese dictionary I used in high school. A star in "Hotohori" is second magnitude, and the brightest star is Suzaku (Alpha Hadrae, also known as Alphard or the Solitary One. – Ed.)

The names for the Four Gods were taken from these constellation listings. The Southern Seven Star Constellations look like they have short tails so the ancients called them a bird, the Western Seven Star Constellations resemble a tiger, and so on.

Between February and May, you can see the Suzaku constellations appear in the night sky. The brightest star in Cancer is Tamahome.

I love the cosmos, so I get a kick out of naming my characters after constellations.

I've also been told that "Nuriko" is "Meriko," but I think it can be named both ways (most of the time it's called Nuriko). Also, Mitsukake can be read both as Mitsukake and Mitsuuchi. Some said that Tamahome and crew were part of Byakko, but they're mistaken.

Genbu is pretty sad. Dragons like Seiryu are kind of cool, but the idea of a turtle and snake copulating!! Blech! I am not into that!!

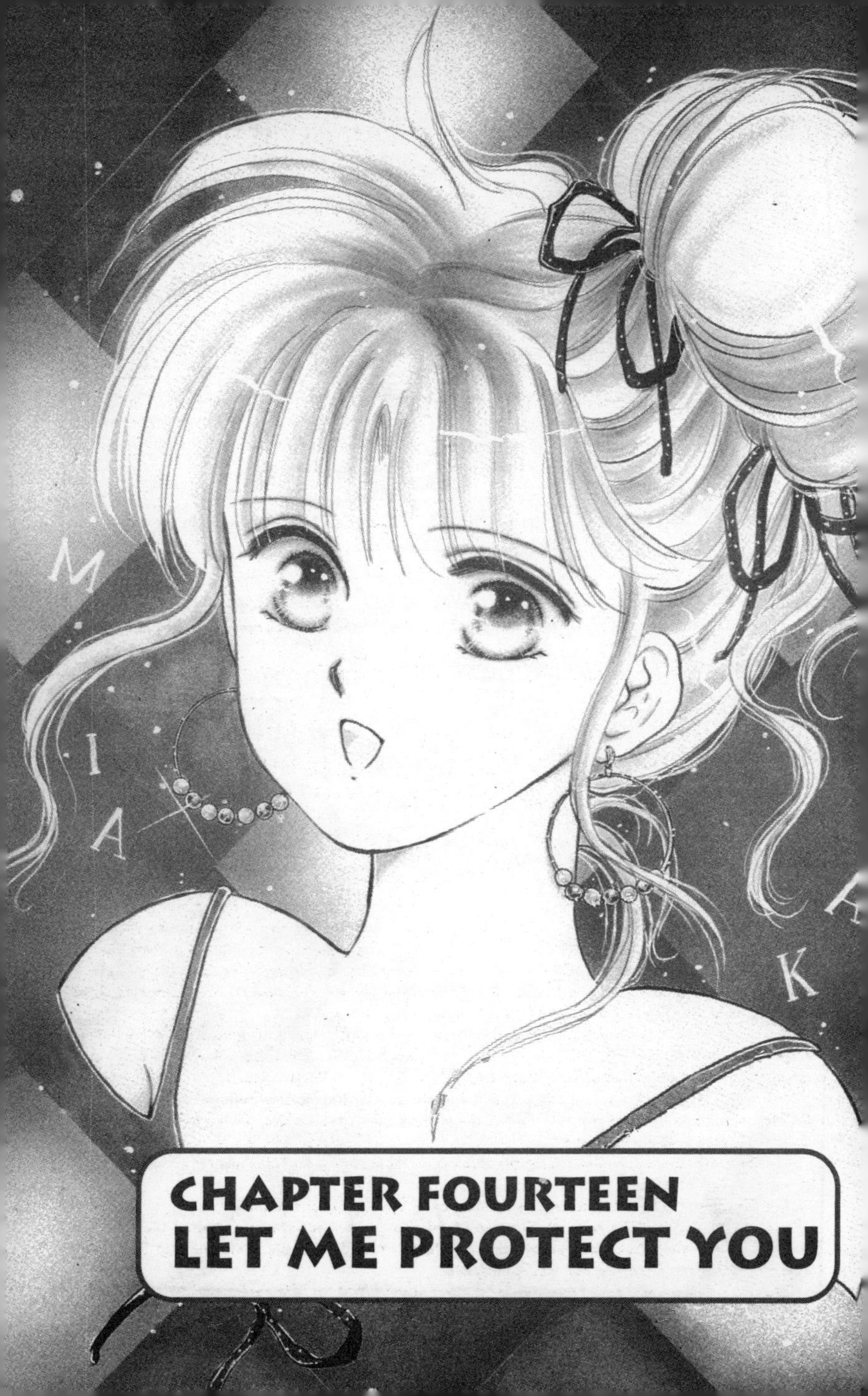
MIAKA
CHAPTER FOURTEEN
LET ME PROTECT YOU

MEOW MEOW

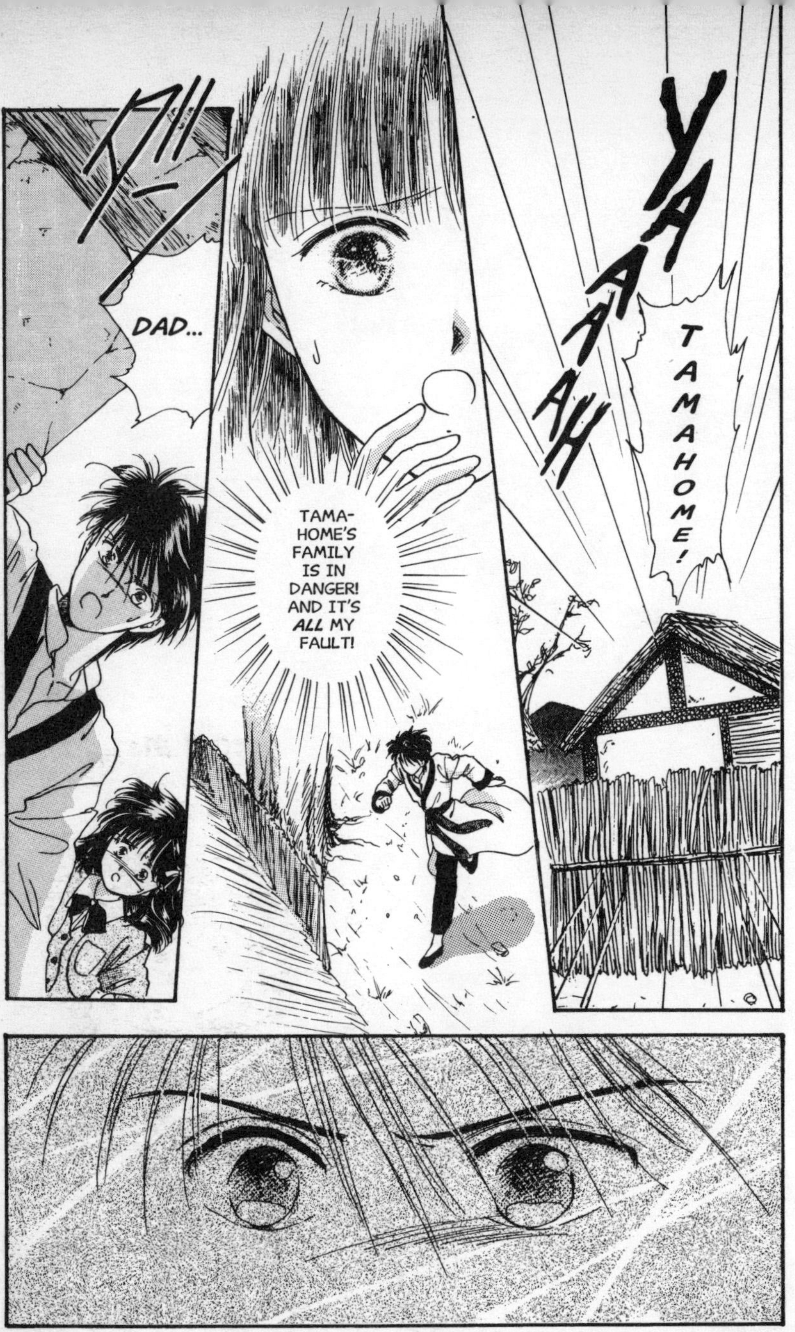
YAAAAAH
TAMAHOME!
TAMA-HOME'S FAMILY IS IN DANGER! AND IT'S ALL MY FAULT!
DAD...

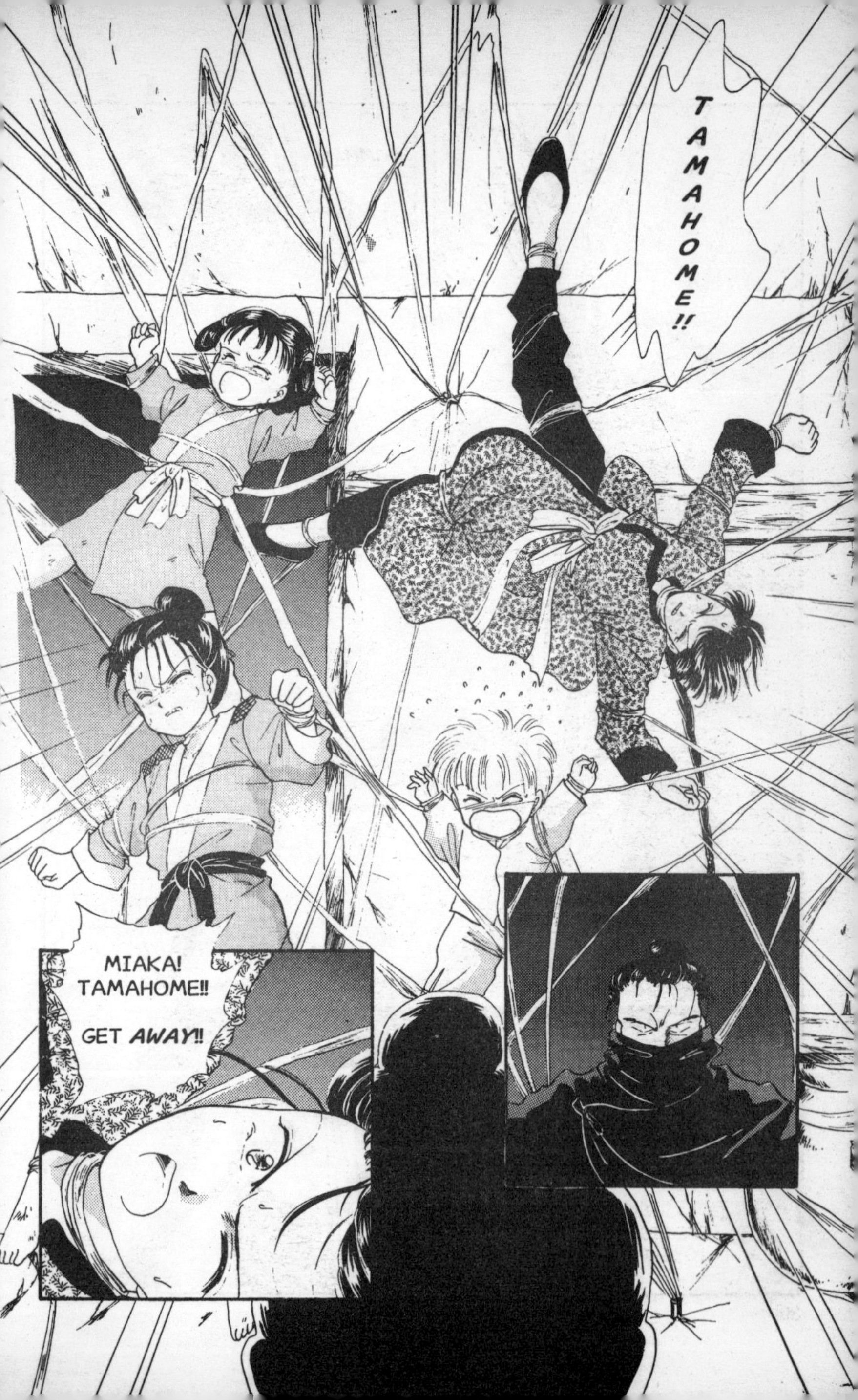
TAMAHOME!!
MIAKA! TAMAHOME!!
GET AWAY!!

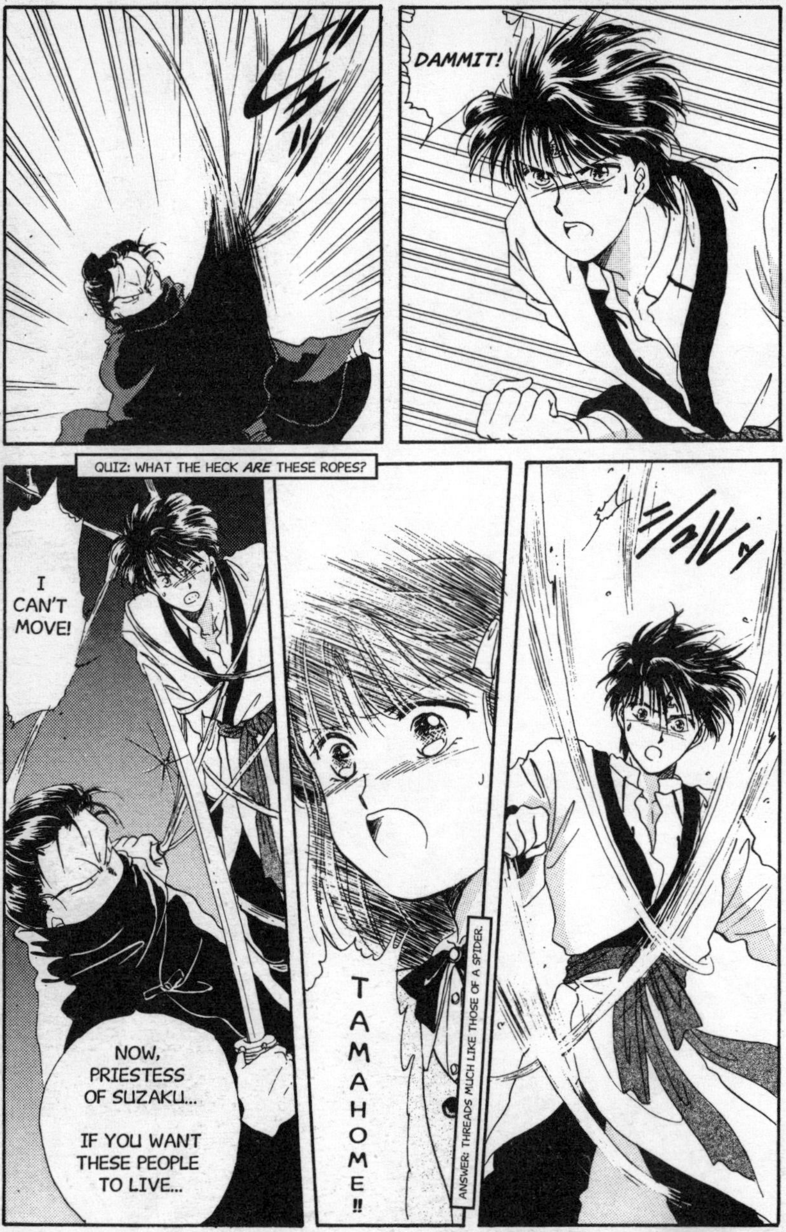
DAMMIT!
QUIZ: WHAT THE HECK *ARE* THESE ROPES?
ANSWER: THREADS MUCH LIKE THOSE OF A SPIDER.
TAMAHOME!!
I CAN'T MOVE!
NOW, PRIESTESS OF SUZAKU...
IF YOU WANT THESE PEOPLE TO LIVE...

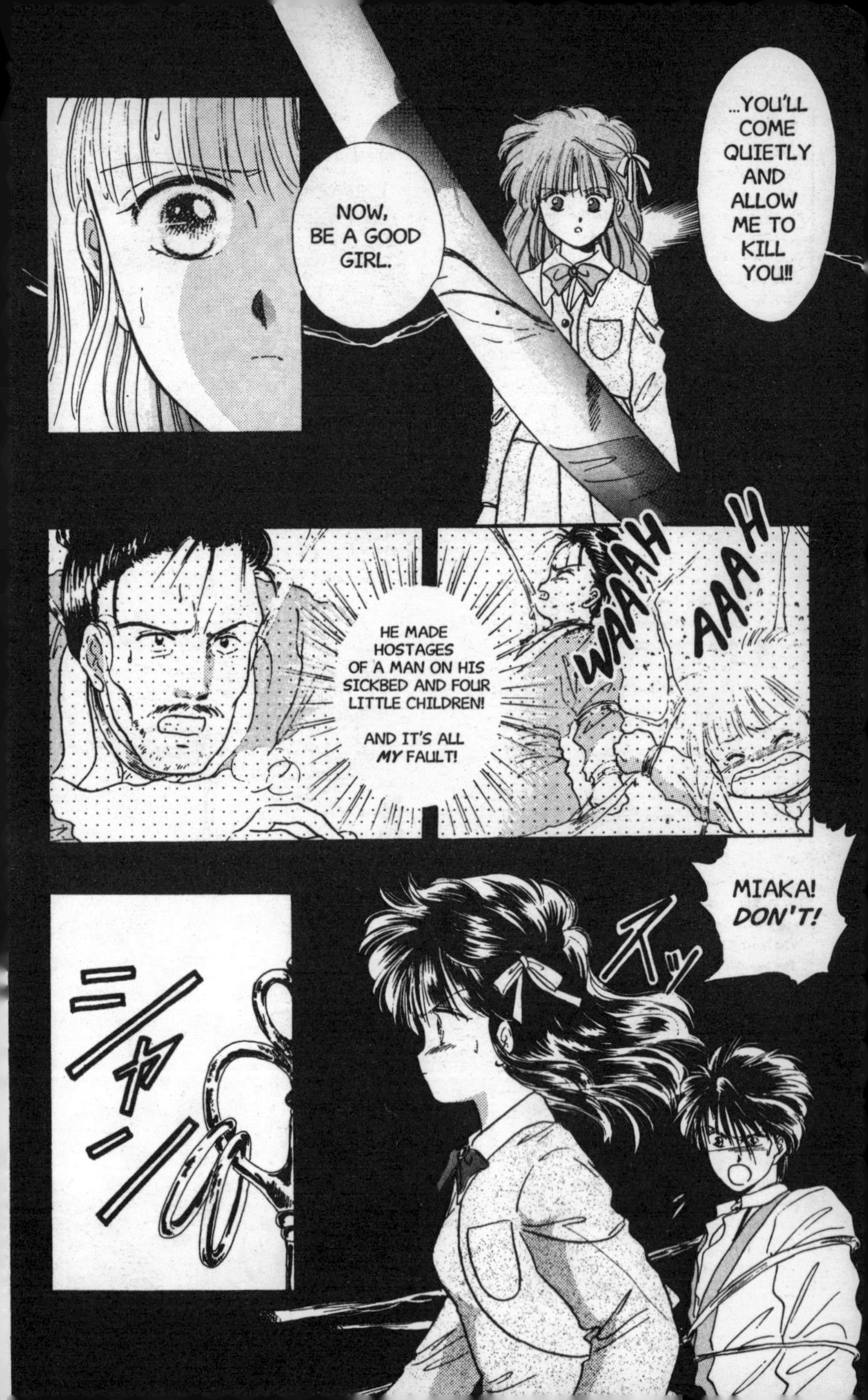
...YOU'LL COME QUIETLY AND ALLOW ME TO KILL YOU!!
NOW, BE A GOOD GIRL.
WAAAH
AAAH
HE MADE HOSTAGES OF A MAN ON HIS SICKBED AND FOUR LITTLE CHILDREN!
AND IT'S ALL *MY* FAULT!
MIAKA! *DON'T!*

I mentioned before how I've been reading your fan mail, and I'm surprised at the huge number of questions. You're all so concerned about the remaining warriors in the constellations of Suzaku. Some of you have even sent me illustrations and suggestions for the rest of the warriors. But to tell the truth, I decided on all seven characters before I even started drawing the comic. So I'll introduce them one by one, the same way I envisioned them.

I find it fascinating how all the characters get their own fans. The Tamahome fans don't like Hotohori, and the Hotohori fans look down on Tamahome. Nuriko's been gaining popularity. Keisuke, Miaka's brother, has a set of fans, too. Well, they're all cute so I don't mind. All of my assistants rate their favorites differently. Sometimes they play "Who'd be the best voice actor for each character?" and everyone gets all worked up. Fans have suggested some in their letters, but most of them don't seem right to me. (Sorry!). That's not to say my ideas are any better. We had a dramatic section in "Toy Box '93" so I was allowed to choose the actors for Miaka and Tamahome (but only them). I talked it over with my assistants then made my decision. Give it a listen and see what you think. I like voices that are mature and masculine (and a little erotic). What else? Oh, yes, I heard that all the merchandise at the Animate store sold out!

And we got a lot of complaints! I never got any myself!! The least they could do is save a sample for me!! Did you hear there was a bonus poster with every ¥2,000 purchase!? Gimme!! Calendars are posted in bookstores without my knowledge. And I never knew it had been printed!! Speaking of calendars, I think you should know that I had to fight to get an original drawing into that calendar. It also took a lot of work to convince my editor that I should draw for the CD book, too.

There are really very few who like both!

Supposedly, they only display July and August

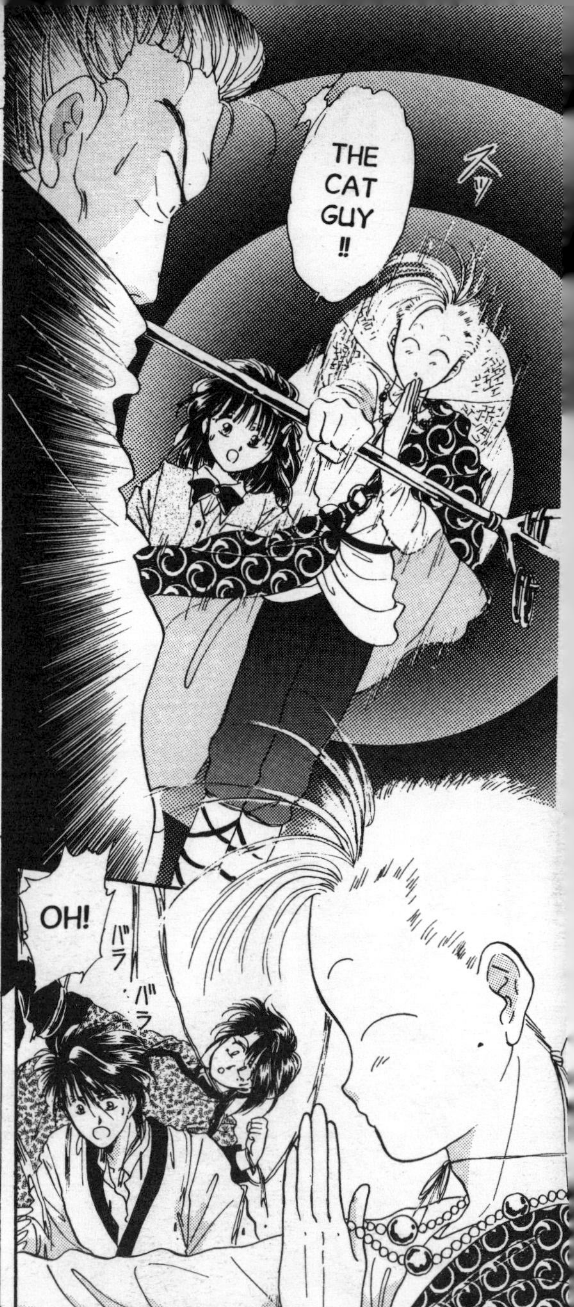

スッ
THE CAT GUY!!
OH!
バラ
バラ

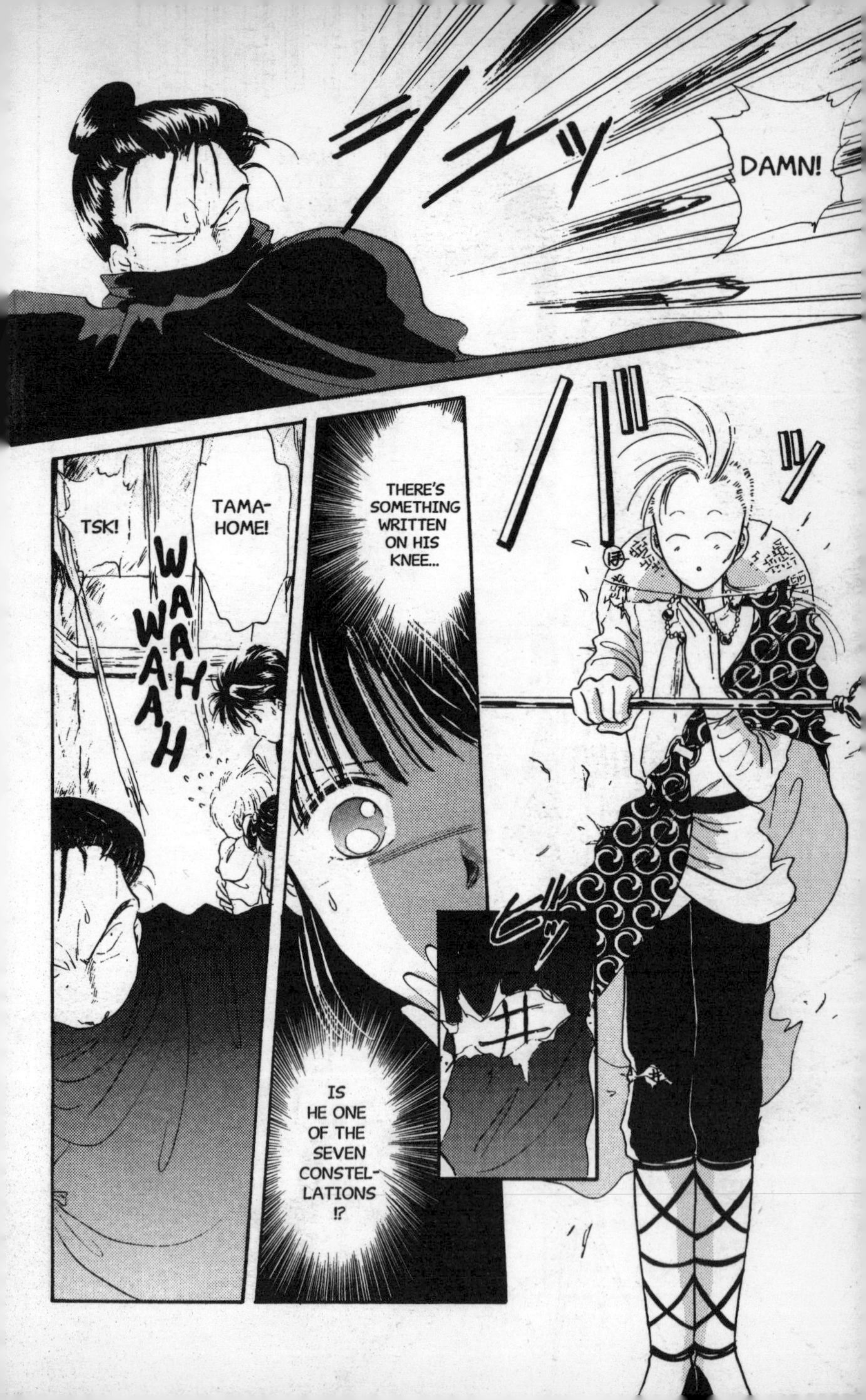
DAMN!
THERE'S SOMETHING WRITTEN ON HIS KNEE...
IS HE ONE OF THE SEVEN CONSTEL-LATIONS!?
TAMA-HOME!
TSK!
WAAH
WAAAH

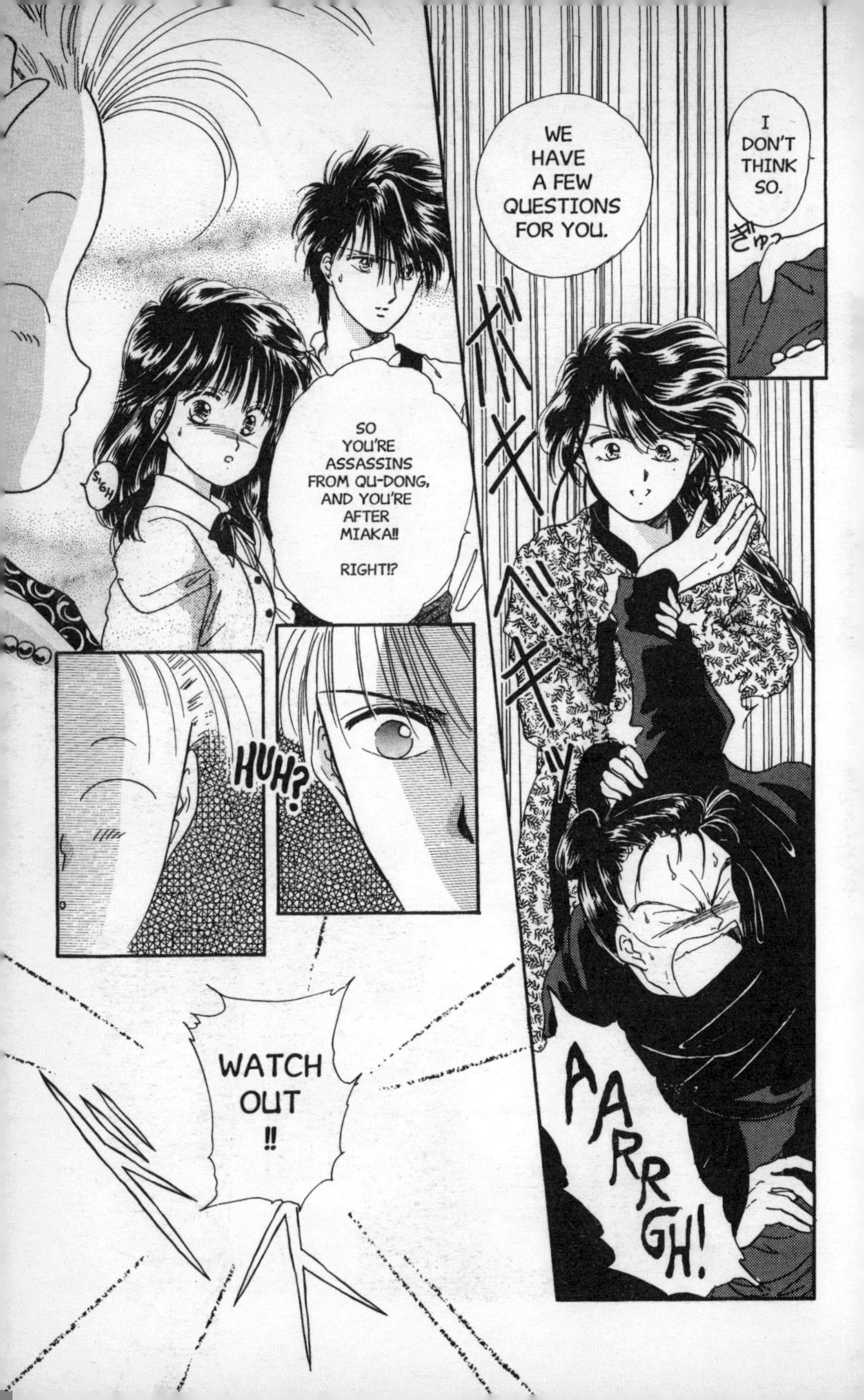

I DON'T THINK SO.
WE HAVE A FEW QUESTIONS FOR YOU.
AARRGH!
SO YOU'RE ASSASSINS FROM QU-DONG, AND YOU'RE AFTER MIAKA!! RIGHT!?
SIGH
HUH?
WATCH OUT !!

OH, ANYBODY COULD'VE DONE THAT!

TAMAHOME, I GOTTA SAY YOU READ THAT ATTACK WELL!

YOU'RE ALL RIGHT AFTER ALL!

NO DA!

MAYBE *SOMEBODY* COULDA PROTECTED *ME*.

URK

DEAD SPIES TELL NO TALES.

ONCE WE FIND THE...

PRIESTESS OF SEIRYU...

YOUR COUNTRY WILL BE...

FINISHED...

≥COUGH≥

HEH HEH COUGH

YOU...

GUYS ARE...

NOTHING!

WHAT DO YOU MEAN!?

ANSWER ME!!

THE PRIESTESS OF SEIRYU!?

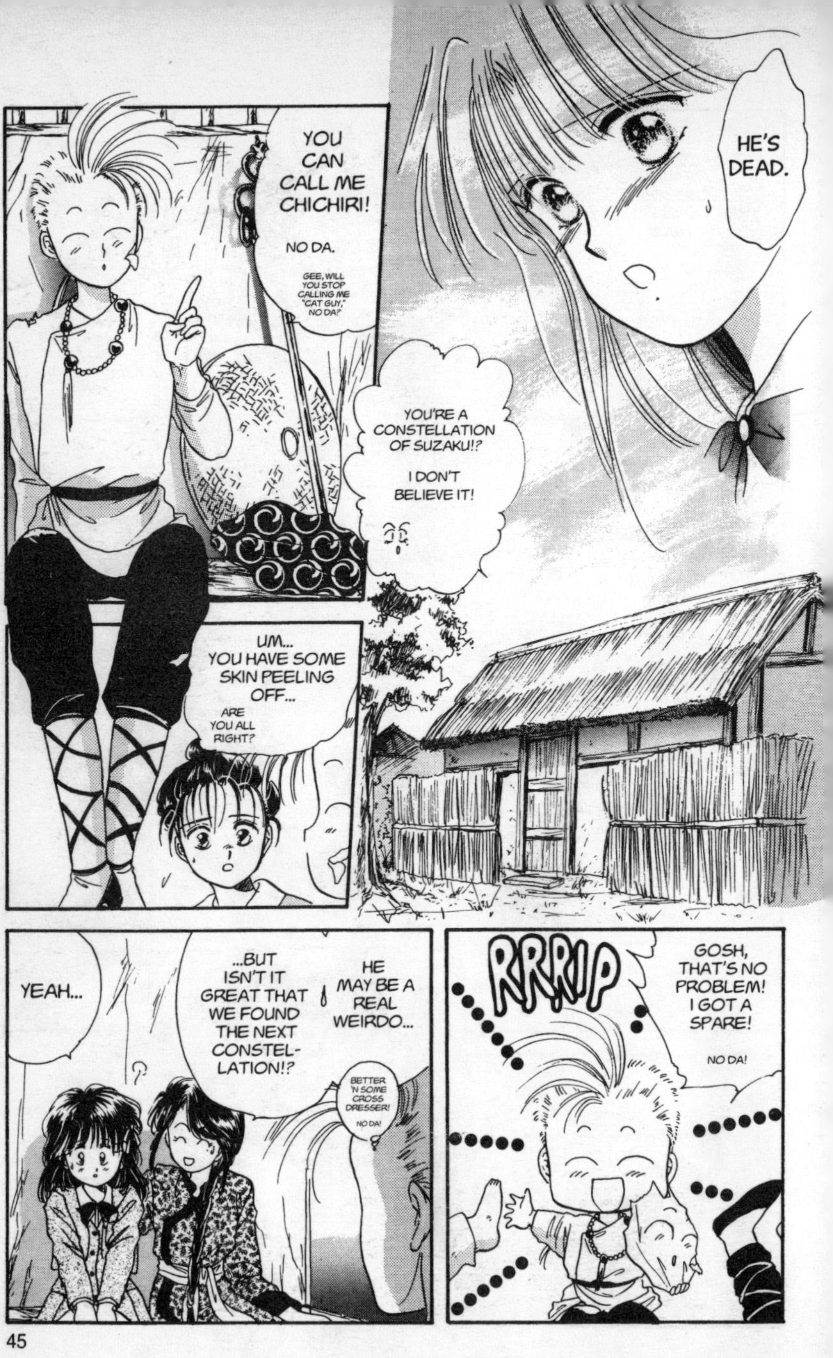
YOU CAN CALL ME CHICHIRI!
NO DA.
GEE, WILL YOU STOP CALLING ME "CAT GUY," NO DA?
YOU'RE A CONSTELLATION OF SUZAKU!?
I DON'T BELIEVE IT!
HE'S DEAD.
UM... YOU HAVE SOME SKIN PEELING OFF...
ARE YOU ALL RIGHT?
YEAH...
HE MAY BE A REAL WEIRDO...
...BUT ISN'T IT GREAT THAT WE FOUND THE NEXT CONSTEL-LATION!?
BETTER 'N SOME CROSS DRESSER! NO DA!
RRRIP
GOSH, THAT'S NO PROBLEM! I GOT A SPARE!
NO DA!

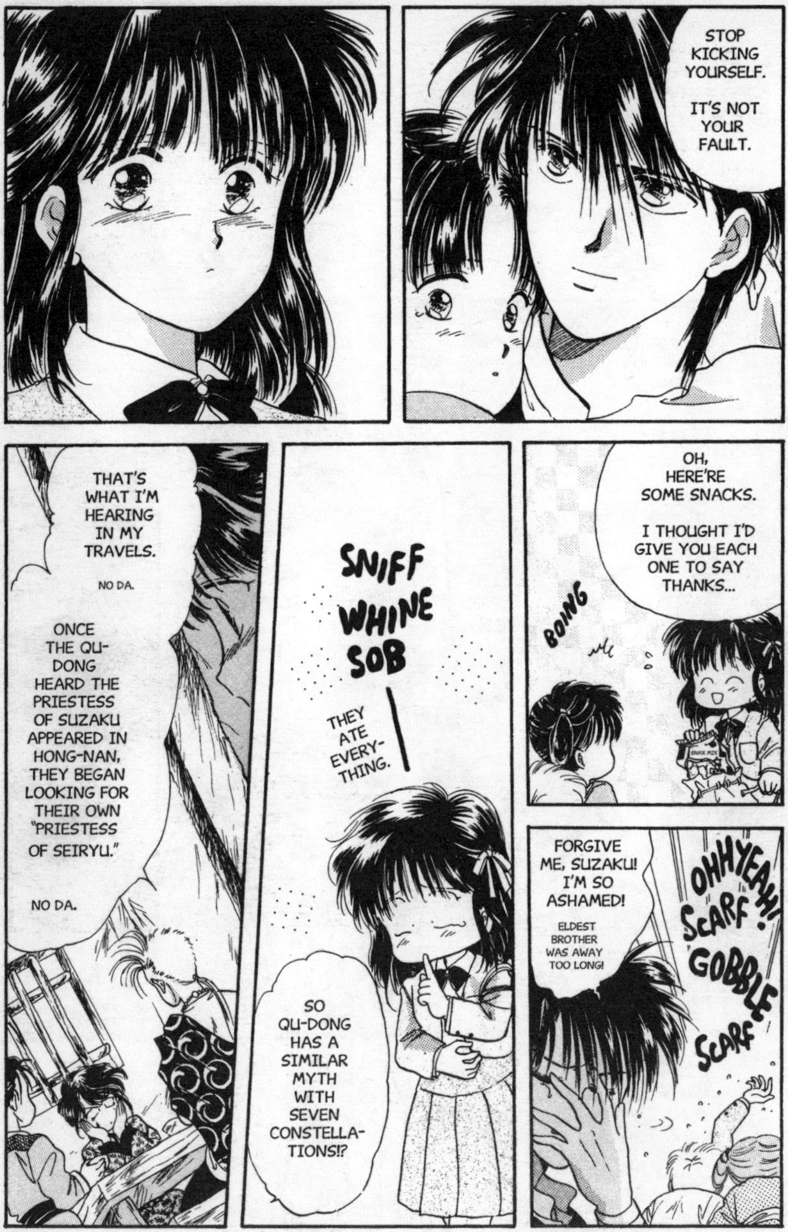
STOP KICKING YOURSELF.
IT'S NOT YOUR FAULT.
THAT'S WHAT I'M HEARING IN MY TRAVELS.
NO DA.
ONCE THE QU-DONG HEARD THE PRIESTESS OF SUZAKU APPEARED IN HONG-NAN, THEY BEGAN LOOKING FOR THEIR OWN "PRIESTESS OF SEIRYU."
NO DA.
SNIFF WHINE SOB
THEY ATE EVERY-THING.
SO QU-DONG HAS A SIMILAR MYTH WITH SEVEN CONSTELLA-TIONS!?
OH, HERE'RE SOME SNACKS.
I THOUGHT I'D GIVE YOU EACH ONE TO SAY THANKS...
BOING
SNAX MIX
FORGIVE ME, SUZAKU! I'M SO ASHAMED!
ELDEST BROTHER WAS AWAY TOO LONG!
OHHYEAH!
SCARF
GOBBLE
SCARF

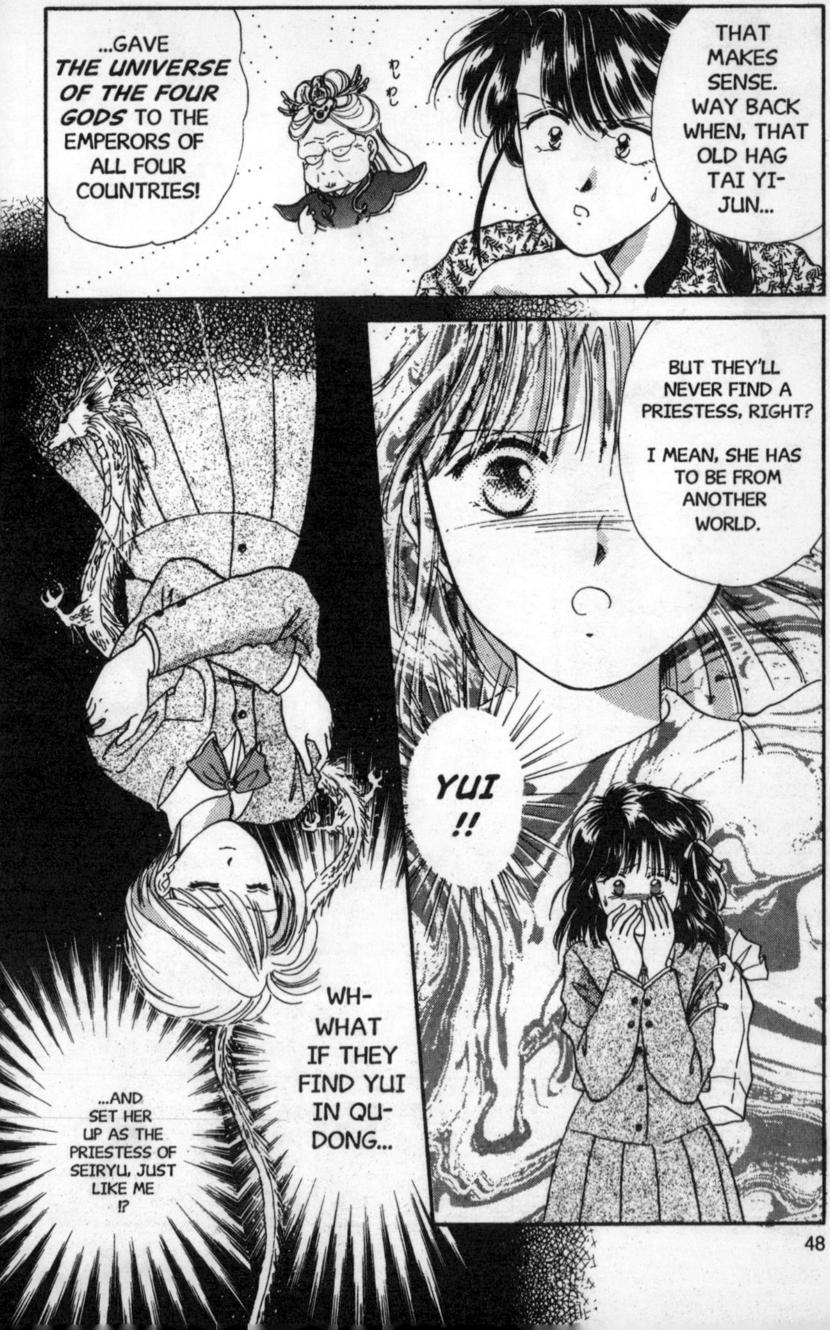
THAT MAKES SENSE. WAY BACK WHEN, THAT OLD HAG TAI YI-JUN...
...GAVE *THE UNIVERSE OF THE FOUR GODS* TO THE EMPERORS OF ALL FOUR COUNTRIES!
BUT THEY'LL NEVER FIND A PRIESTESS, RIGHT?
I MEAN, SHE HAS TO BE FROM ANOTHER WORLD.
YUI !!
WH- WHAT IF THEY FIND YUI IN QU-DONG...
...AND SET HER UP AS THE PRIESTESS OF SEIRYU, JUST LIKE ME !?

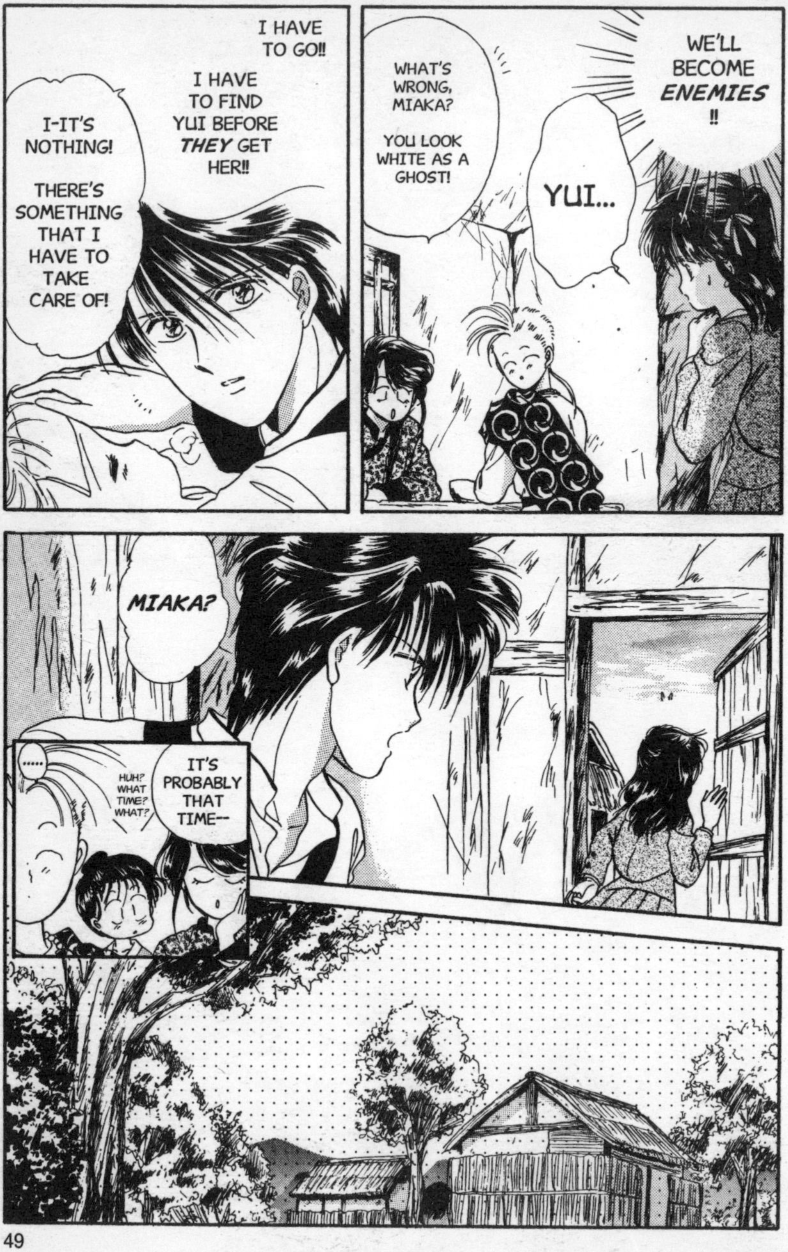

WE'LL BECOME ENEMIES!!
YUI...
WHAT'S WRONG, MIAKA?
YOU LOOK WHITE AS A GHOST!
I HAVE TO GO!!
I HAVE TO FIND YUI BEFORE THEY GET HER!!
I-IT'S NOTHING!
THERE'S SOMETHING THAT I HAVE TO TAKE CARE OF!
MIAKA?
IT'S PROBABLY THAT TIME--
HUH? WHAT TIME? WHAT?
......

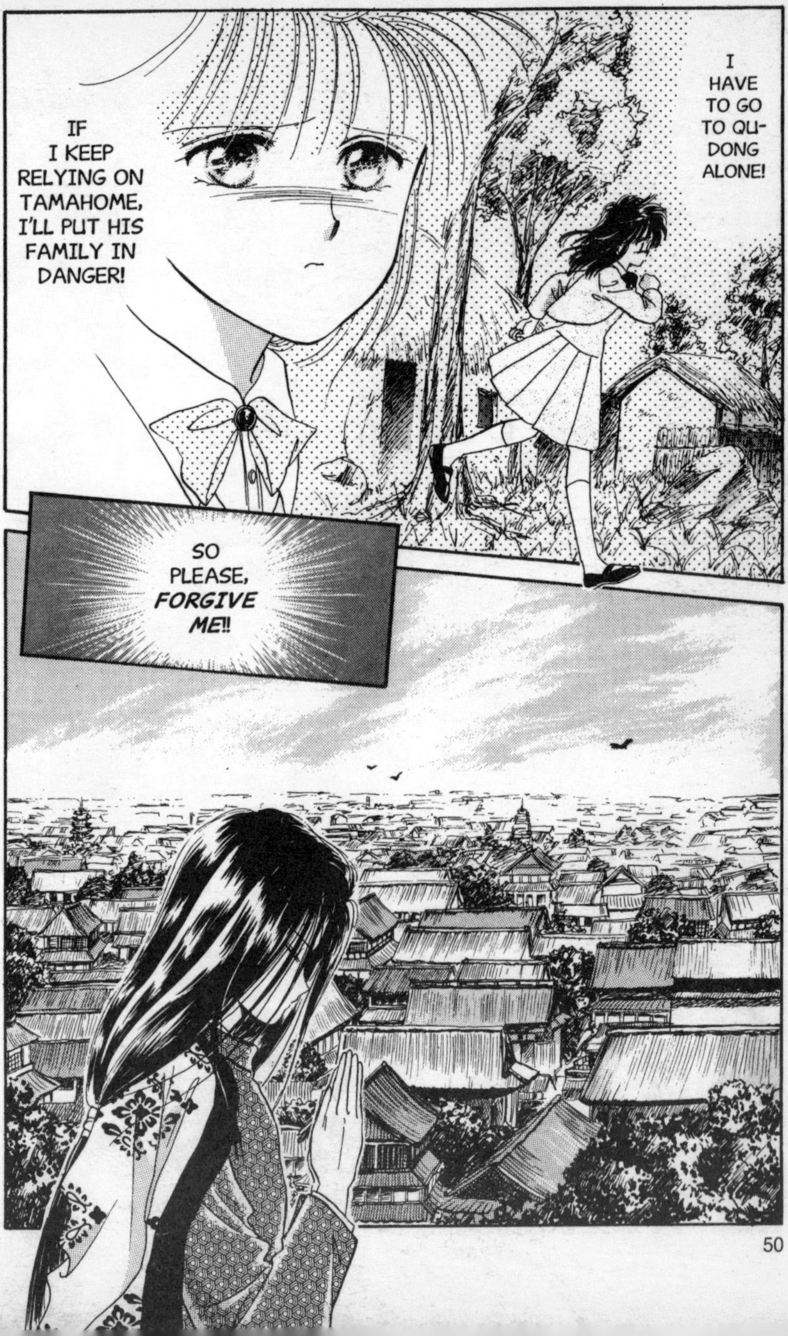
IF I KEEP RELYING ON TAMAHOME, I'LL PUT HIS FAMILY IN DANGER!
I HAVE TO GO TO QU-DONG ALONE!
SO PLEASE, *FORGIVE ME!!*

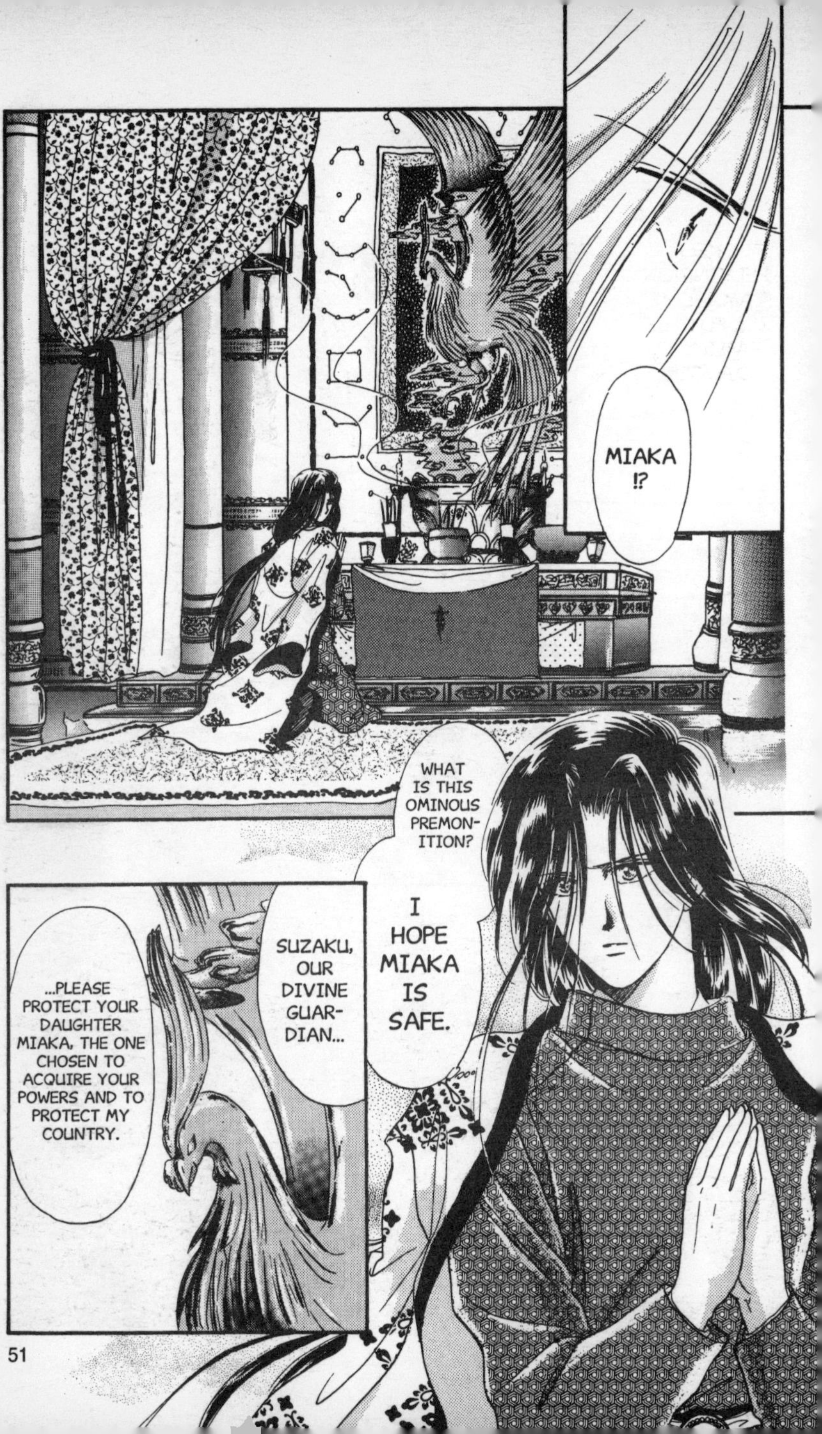
MIAKA !?
WHAT IS THIS OMINOUS PREMON- ITION?
I HOPE MIAKA IS SAFE.
SUZAKU, OUR DIVINE GUAR- DIAN...
...PLEASE PROTECT YOUR DAUGHTER MIAKA, THE ONE CHOSEN TO ACQUIRE YOUR POWERS AND TO PROTECT MY COUNTRY.

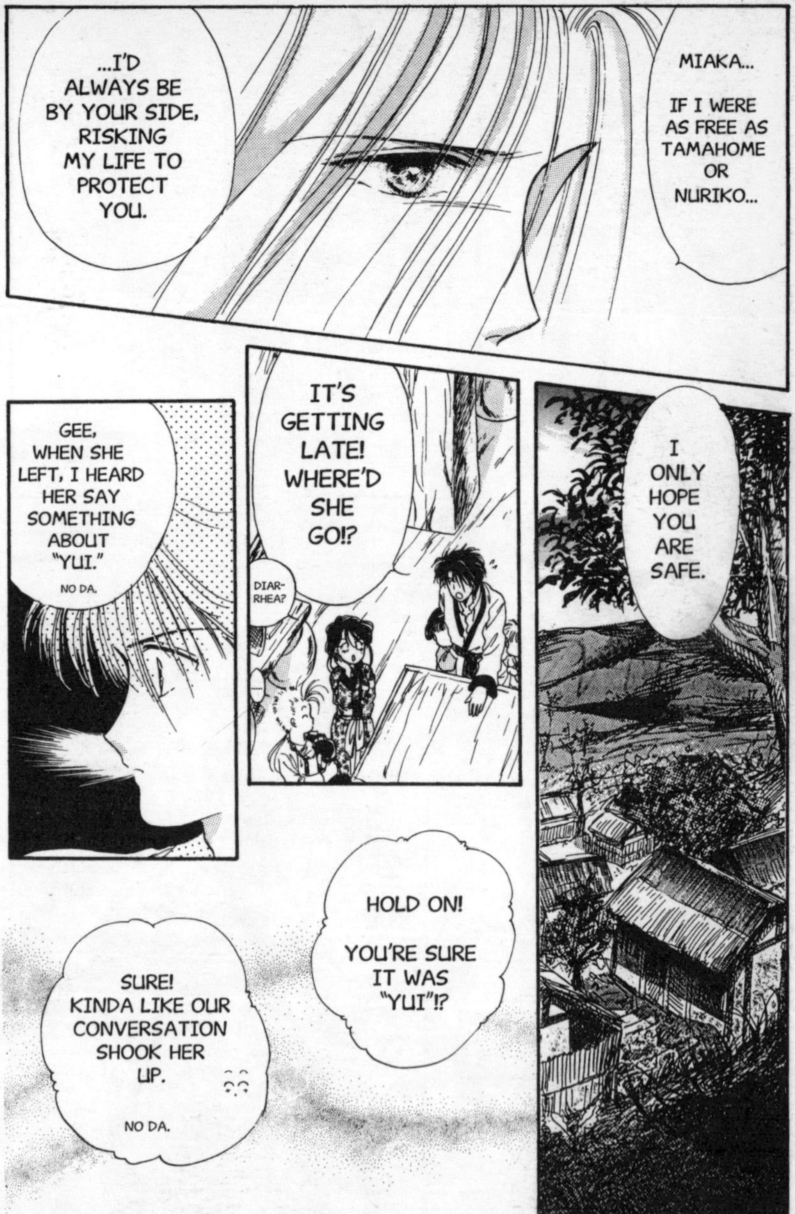
MIAKA...
IF I WERE AS FREE AS TAMAHOME OR NURIKO...
...I'D ALWAYS BE BY YOUR SIDE, RISKING MY LIFE TO PROTECT YOU.
I ONLY HOPE YOU ARE SAFE.
IT'S GETTING LATE! WHERE'D SHE GO!?
DIARRHEA?
GEE, WHEN SHE LEFT, I HEARD HER SAY SOMETHING ABOUT "YUI."
NO DA.
HOLD ON!
YOU'RE SURE IT WAS "YUI"!?
SURE! KINDA LIKE OUR CONVERSATION SHOOK HER UP.
NO DA.

GASP

YUI...

WAS SHE THE ONE WITH MIAKA WHEN WE FIRST MET?

SO SHE MAY BE IN THIS WORLD, TOO?

TAMAHOME!?

NURIKO, CHICHIRI!!

LOOK AFTER MY FAMILY!!

GOSH, LOOKS LIKE I'LL HAVE TO CHECK THIS OUT, TOO.

NO DA.

WHAT'S GOING ON!?

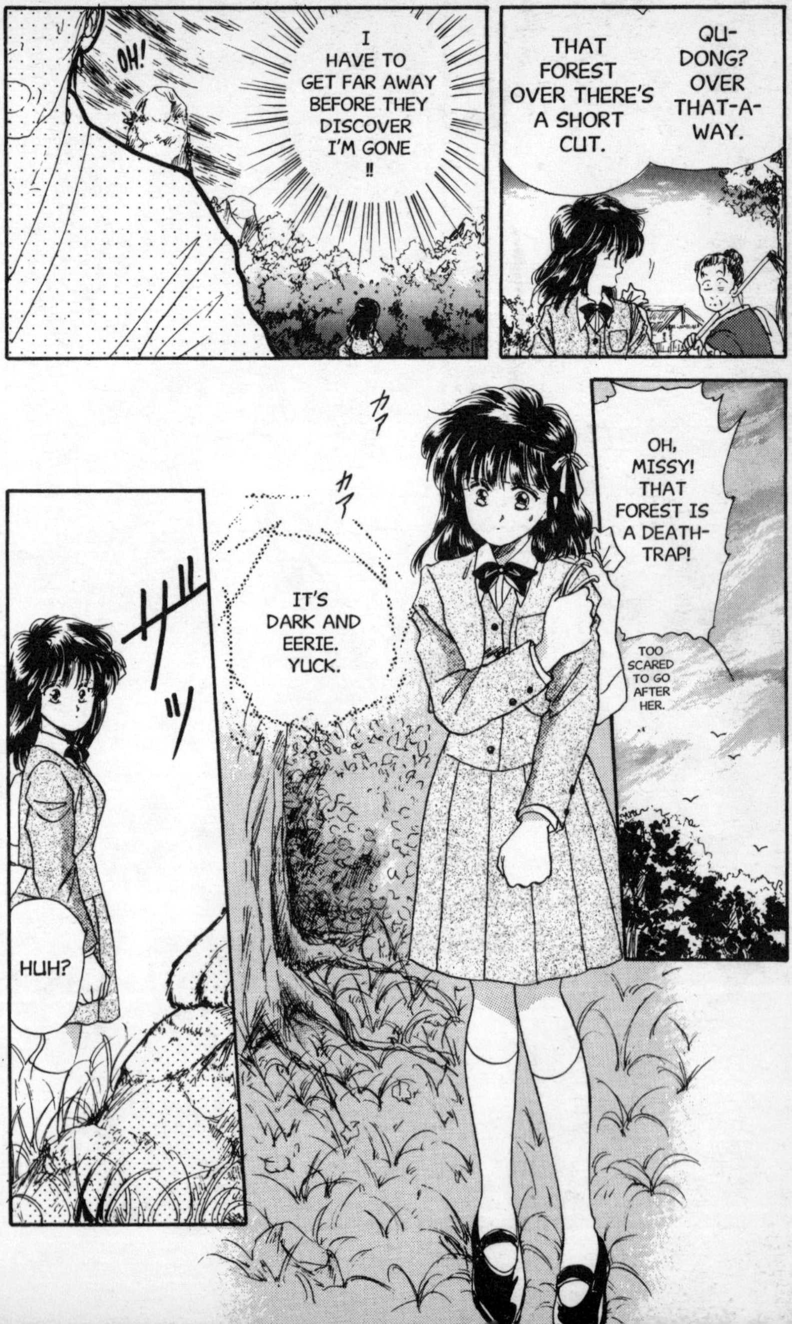
QU-DONG? OVER THAT-A-WAY.
THAT FOREST OVER THERE'S A SHORT CUT.
OH!
I HAVE TO GET FAR AWAY BEFORE THEY DISCOVER I'M GONE!!
OH, MISSY! THAT FOREST IS A DEATH-TRAP!
TOO SCARED TO GO AFTER HER.
カァ
カァ
IT'S DARK AND EERIE. YUCK.
ザッ
HUH?

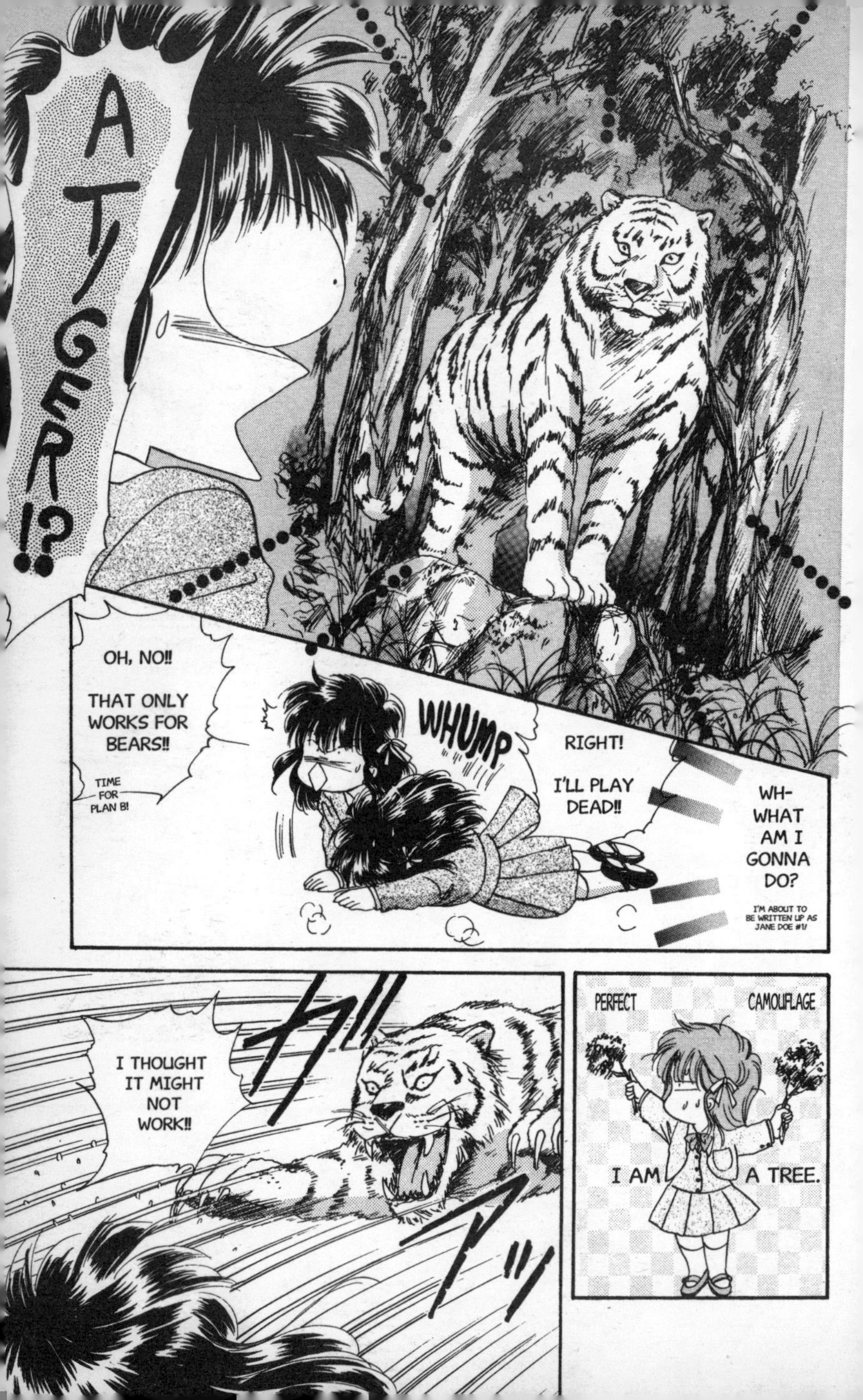
A TIGER!?
OH, NO!!
THAT ONLY WORKS FOR BEARS!!
TIME FOR PLAN B!
WHUMP
RIGHT!
I'LL PLAY DEAD!!
WH-WHAT AM I GONNA DO?
I'M ABOUT TO BE WRITTEN UP AS JANE DOE #1!
PERFECT CAMOUFLAGE
I AM A TREE.
I THOUGHT IT MIGHT NOT WORK!!

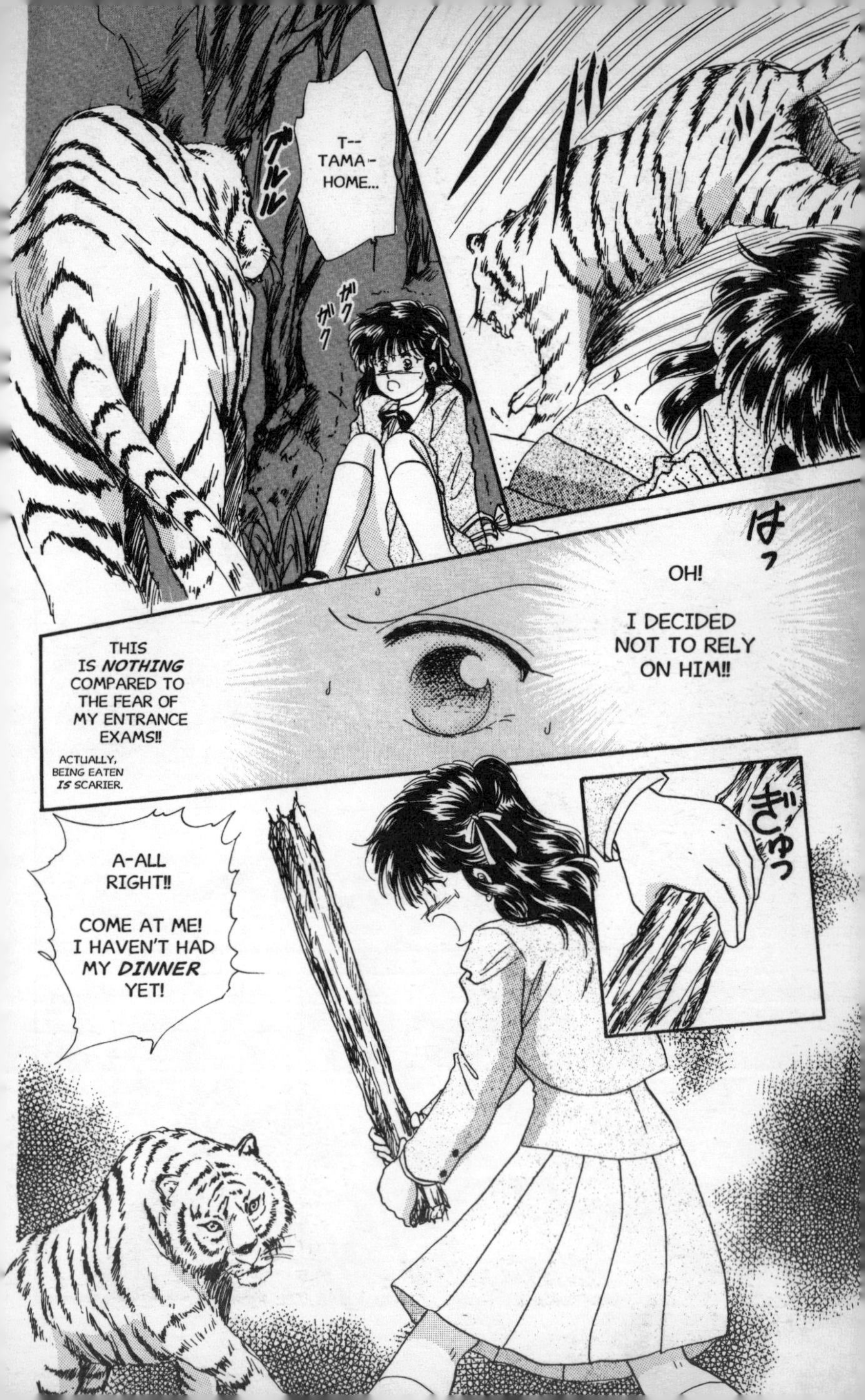

グルル
T-- TAMA-HOME...
ガクガク
はっ
OH!
I DECIDED NOT TO RELY ON HIM!!
THIS IS *NOTHING* COMPARED TO THE FEAR OF MY ENTRANCE EXAMS!!
ACTUALLY, BEING EATEN *IS* SCARIER.
ぎゅっ
A-ALL RIGHT!!
COME AT ME! I HAVEN'T HAD MY *DINNER* YET!

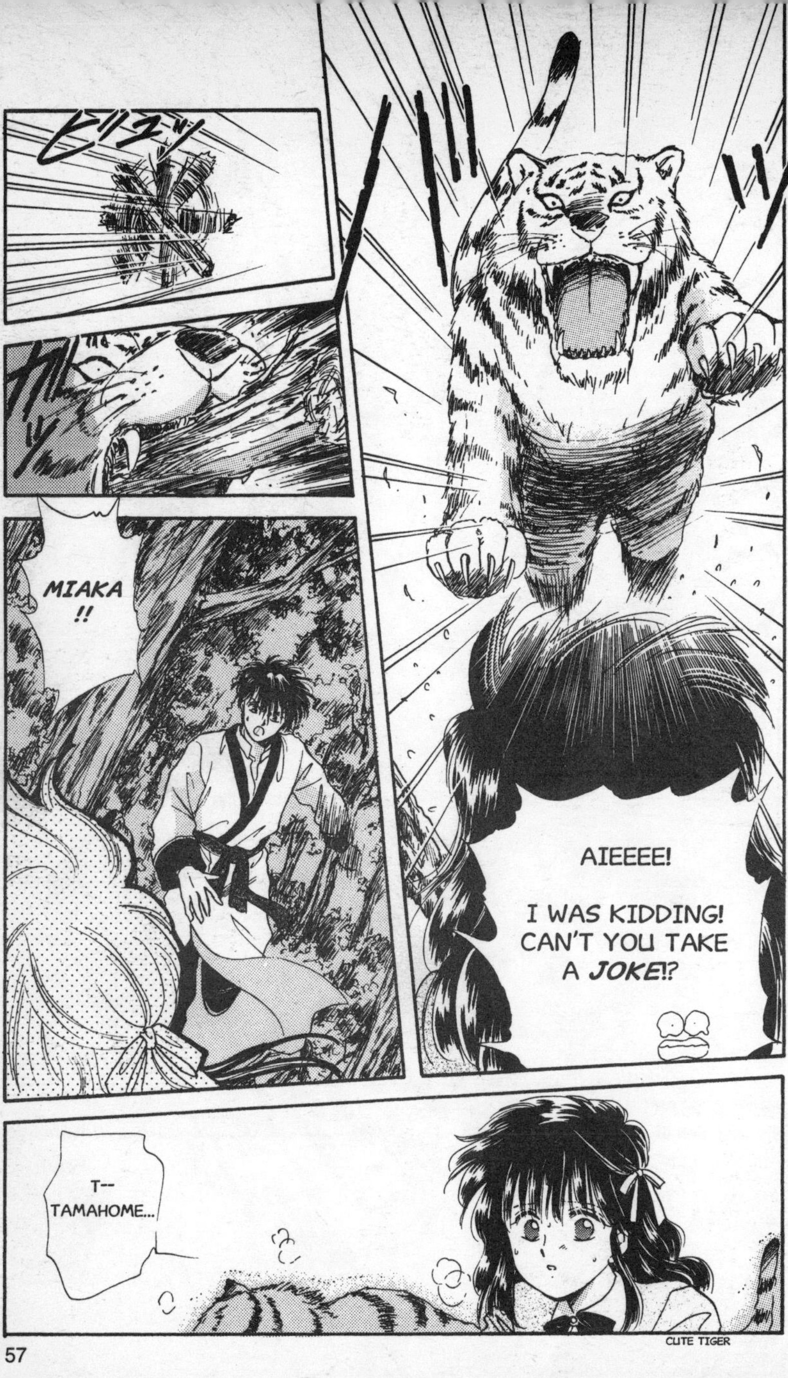
AIEEEE!
I WAS KIDDING! CAN'T YOU TAKE A *JOKE*!?
MIAKA !!
T-- TAMAHOME...

CUTE TIGER

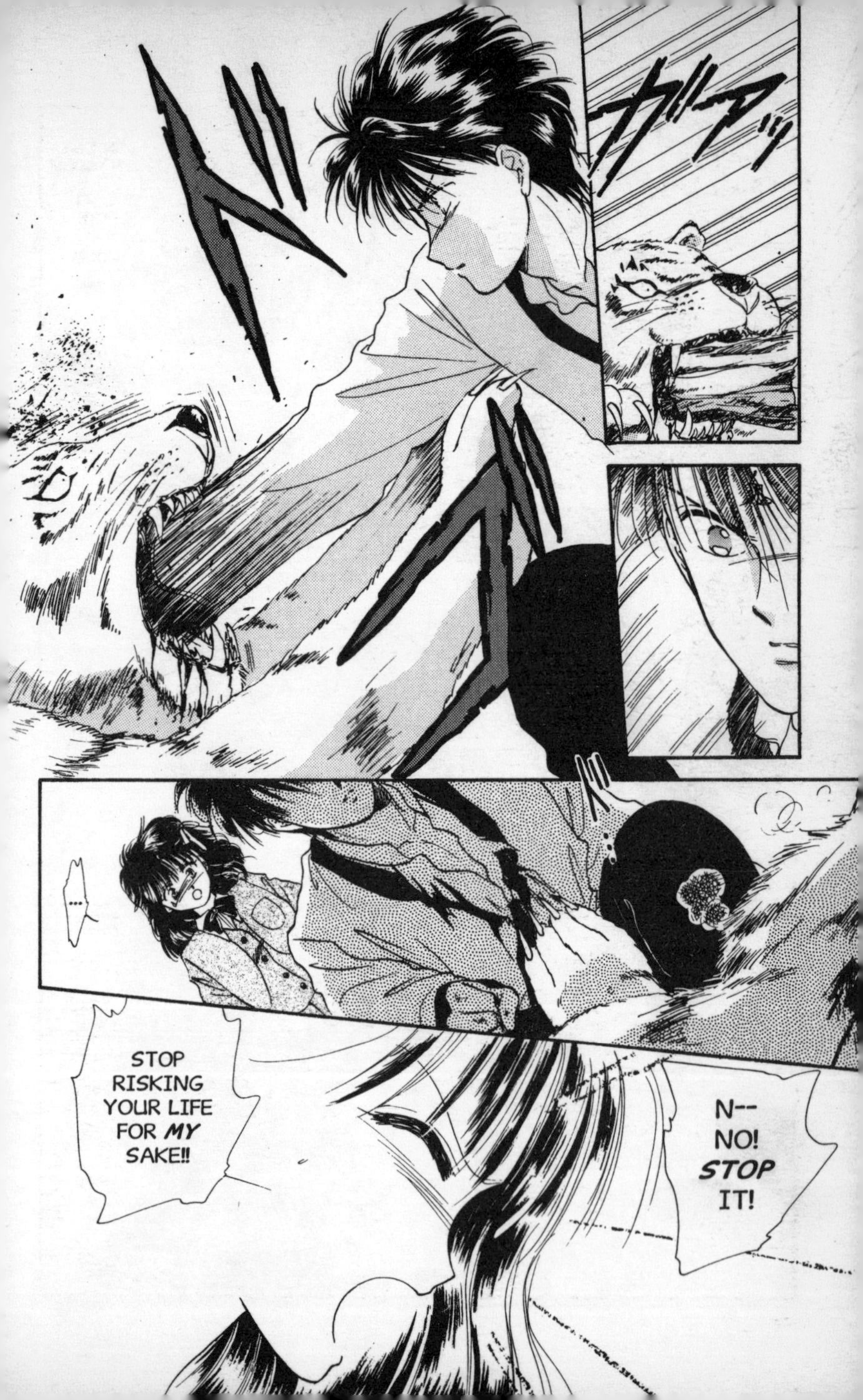
...
N-- NO! *STOP* IT!
STOP RISKING YOUR LIFE FOR *MY* SAKE!!

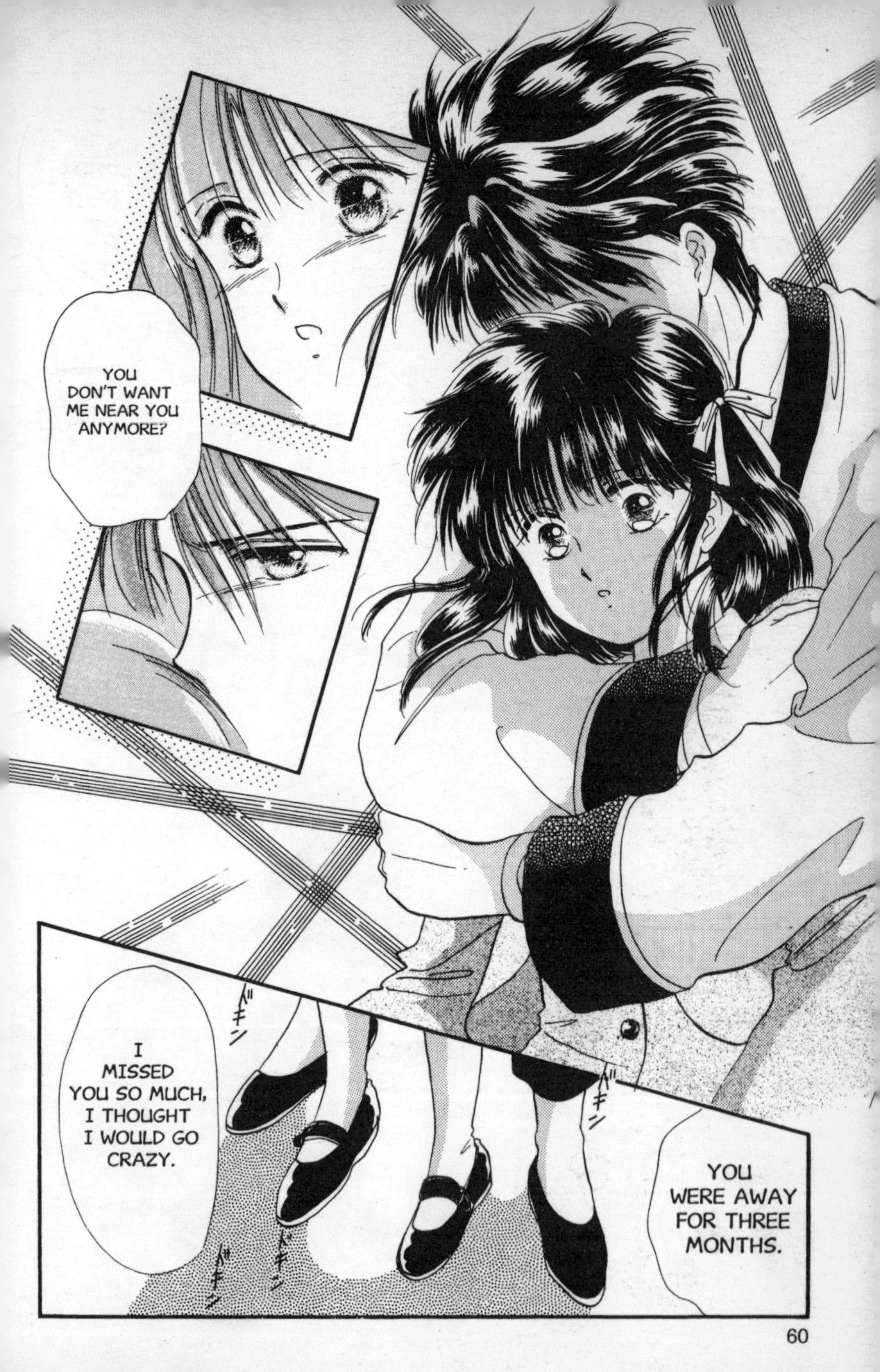
YOU DON'T WANT ME NEAR YOU ANYMORE?
YOU WERE AWAY FOR THREE MONTHS.
I MISSED YOU SO MUCH, I THOUGHT I WOULD GO CRAZY.

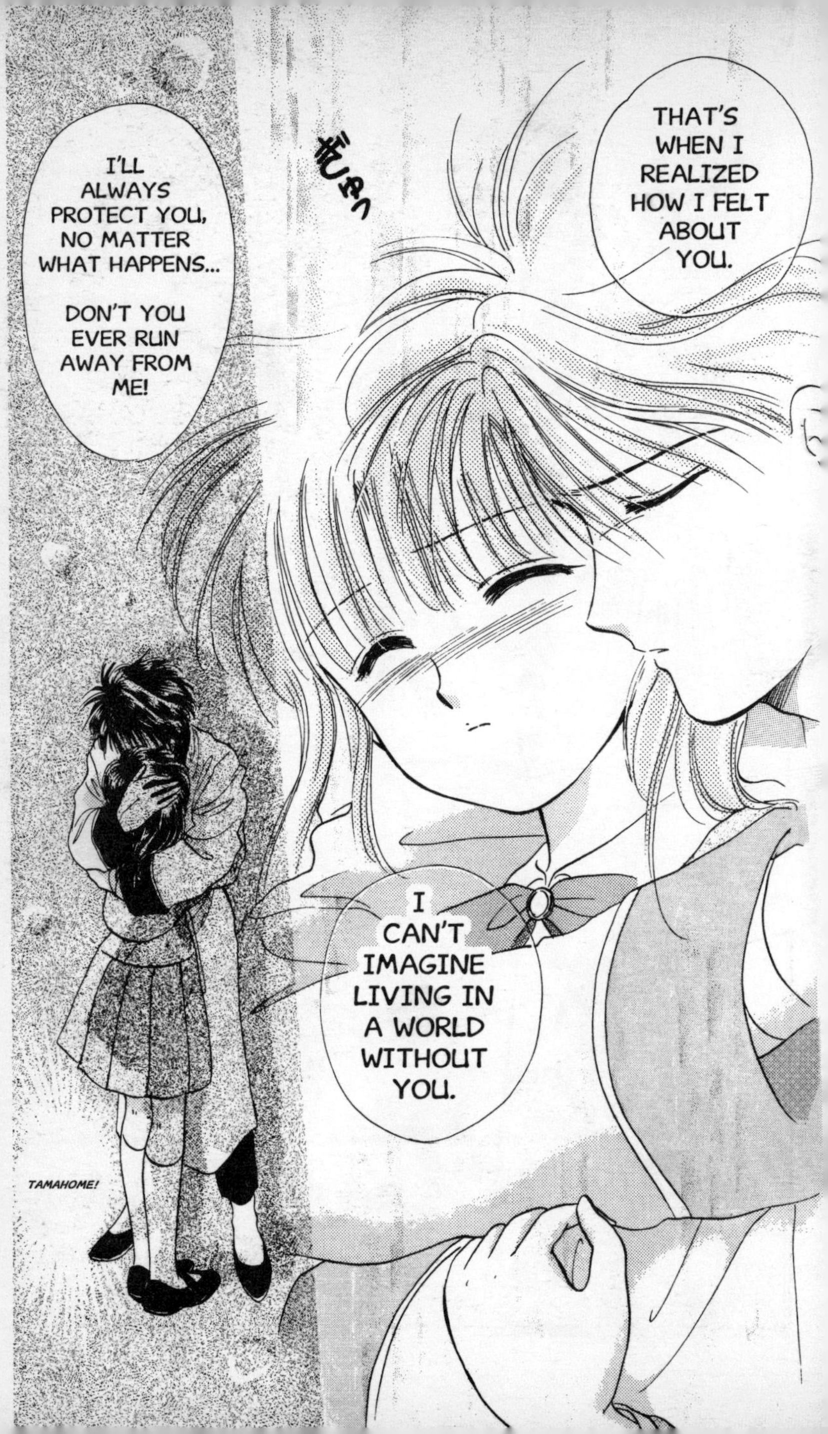
THAT'S WHEN I REALIZED HOW I FELT ABOUT YOU.
ぎゅっ
I'LL ALWAYS PROTECT YOU, NO MATTER WHAT HAPPENS...
DON'T YOU EVER RUN AWAY FROM ME!
I CAN'T IMAGINE LIVING IN A WORLD WITHOUT YOU.
TAMAHOME!

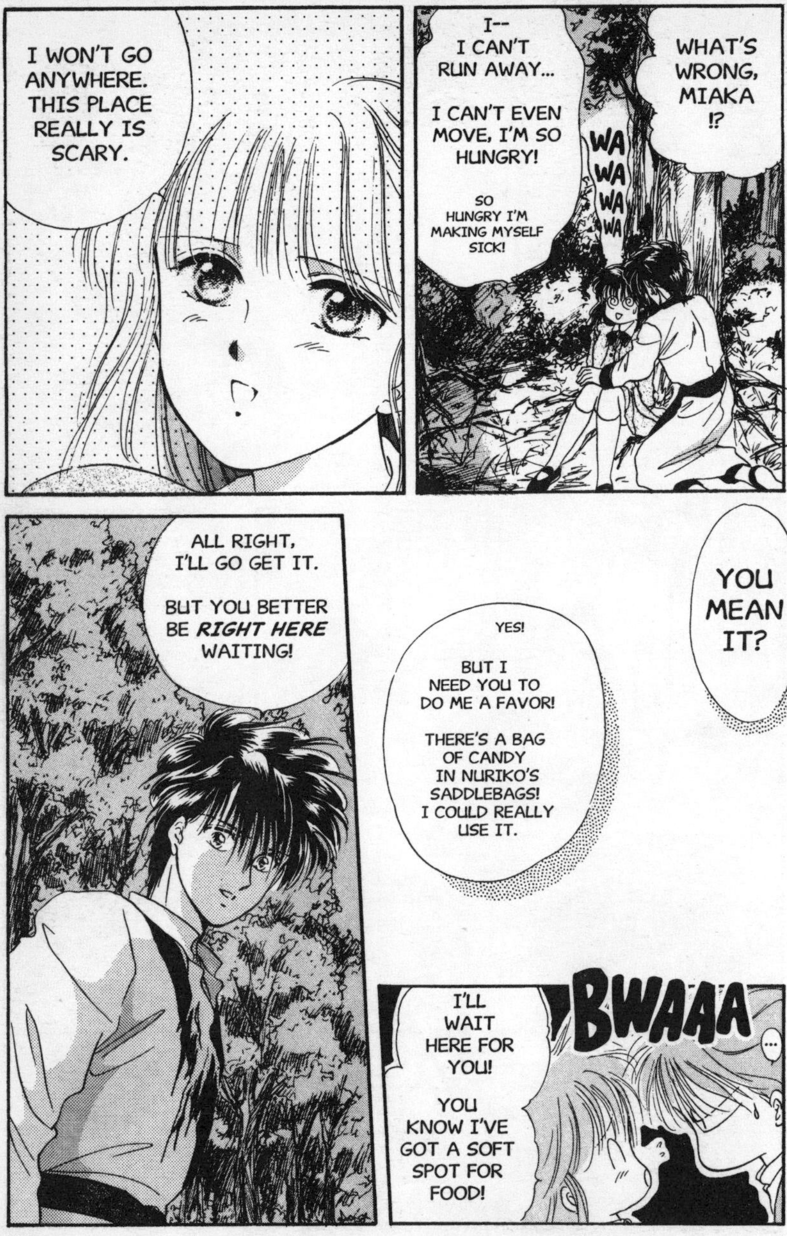

I WON'T GO ANYWHERE. THIS PLACE REALLY IS SCARY.
WHAT'S WRONG, MIAKA !?
I-- I CAN'T RUN AWAY... I CAN'T EVEN MOVE, I'M SO HUNGRY!
WA WA WA WA
SO HUNGRY I'M MAKING MYSELF SICK!
YOU MEAN IT?
YES! BUT I NEED YOU TO DO ME A FAVOR! THERE'S A BAG OF CANDY IN NURIKO'S SADDLEBAGS! I COULD REALLY USE IT.
ALL RIGHT, I'LL GO GET IT. BUT YOU BETTER BE *RIGHT HERE* WAITING!
I'LL WAIT HERE FOR YOU! YOU KNOW I'VE GOT A SOFT SPOT FOR FOOD!
BWAAA
...

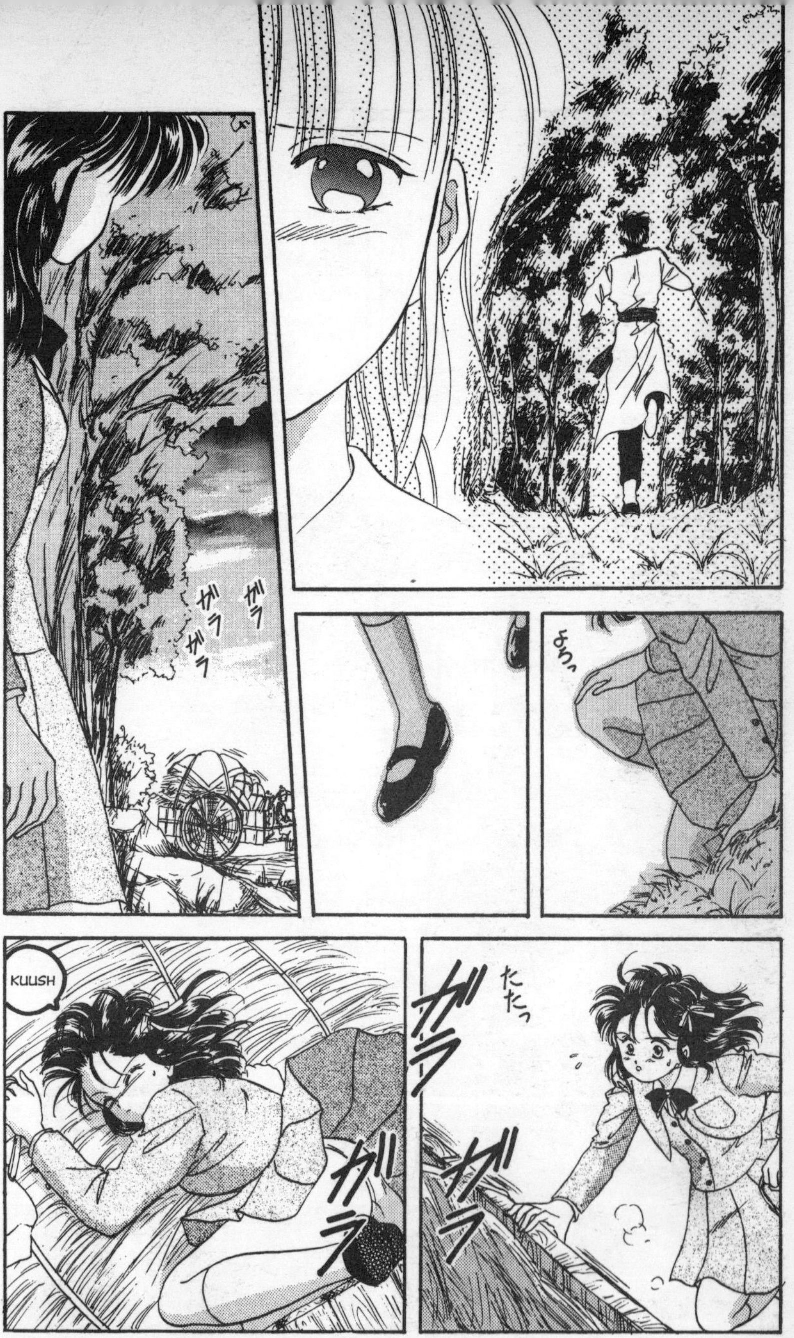
ガラ
ガラ
ガラ
よろっ
KUUSH
たたっ
ガラ
ガラ
ガラ
ガラ

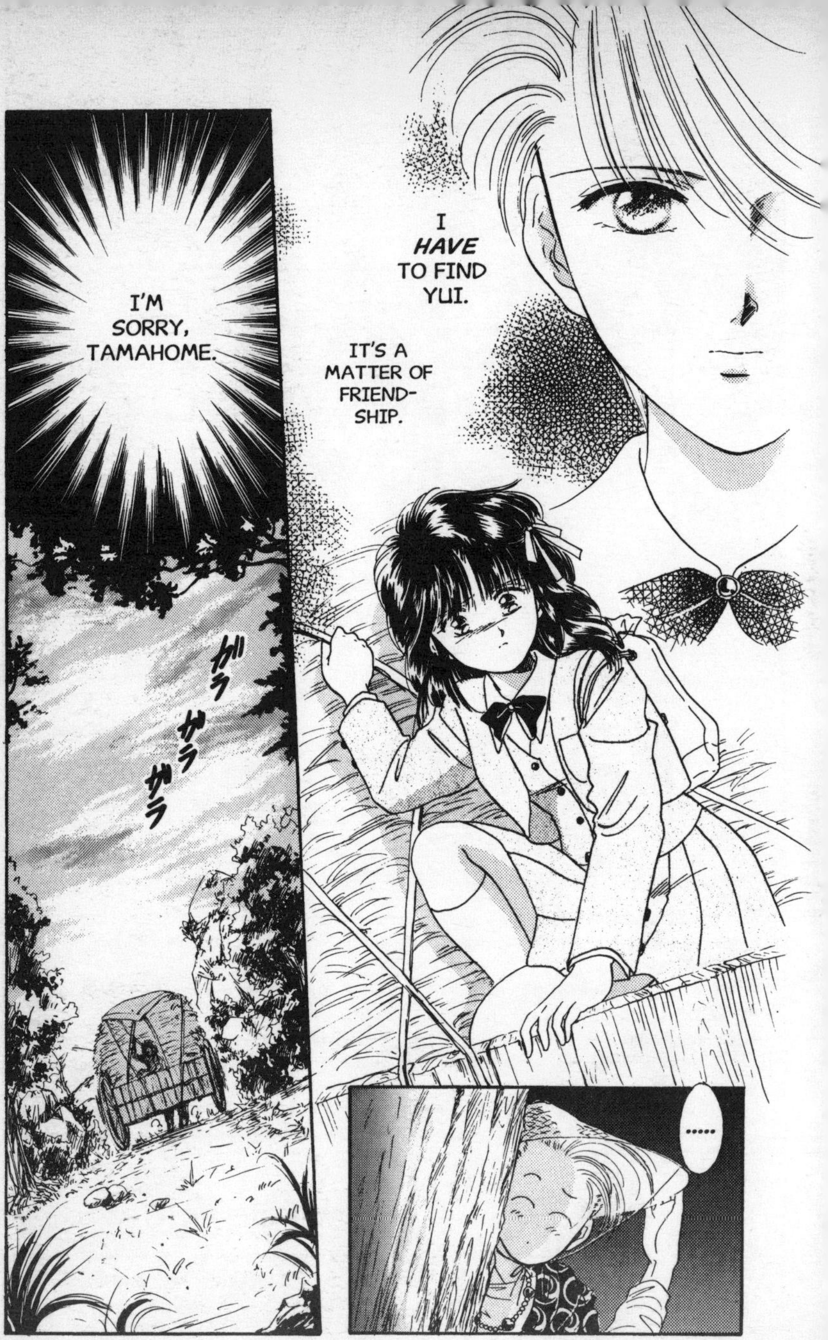
I *HAVE* TO FIND YUI.
IT'S A MATTER OF FRIEND-SHIP.
I'M SORRY, TAMAHOME.
ガラ ガラ ガラ
......

Xong 琼　Gui 鬼　Siu 宿

Cancer

T A M A H O M E

A natural-born talent

- Born in Bai-Jiang Village, Shou-Shuang Prefecture, Hong-Nan.
  Birthday is sometime between February and May (Because he's a constellation of Suzaku).
  Presently 17 years old.
- Relations: father, 2 brothers, 2 sisters. Mother: Died when he was 12 years old. Strengths: Martial arts
- Height: 5'9"　　　Blood type: O　　　Hobby: Making money
- Eldest son taking the place of his ill father to support his family. Whatta great big brother! He's very caring, but at the same time, he can cause a lot of trouble for others. But everyone cuts him a break. On the outside, he is very chipper, and that leads to some comic expressions. But he's tough on the inside (so he thinks). On the other hand, he is very shy. (He had to become stoic for his family's sake.) That's why he was hard on Miaka in the first issue. Sacrifices himself for the sake of others, and won't back down against an enemy.

It looks like you've all become accustomed to the Tamahome with short hair, but have you noticed how his hair's grown since graphic novel #2? My assistants and I complain about how none of the readers wrote in concerning it.

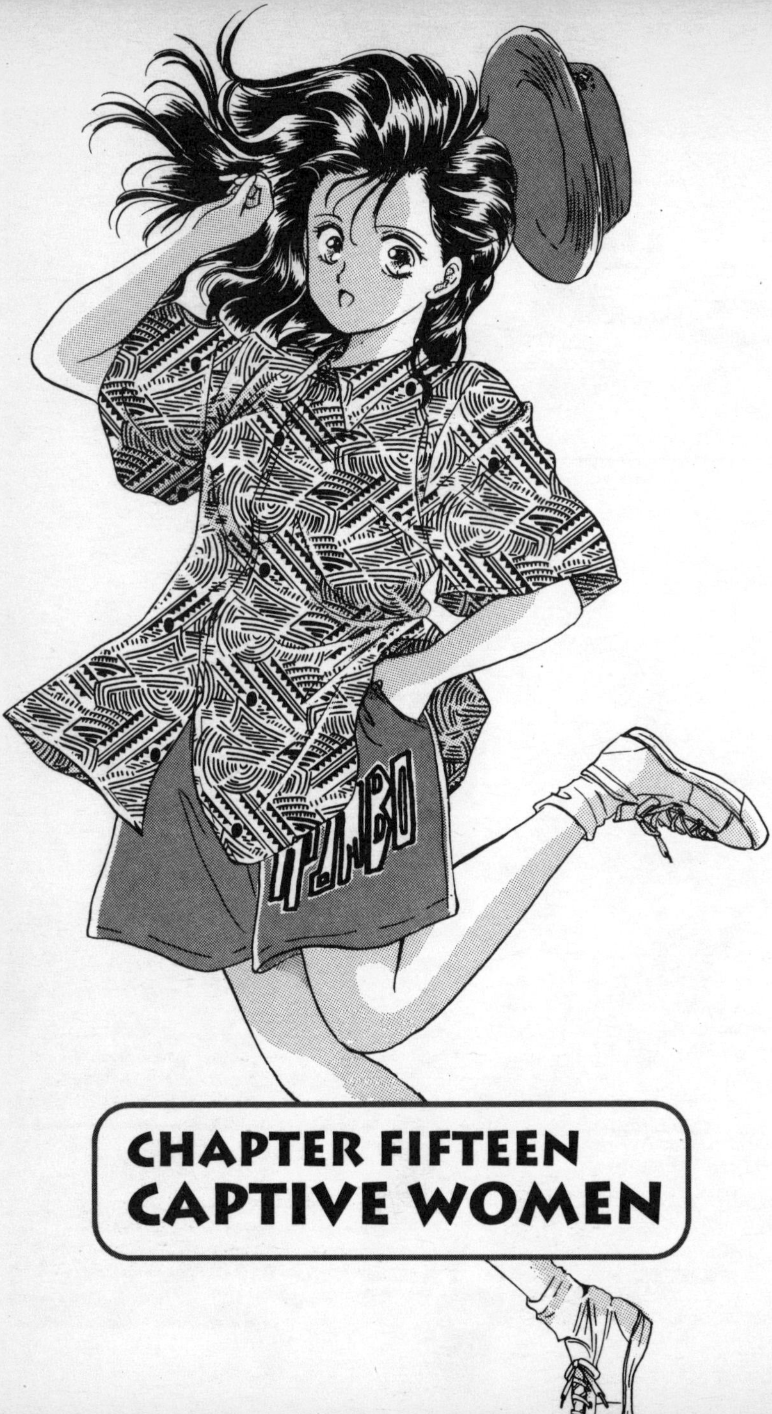

CHAPTER FIFTEEN
CAPTIVE WOMEN

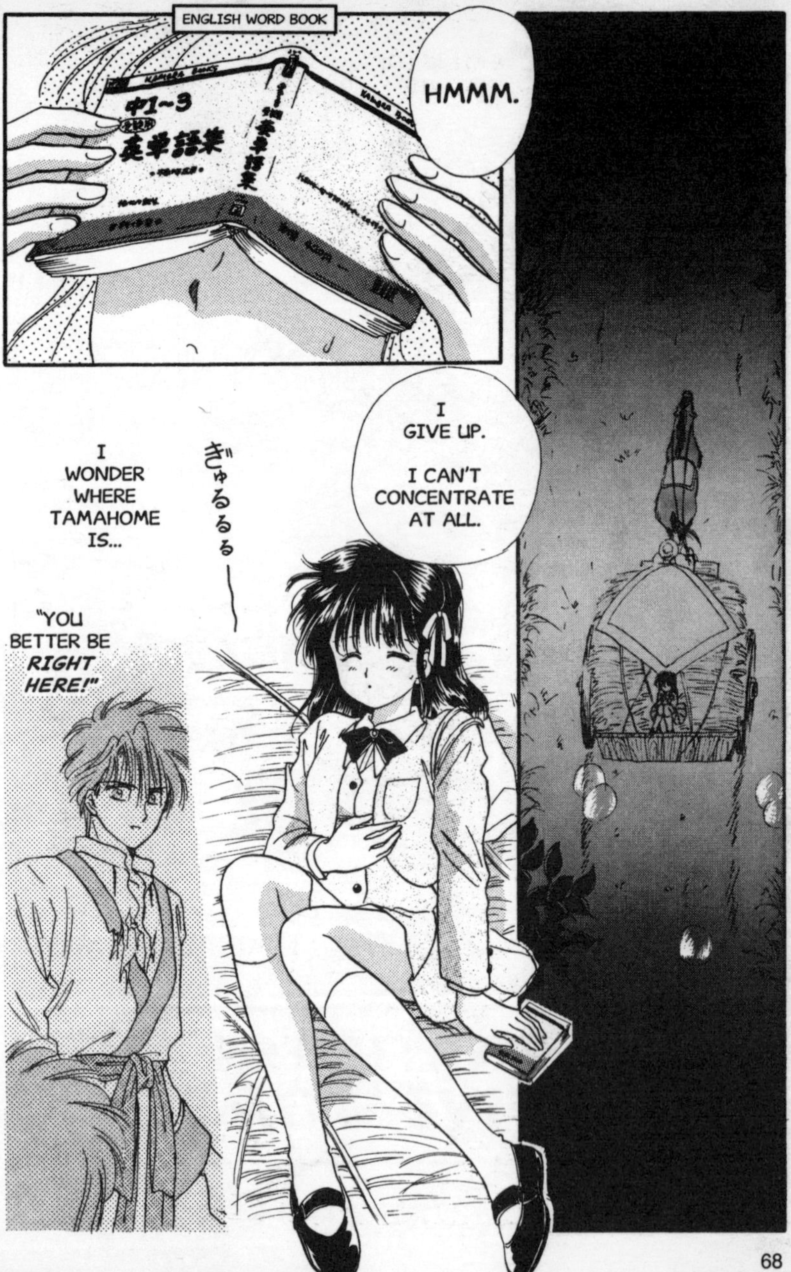
ENGLISH WORD BOOK
HMMM.
I GIVE UP. I CAN'T CONCENTRATE AT ALL.
ぎゅるるる――
I WONDER WHERE TAMAHOME IS...
"YOU BETTER BE *RIGHT HERE!*"

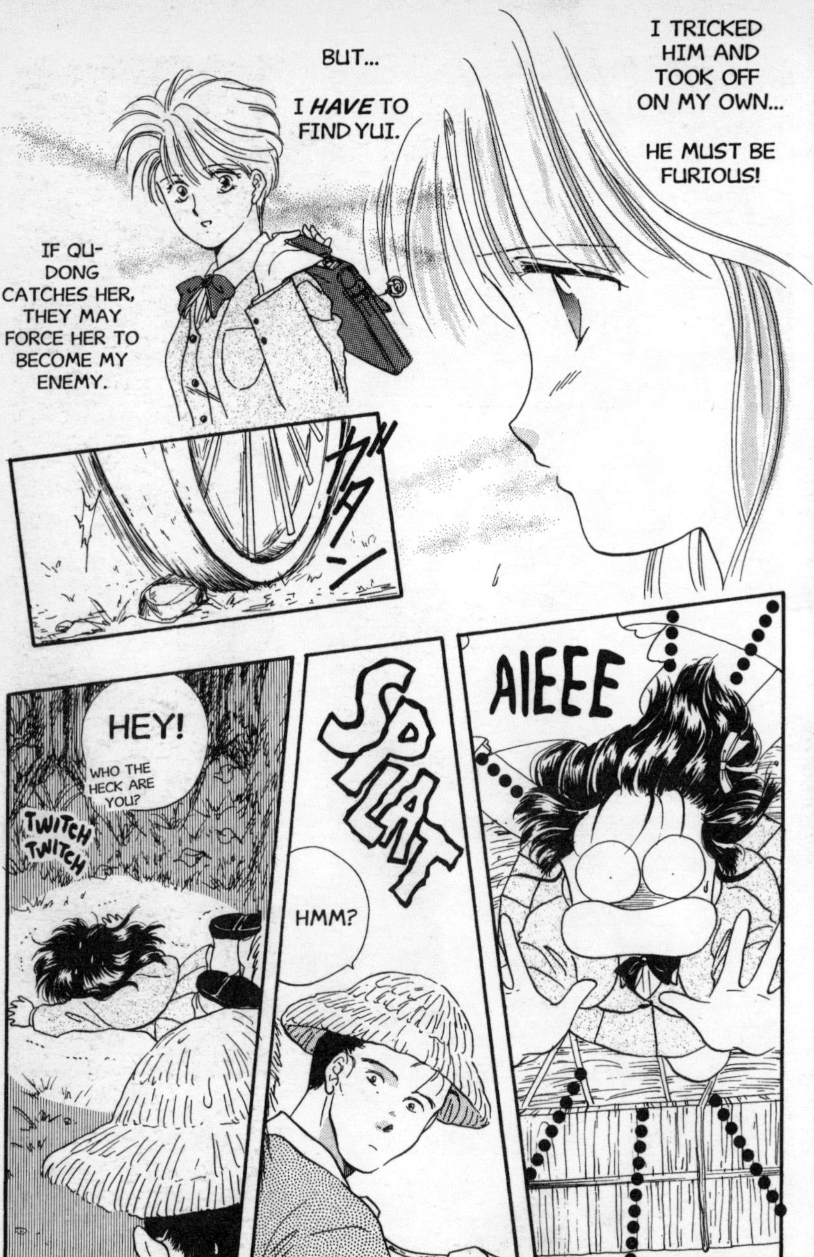

I TRICKED HIM AND TOOK OFF ON MY OWN...
HE MUST BE FURIOUS!
BUT...
I *HAVE* TO FIND YUI.
IF QU-DONG CATCHES HER, THEY MAY FORCE HER TO BECOME MY ENEMY.
ガタン
AIEEE
SPLAT
HMM?
HEY!
WHO THE HECK ARE YOU?
TWITCH TWITCH

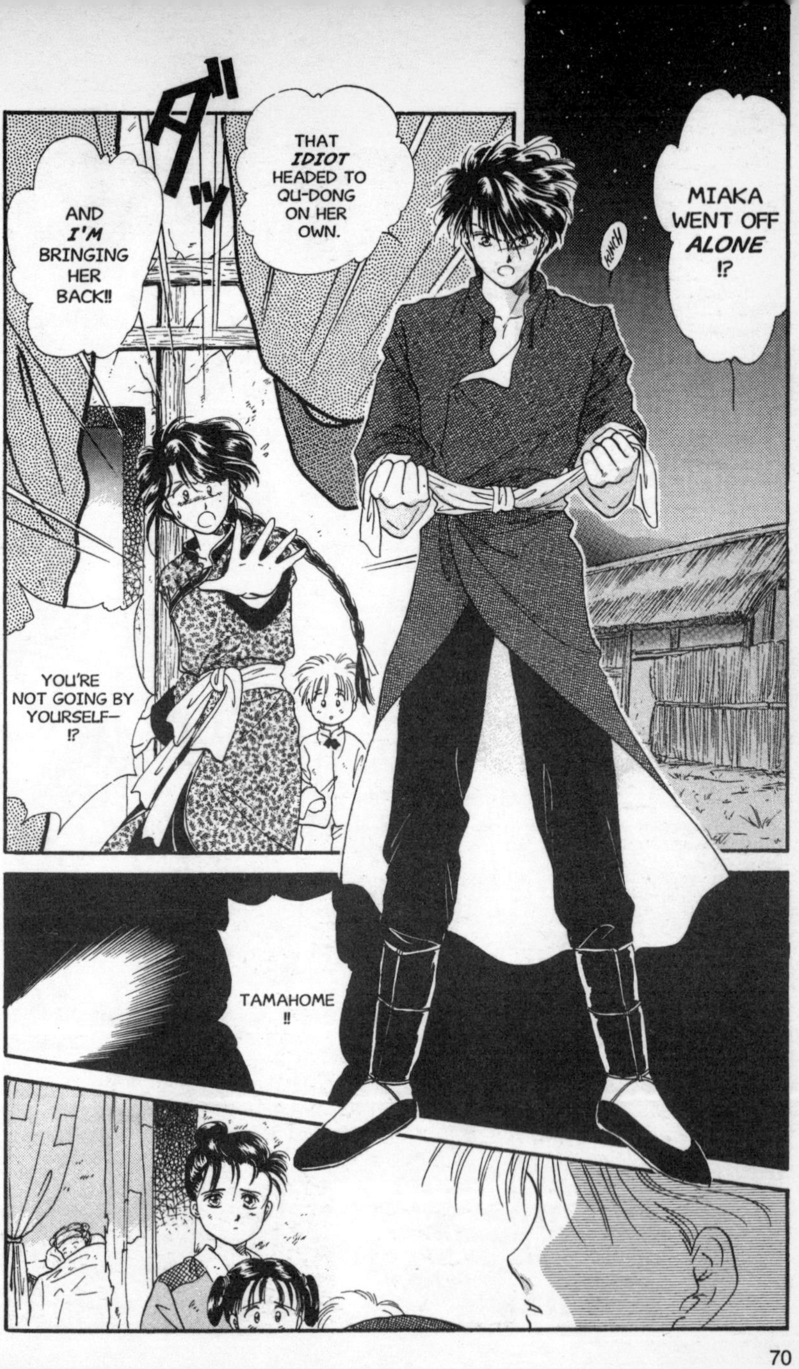
MIAKA WENT OFF *ALONE* !?
KINCH
THAT *IDIOT* HEADED TO QU-DONG ON HER OWN.
AND *I'M* BRINGING HER BACK!!
YOU'RE NOT GOING BY YOURSELF— !?
TAMAHOME !!

I was so busy this year, I wasn't able to go home for the annual festival. But much to my amazement, even though I was in Tokyo, the festivals were given a lot of coverage on TV!! I used to think my area was the middle of the boonies, but I guess it's becoming famous. But I couldn't look when one of the ceremonial wagons went crashing into a telephone pole, killing seven people! Things were out of control! What's going on Kishi---da!? (Must remain anonymous.)

If I'd gone home, I would've been both furious and terrified. But I have no problem watching it on TV. Hmm. Maybe I should have promoted myself more when I lived there. (Promoted what!?) My little brother really wanted to go back, but my mom isn't too thrilled with the idea. (She's scared.)

My parents were born in Osaka so they're not actually from the town. But the minute I hear the sound of those taiko drums, it starts my blood flowing.

When I was a senior in high school, I always went to the festival wearing a happi coat, but I didn't pull the float. Now guys look pretty good in happi coats. The designs vary from town to town, but our town's design was simple (white lettering on black cloth). The whole town preferred that festival even to New Year's. Town natives who moved away to places over the country take vacations to come home for the festival. (I didn't. Sorry!) They even close down the grade schools for it. Amazing, really! The downtown district has its festival in September, and the uptown district has its in October. The uptown kids (like me) had vacation days for both. The year after I moved to Tokyo when I came back for the festival, my cousin (♀) was pulling the float when she fell, but she held onto the rope for a couple dozen meters. Even though she was scraped and bleeding, she caught her feet and still helped out. If you let go of the rope, you get run over by the float, so you can't let go even if you fall. Of course, some of the older guys act as guardians to save you in case of an accident. It can be scary. Anyway, a lot of famous people are from the area. Kiyohara of the Seibu Lions, the designers, the Koshinos (former neighbors of mine) and a few actors.... I'm the first manga artist to come from there (I think).

I'll go back next year!

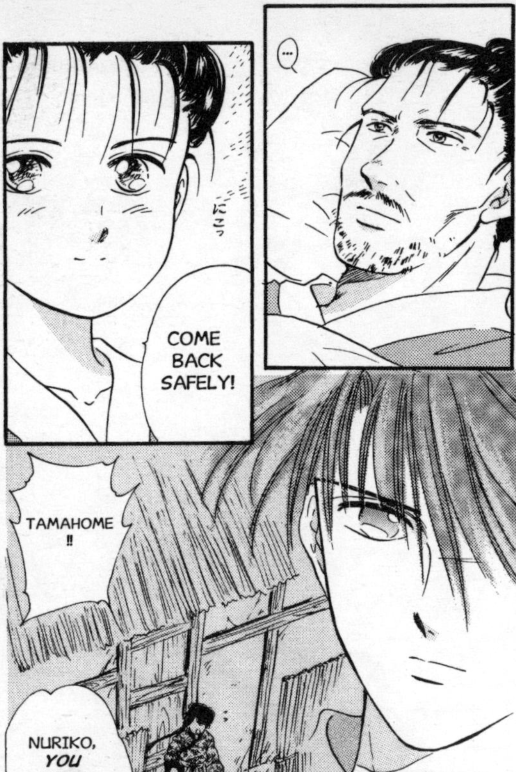

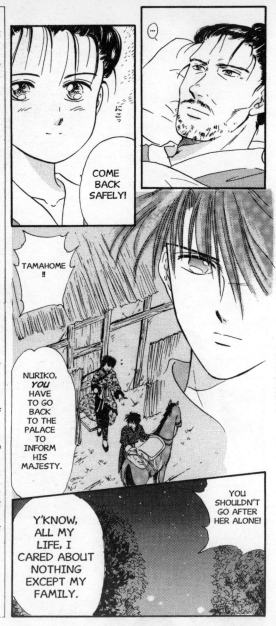

...
にこっ
COME BACK SAFELY!
TAMAHOME !!
NURIKO, YOU HAVE TO GO BACK TO THE PALACE TO INFORM HIS MAJESTY.
YOU SHOULDN'T GO AFTER HER ALONE!
Y'KNOW, ALL MY LIFE, I CARED ABOUT NOTHING EXCEPT MY FAMILY.

73

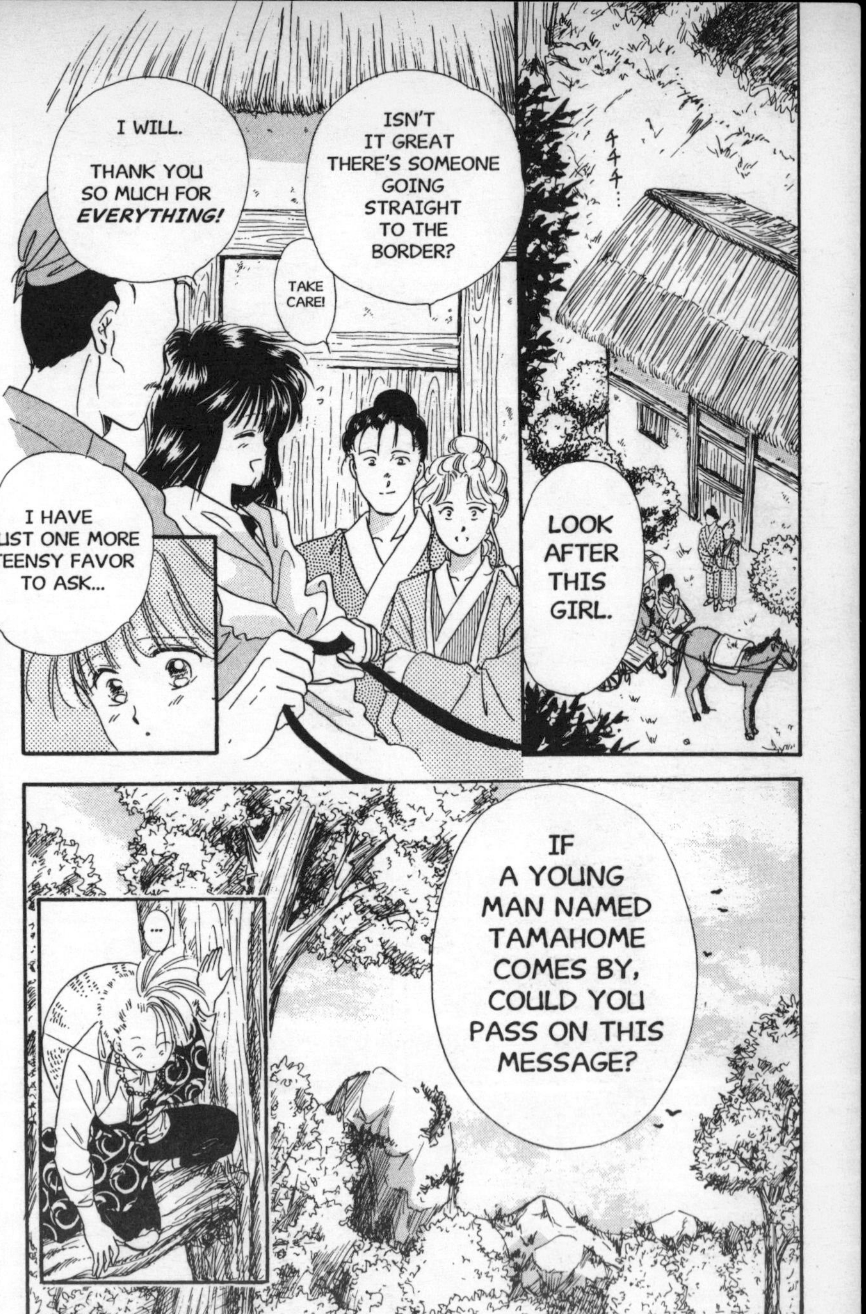
I WILL.
THANK YOU SO MUCH FOR *EVERYTHING!*
ISN'T IT GREAT THERE'S SOMEONE GOING STRAIGHT TO THE BORDER?
TAKE CARE!
I HAVE JUST ONE MORE TEENSY FAVOR TO ASK...
チチチ…
LOOK AFTER THIS GIRL.
...
IF A YOUNG MAN NAMED TAMAHOME COMES BY, COULD YOU PASS ON THIS MESSAGE?

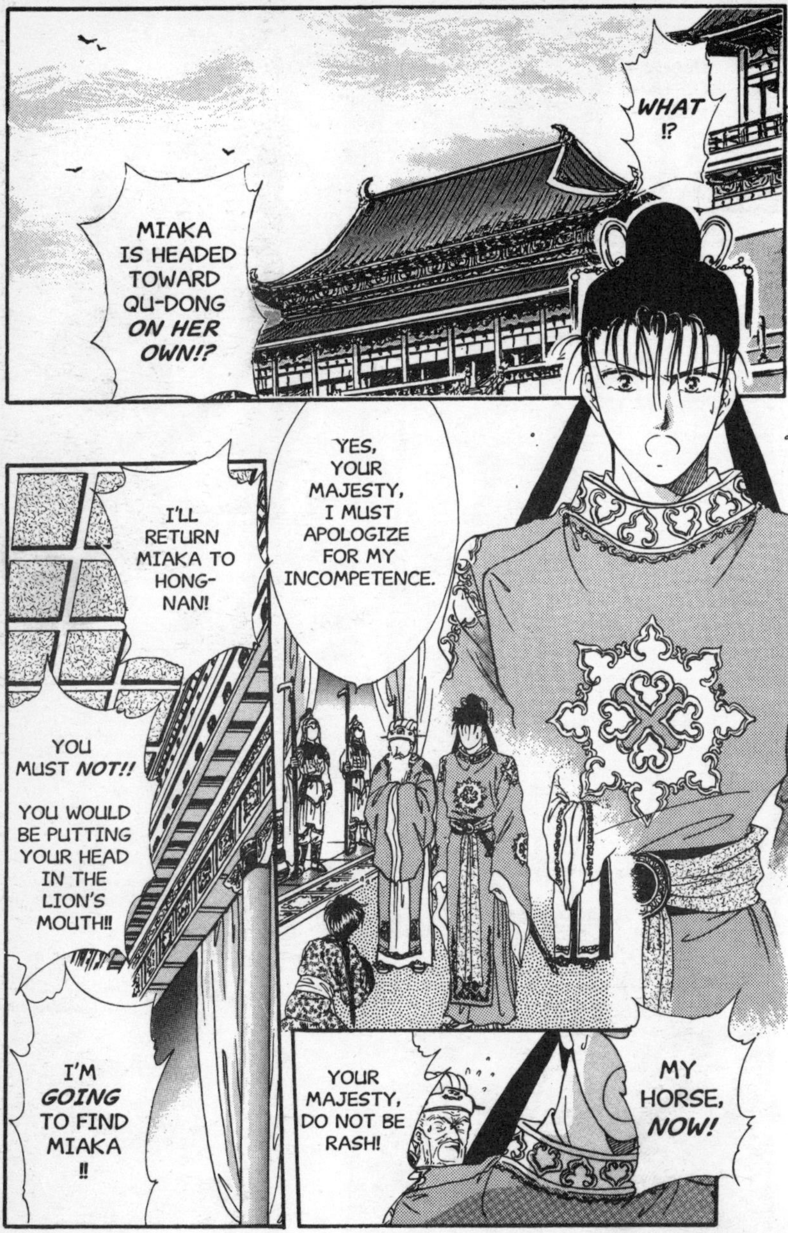
WHAT !?
MIAKA IS HEADED TOWARD QU-DONG ON HER OWN!?
YES, YOUR MAJESTY, I MUST APOLOGIZE FOR MY INCOMPETENCE.
I'LL RETURN MIAKA TO HONG-NAN!
YOU MUST NOT!!
YOU WOULD BE PUTTING YOUR HEAD IN THE LION'S MOUTH!!
MY HORSE, NOW!
YOUR MAJESTY, DO NOT BE RASH!
I'M GOING TO FIND MIAKA !!

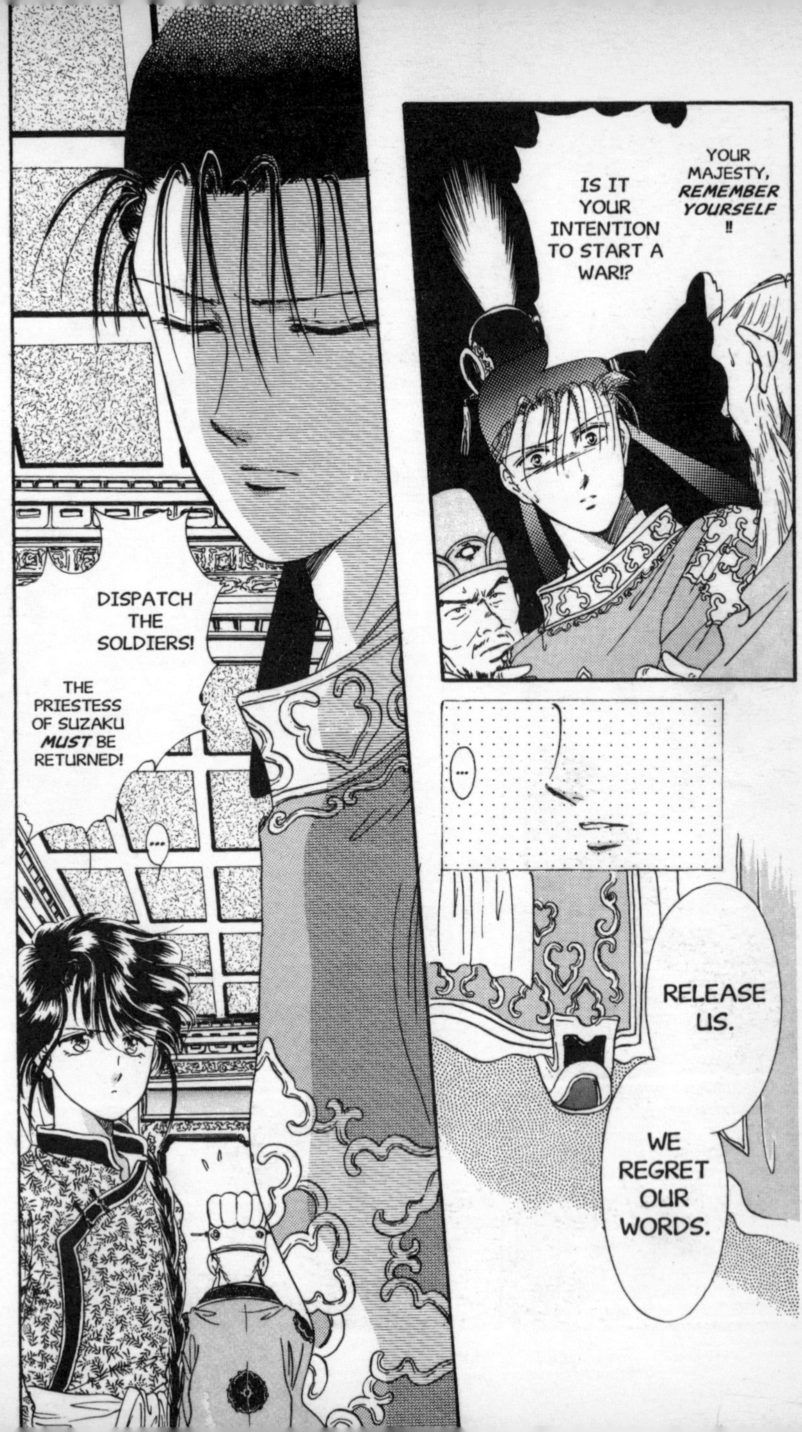
YOUR MAJESTY, REMEMBER YOURSELF!!
IS IT YOUR INTENTION TO START A WAR!?
...
RELEASE US.
WE REGRET OUR WORDS.
DISPATCH THE SOLDIERS!
THE PRIESTESS OF SUZAKU MUST BE RETURNED!
...

KREEK

YOU'D HAVE TO PASS THROUGH THIS VILLAGE TO REACH QU-DONG.

HEY, *YOU* !!

!?

SHE CAN'T HAVE GOTTEN FAR ON HER OWN...

NOW, EVERY YOUNG MAN *HAS* TO BE THIS TAMAHOME CHARACTER.

I'M SORRY, SIR. MY WIFE'S BEEN AT THIS FOR TWO DAYS SINCE A GIRL ASKED US TO PASS ON A MESSAGE.

WHAT, *AGAIN?*

I FOUND HIM!

THIS GUY'S *GOTTA* BE TAMAHOME!!

THIS TIME FOR SURE!

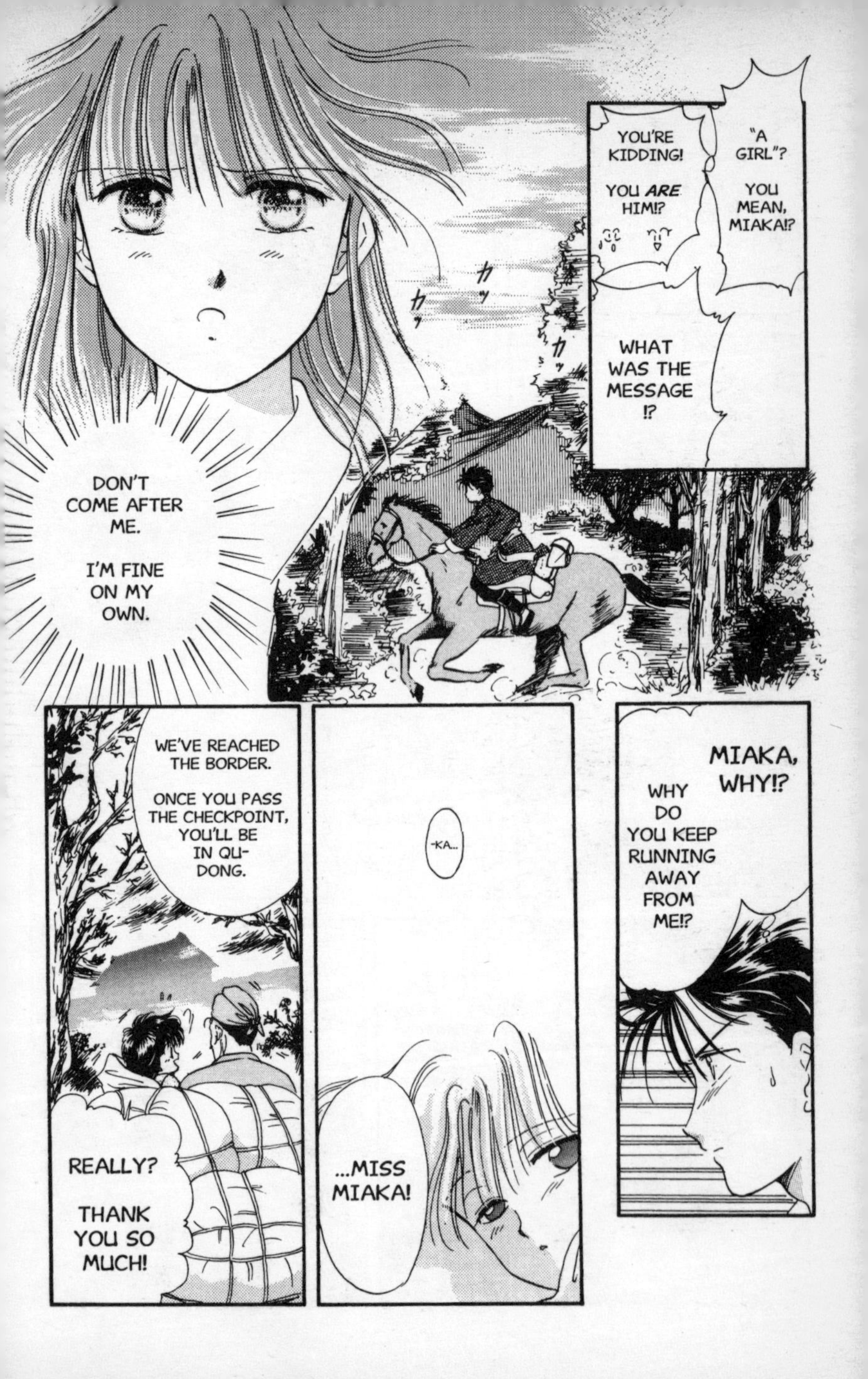
"A GIRL"? YOU MEAN, MIAKA!?
YOU'RE KIDDING! YOU *ARE* HIM!?
WHAT WAS THE MESSAGE !?
カッ
カッ
カッ
DON'T COME AFTER ME.
I'M FINE ON MY OWN.
MIAKA, WHY!?
WHY DO YOU KEEP RUNNING AWAY FROM ME!?
-KA...
...MISS MIAKA!
WE'VE REACHED THE BORDER.
ONCE YOU PASS THE CHECKPOINT, YOU'LL BE IN QU-DONG.
REALLY?
THANK YOU SO MUCH!

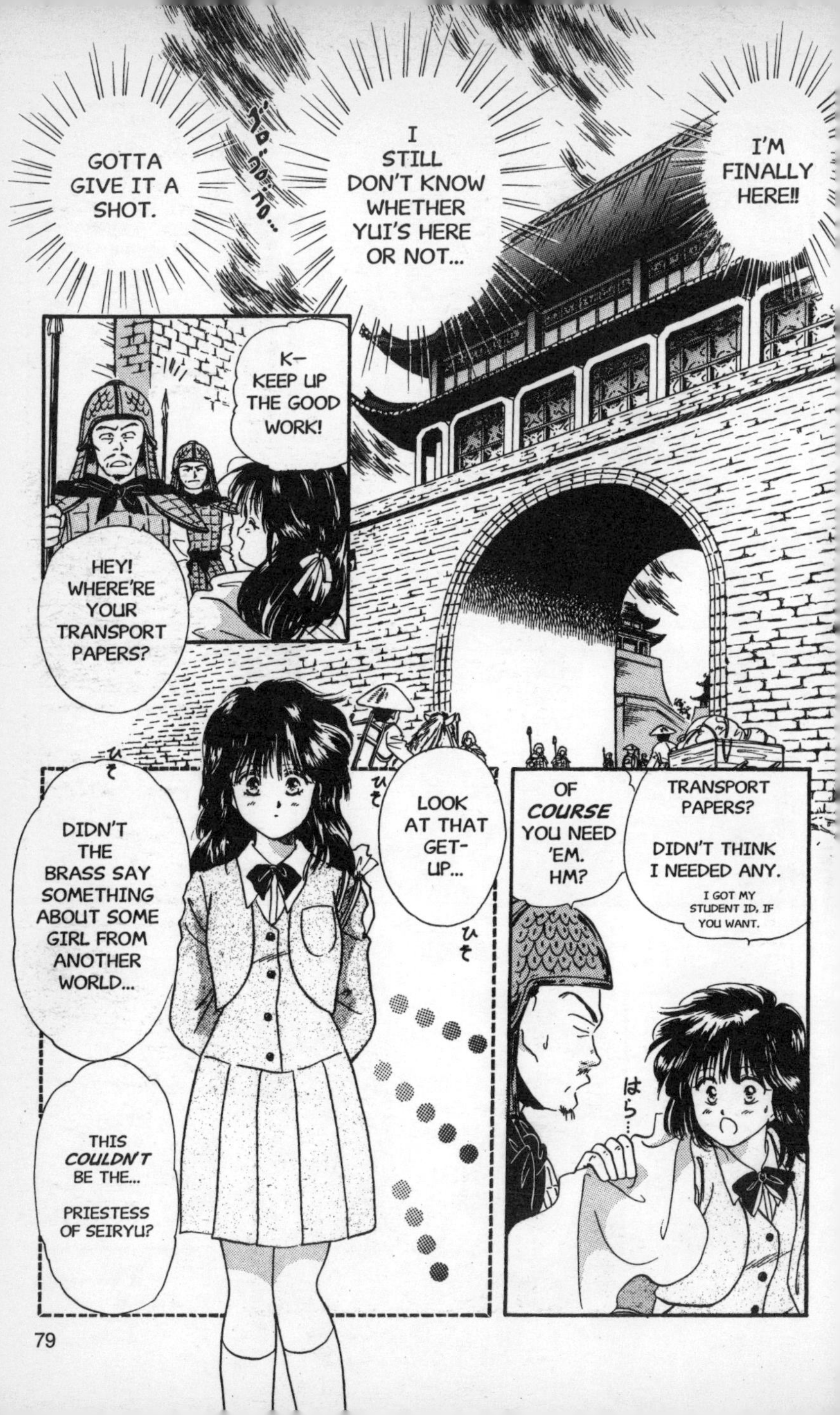
I'M FINALLY HERE!!
I STILL DON'T KNOW WHETHER YUI'S HERE OR NOT...
GOTTA GIVE IT A SHOT.
K— KEEP UP THE GOOD WORK!
HEY! WHERE'RE YOUR TRANSPORT PAPERS?
TRANSPORT PAPERS? DIDN'T THINK I NEEDED ANY.
I GOT MY STUDENT ID, IF YOU WANT.
OF *COURSE* YOU NEED 'EM. HM?
はら…
LOOK AT THAT GET-UP...
ひそ
ひそ
ひそ
DIDN'T THE BRASS SAY SOMETHING ABOUT SOME GIRL FROM ANOTHER WORLD...
THIS *COULDN'T* BE THE... PRIESTESS OF SEIRYU?

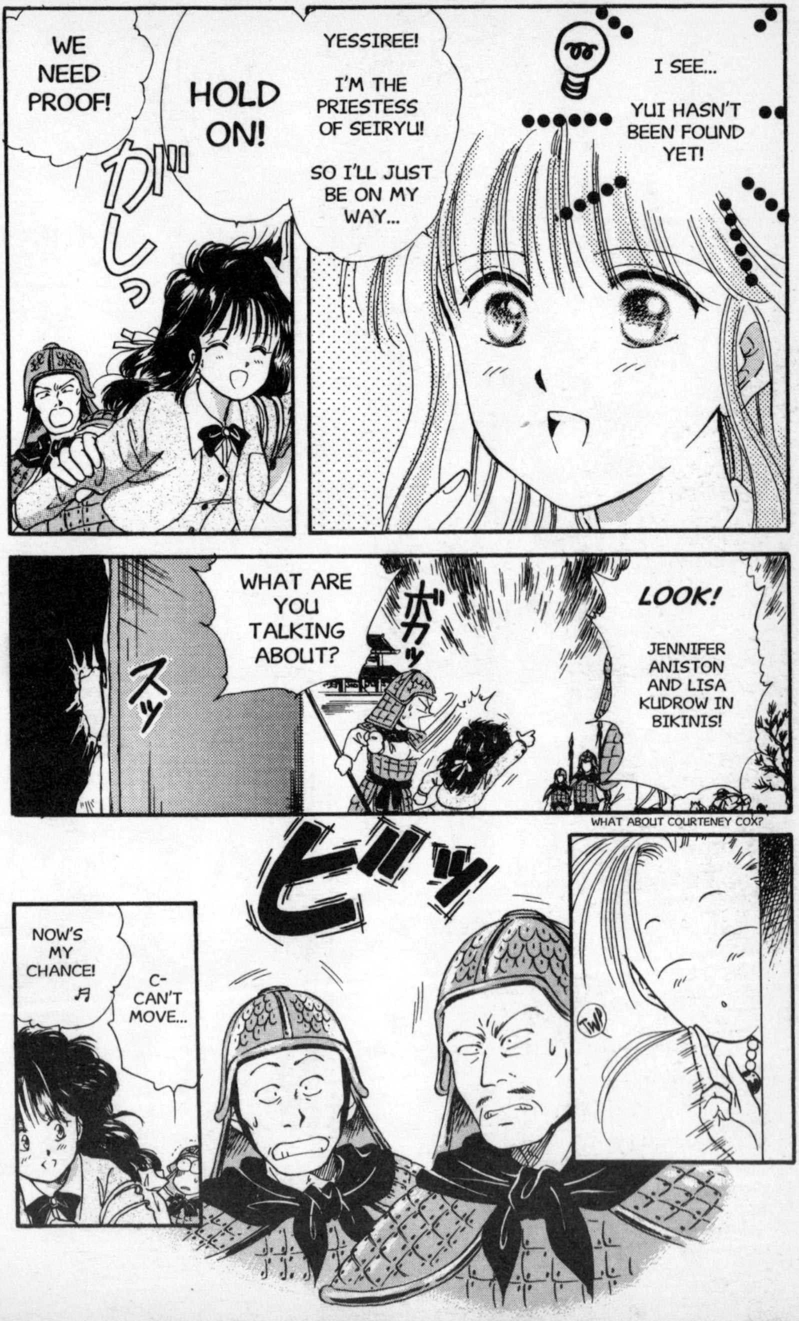
I SEE...
YUI HASN'T BEEN FOUND YET!
YESSIREE!
I'M THE PRIESTESS OF SEIRYU!
SO I'LL JUST BE ON MY WAY...
HOLD ON!
WE NEED PROOF!
がしっ
LOOK!
JENNIFER ANISTON AND LISA KUDROW IN BIKINIS!
ボカッ
WHAT ARE YOU TALKING ABOUT?
スッ
WHAT ABOUT COURTENEY COX?
NOW'S MY CHANCE! ♬
C-CAN'T MOVE...

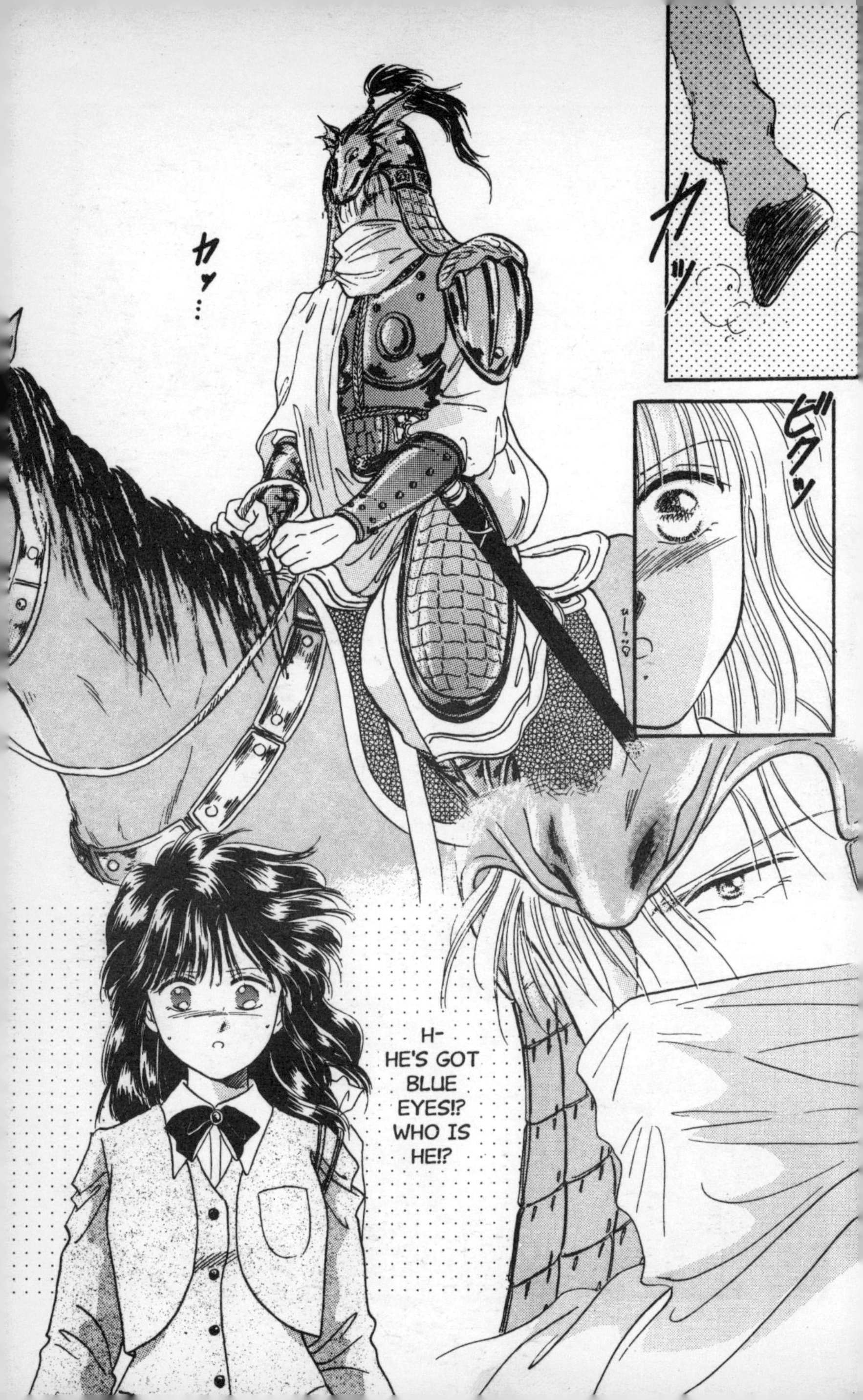
カッ
ビクッ
カッ…
H-
HE'S GOT
BLUE
EYES!?
WHO IS
HE!?

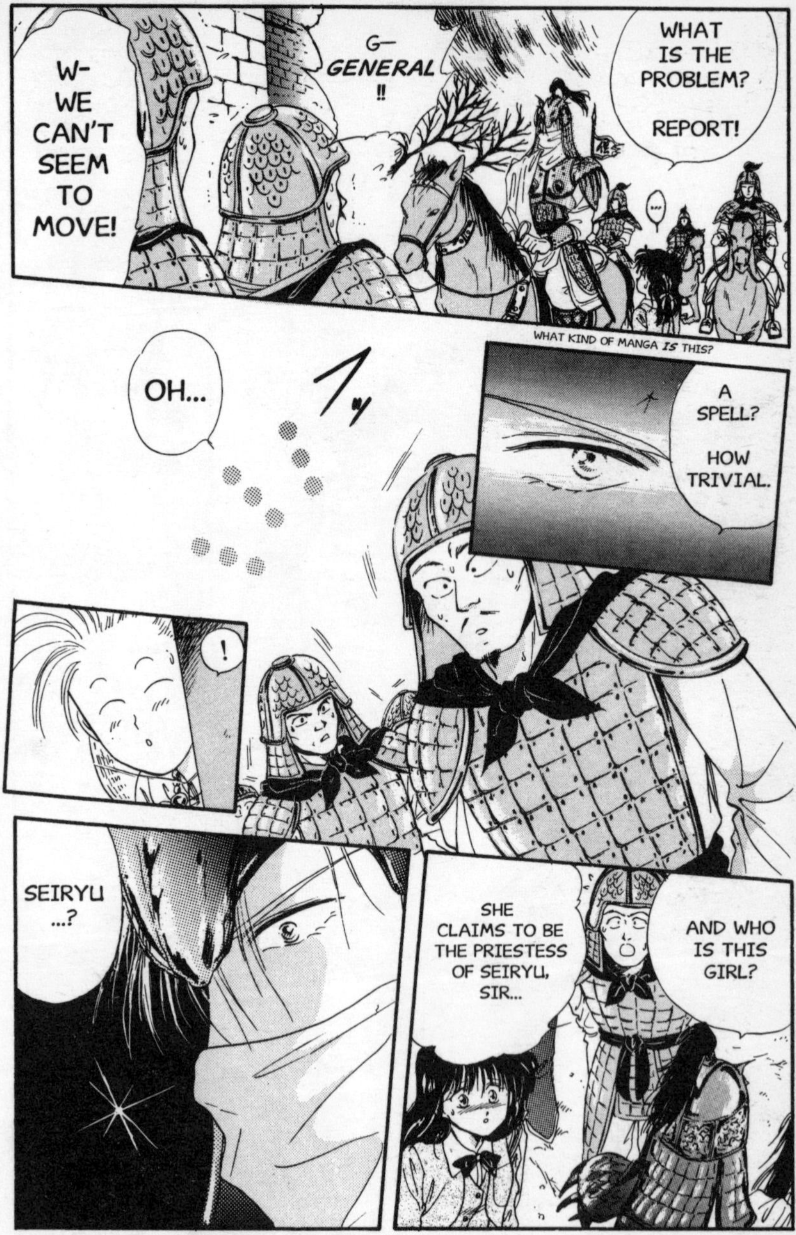
WHAT IS THE PROBLEM? REPORT!
G— GENERAL !!
W- WE CAN'T SEEM TO MOVE!
WHAT KIND OF MANGA IS THIS?
A SPELL? HOW TRIVIAL.
OH...
!
AND WHO IS THIS GIRL?
SHE CLAIMS TO BE THE PRIESTESS OF SEIRYU, SIR...
SEIRYU ...?

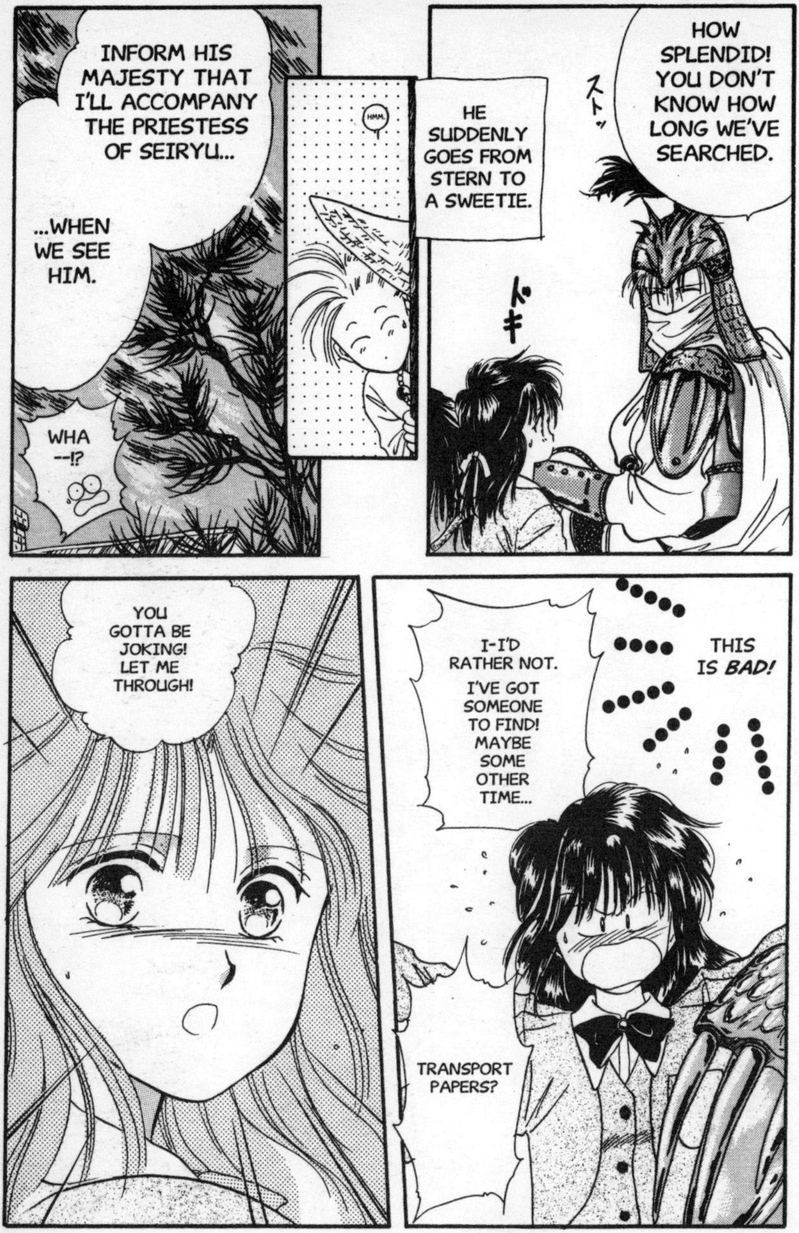
HOW SPLENDID! YOU DON'T KNOW HOW LONG WE'VE SEARCHED.
ストッ
ドキ
HE SUDDENLY GOES FROM STERN TO A SWEETIE.
HMM.
INFORM HIS MAJESTY THAT I'LL ACCOMPANY THE PRIESTESS OF SEIRYU...
...WHEN WE SEE HIM.
WHA --!?
THIS IS *BAD!*
I-I'D RATHER NOT.
I'VE GOT SOMEONE TO FIND! MAYBE SOME OTHER TIME...
TRANSPORT PAPERS?
YOU GOTTA BE JOKING! LET ME THROUGH!

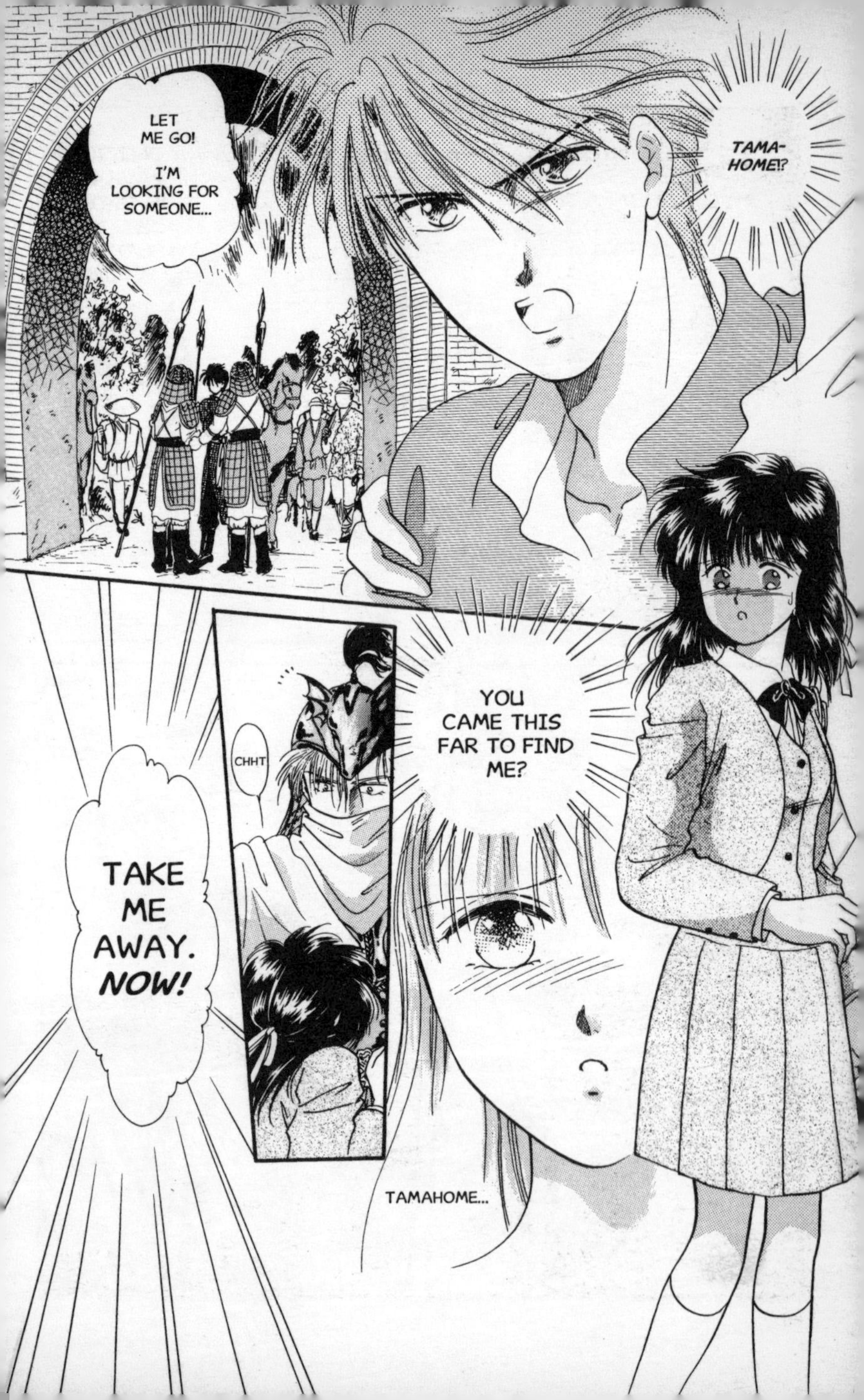
TAMA-HOME!?
LET ME GO! I'M LOOKING FOR SOMEONE...
YOU CAME THIS FAR TO FIND ME?
CHHT
TAKE ME AWAY. NOW!
TAMAHOME...

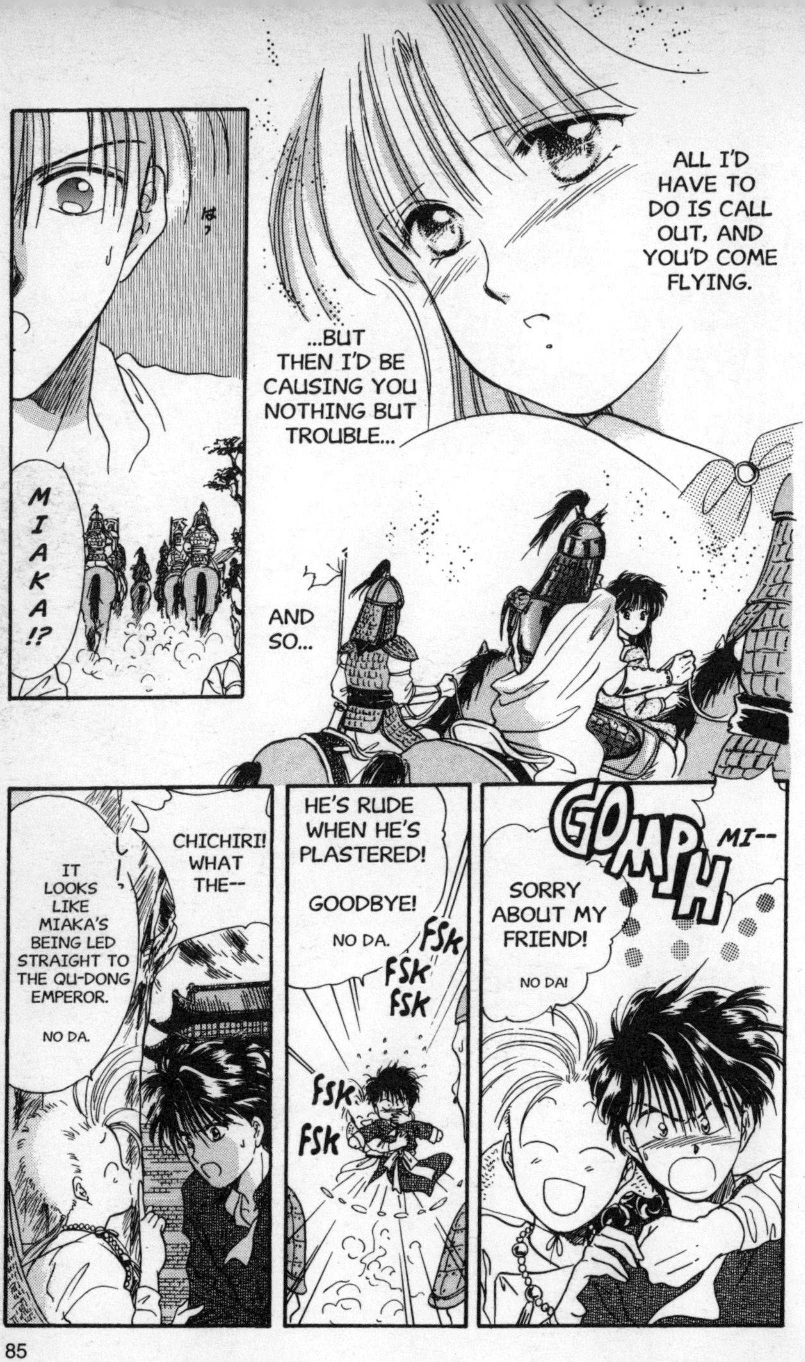

MIAKA!?
ALL I'D HAVE TO DO IS CALL OUT, AND YOU'D COME FLYING.
...BUT THEN I'D BE CAUSING YOU NOTHING BUT TROUBLE...
AND SO...
IT LOOKS LIKE MIAKA'S BEING LED STRAIGHT TO THE QU-DONG EMPEROR.
NO DA.
CHICHIRI! WHAT THE--
HE'S RUDE WHEN HE'S PLASTERED!
GOODBYE!
NO DA.
FSK
FSK
FSK
FSK
FSK
GOMPH
MI--
SORRY ABOUT MY FRIEND!
NO DA!

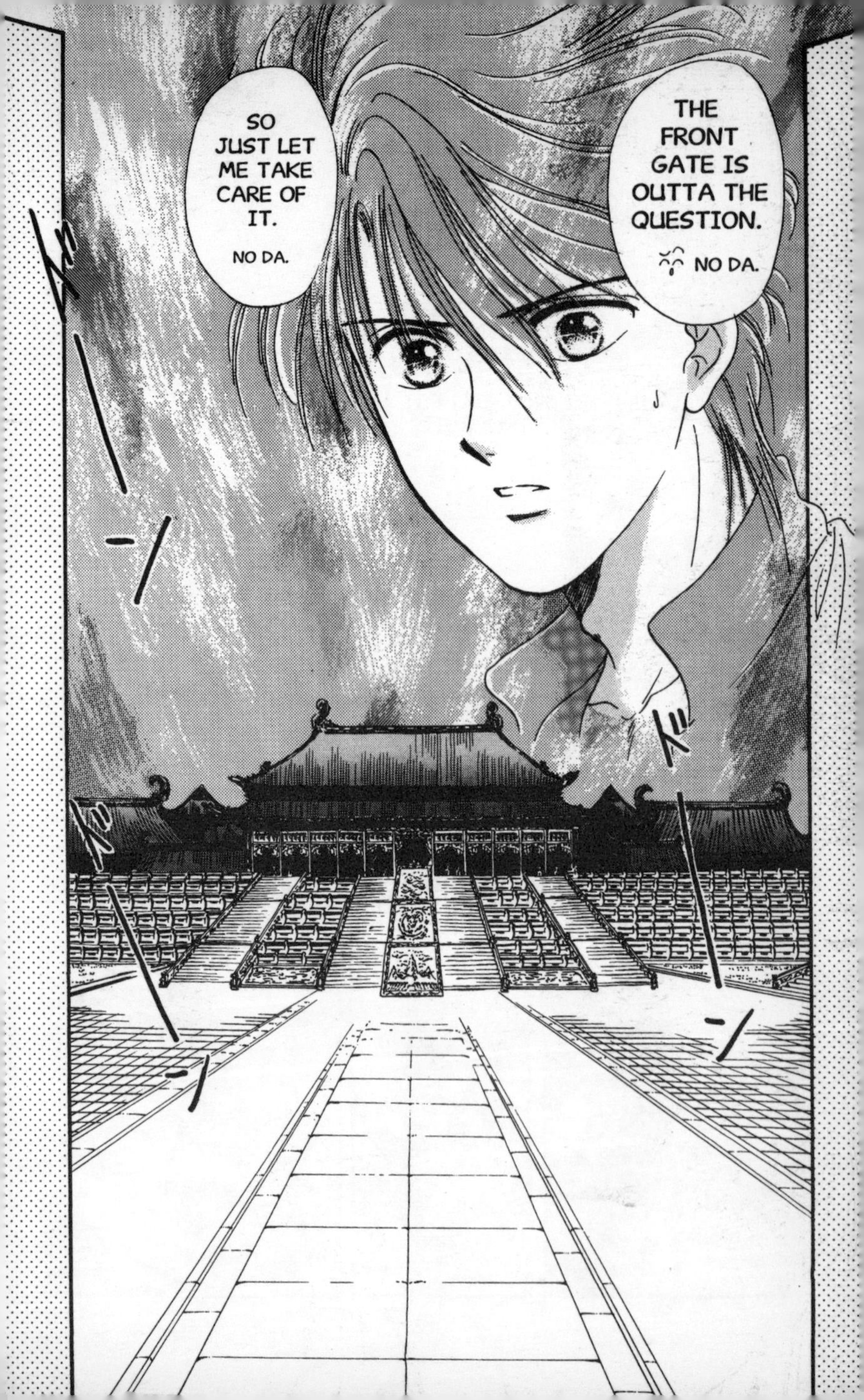
THE FRONT GATE IS OUTTA THE QUESTION.
NO DA.
SO JUST LET ME TAKE CARE OF IT.
NO DA.

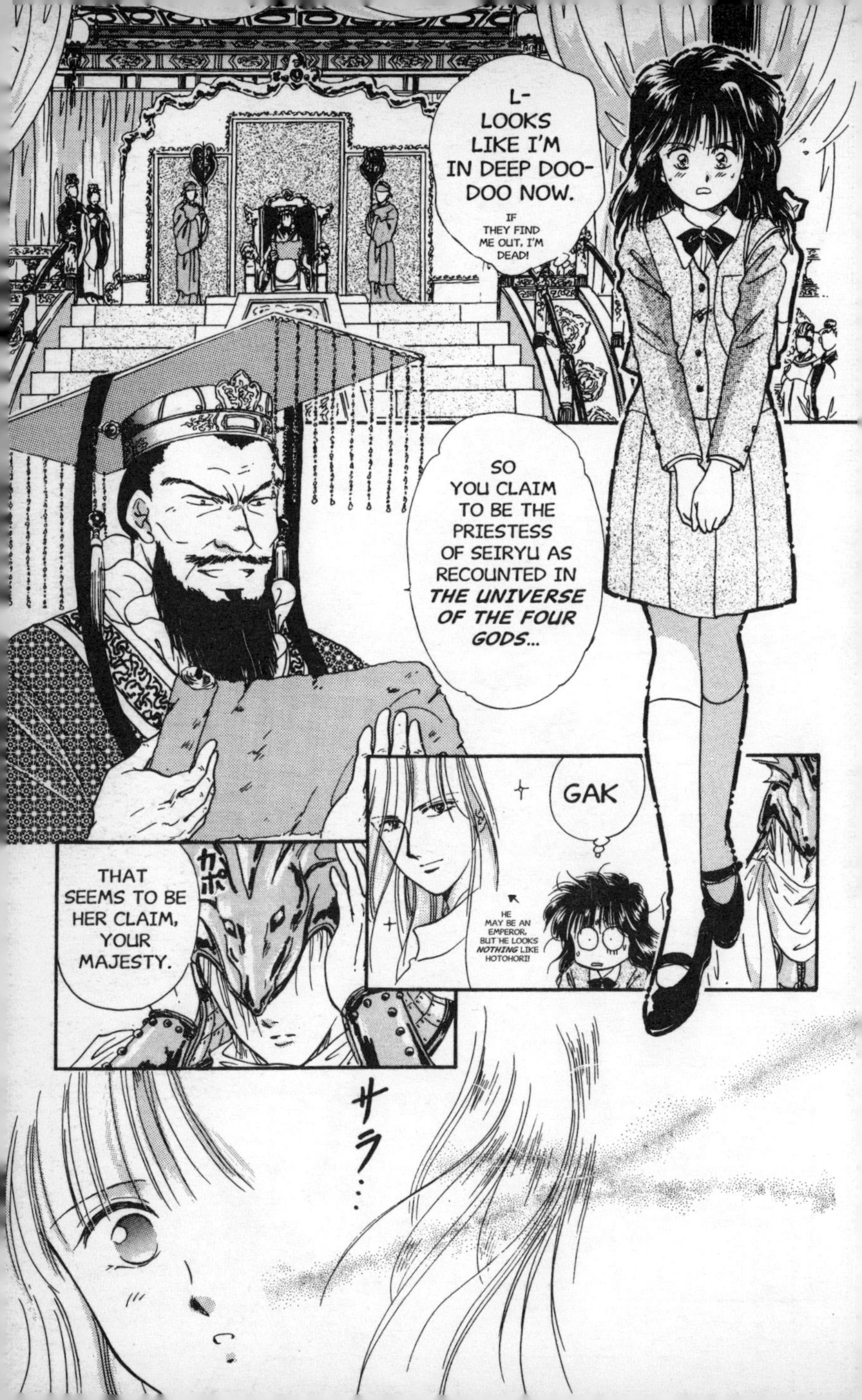
L- LOOKS LIKE I'M IN DEEP DOO-DOO NOW.
IF THEY FIND ME OUT, I'M DEAD!
SO YOU CLAIM TO BE THE PRIESTESS OF SEIRYU AS RECOUNTED IN *THE UNIVERSE OF THE FOUR GODS*...
GAK
HE MAY BE AN EMPEROR, BUT HE LOOKS *NOTHING* LIKE HOTOHORI!
カポ
THAT SEEMS TO BE HER CLAIM, YOUR MAJESTY.
サラ...

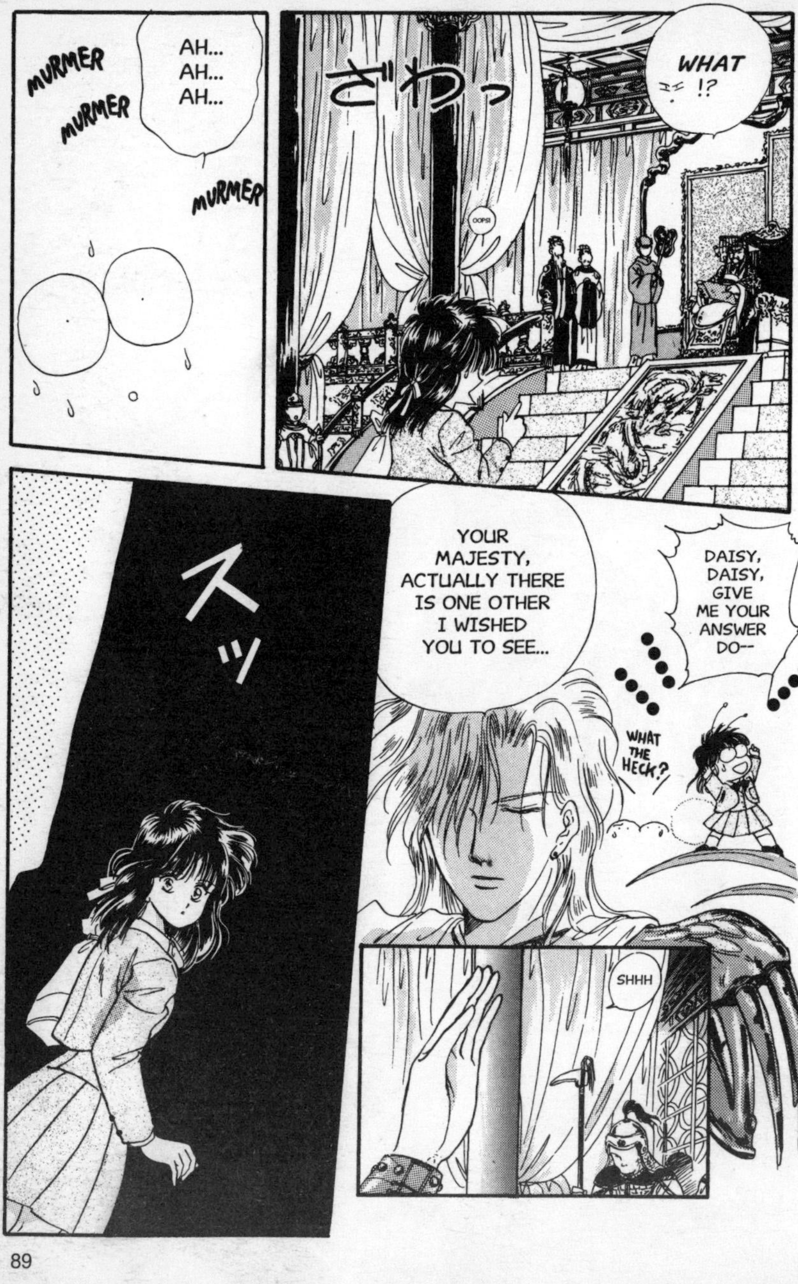
WHAT !?
ざわっ
OOPS!
AH...
AH...
AH...
MURMER
MURMER
MURMER
YOUR MAJESTY, ACTUALLY THERE IS ONE OTHER I WISHED YOU TO SEE...
DAISY, DAISY, GIVE ME YOUR ANSWER DO--
WHAT THE HECK?
SHHH
スッ

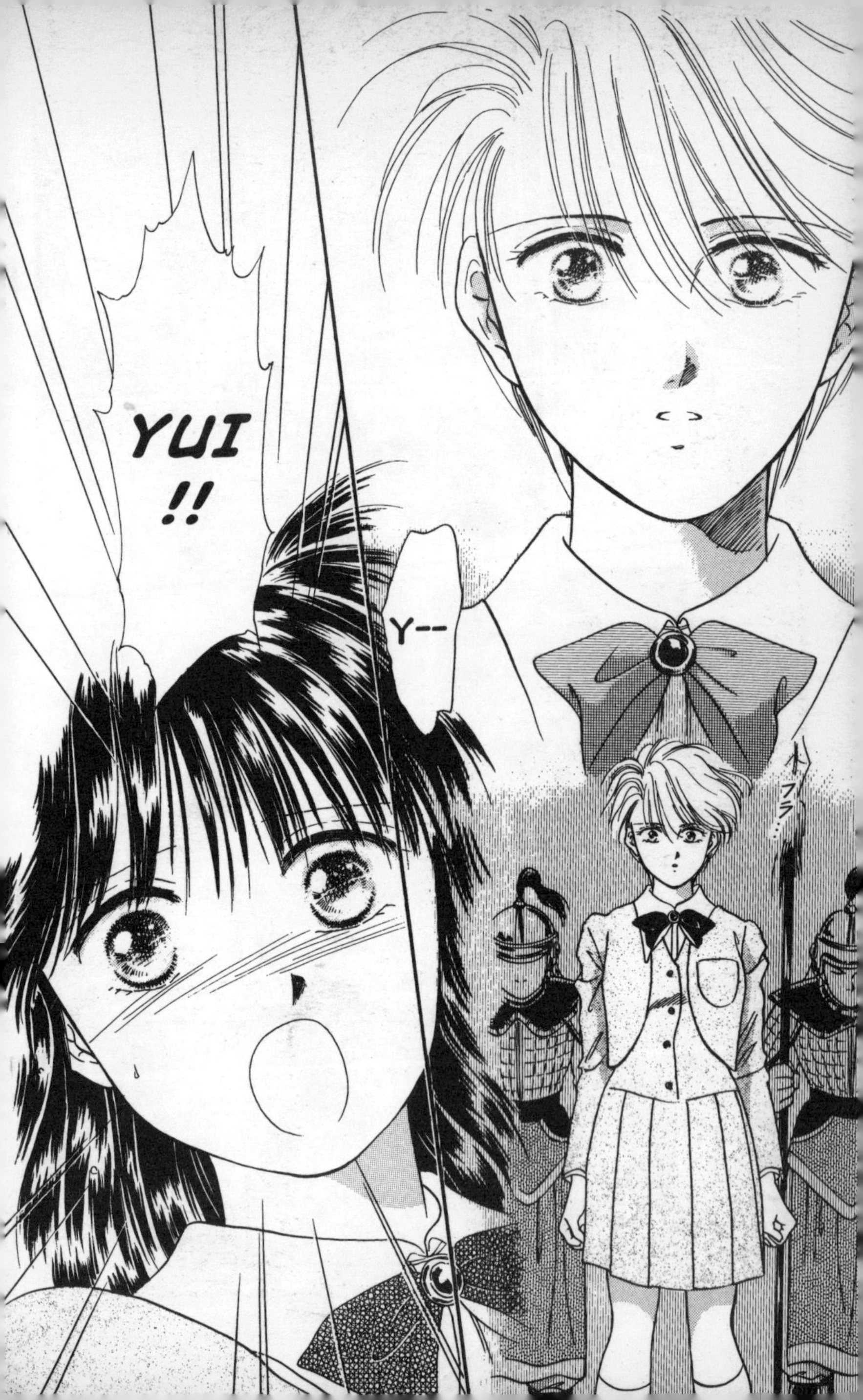
Y--
YUI !!
ホフラ…

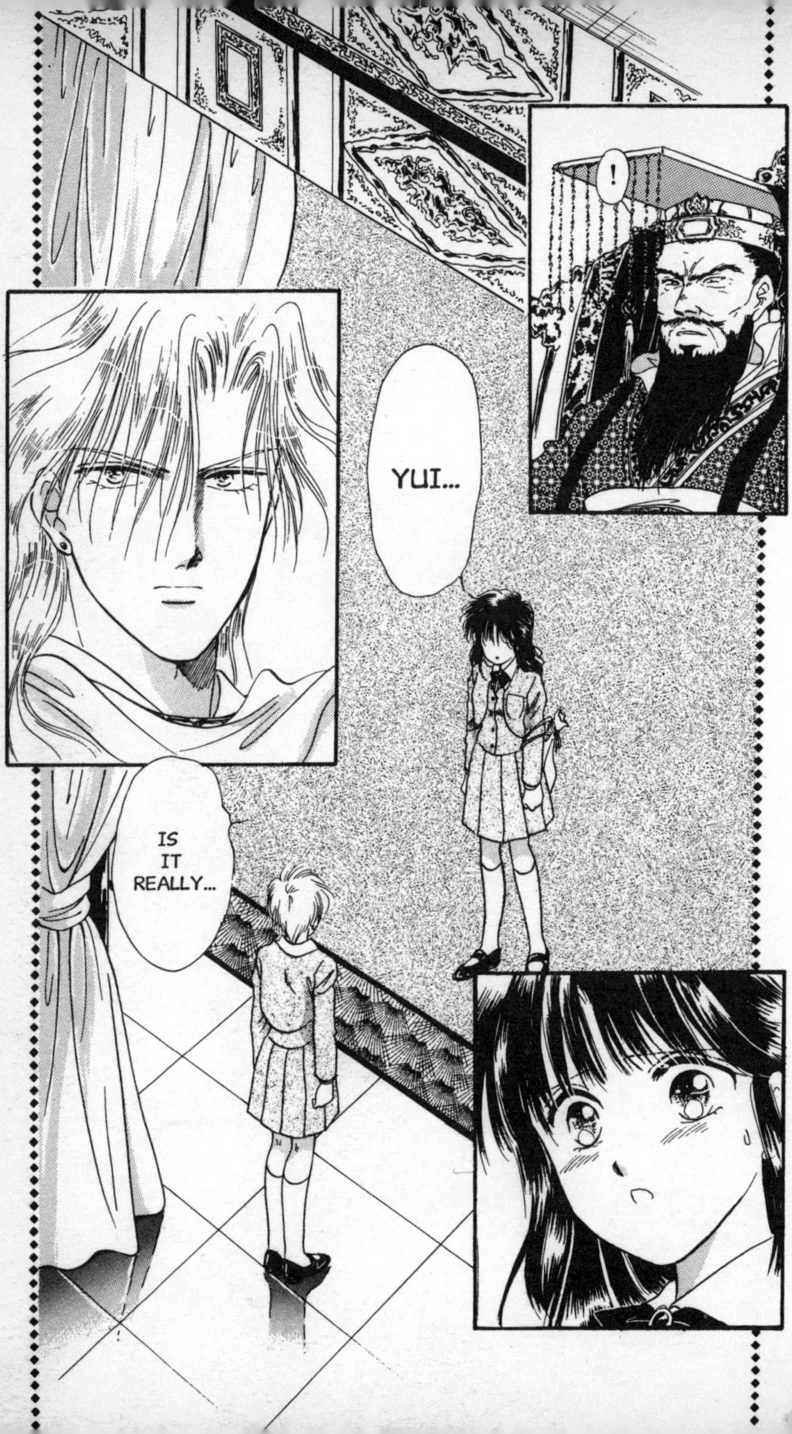
!
YUI...
IS IT REALLY...

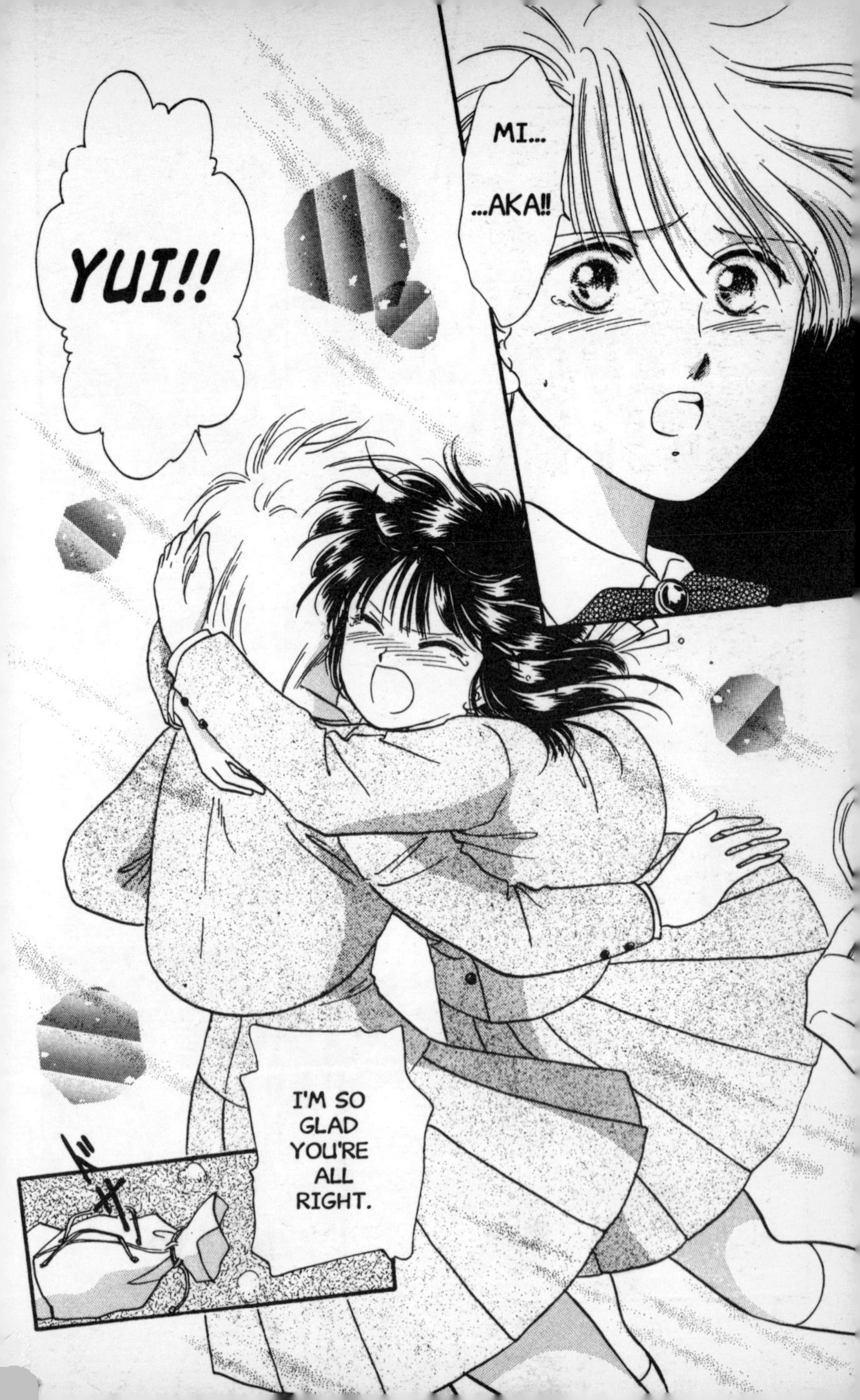
MI...
...AKA!!
YUI!!
I'M SO GLAD YOU'RE ALL RIGHT.

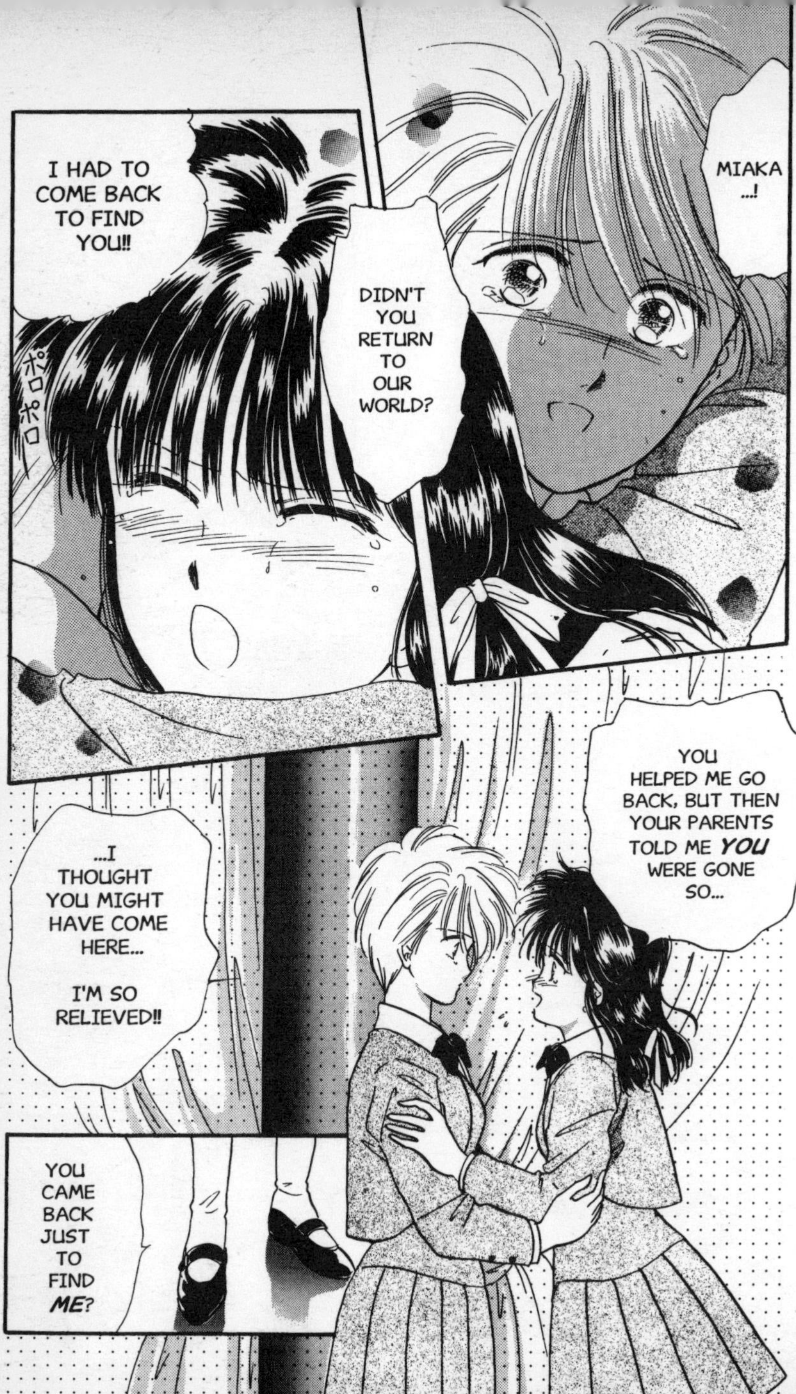
MIAKA ...!
DIDN'T YOU RETURN TO OUR WORLD?
I HAD TO COME BACK TO FIND YOU!!
ポロポロ
YOU CAME BACK JUST TO FIND *ME*?
YOU HELPED ME GO BACK, BUT THEN YOUR PARENTS TOLD ME *YOU* WERE GONE SO...
...I THOUGHT YOU MIGHT HAVE COME HERE...
I'M SO RELIEVED!!

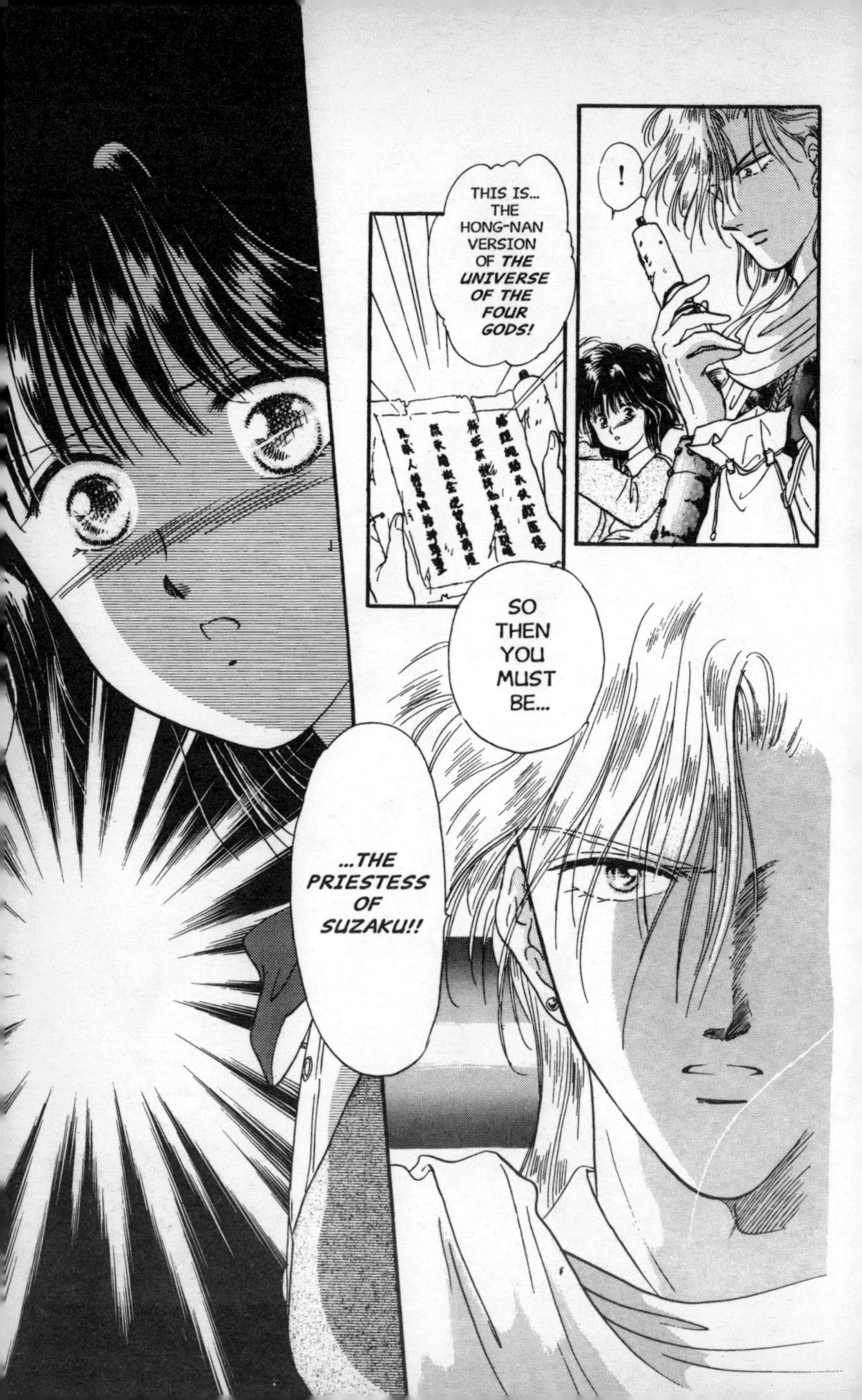
!
THIS IS... THE HONG-NAN VERSION OF *THE UNIVERSE OF THE FOUR GODS!*
SO THEN YOU MUST BE...
...*THE PRIESTESS OF SUZAKU!!*

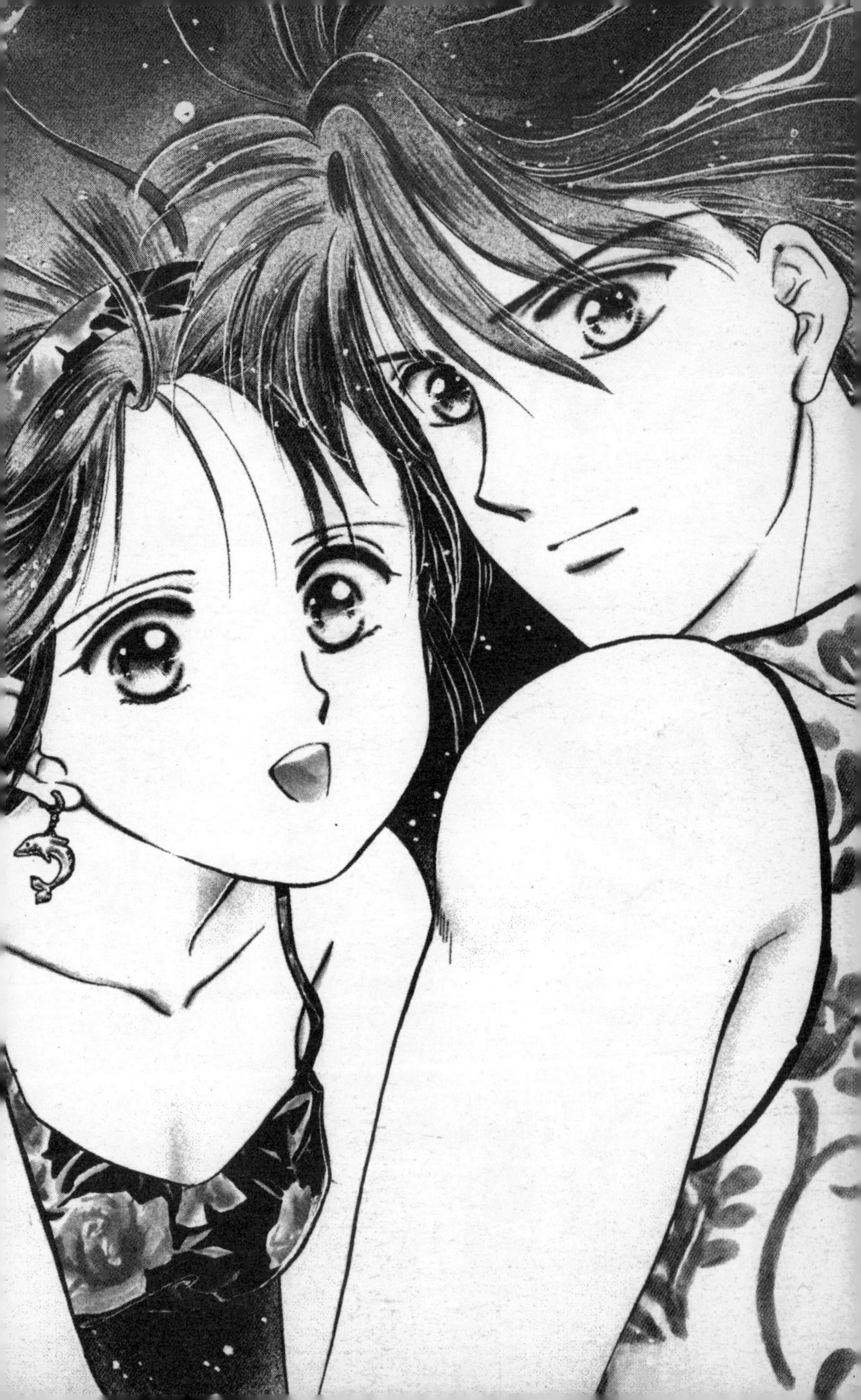

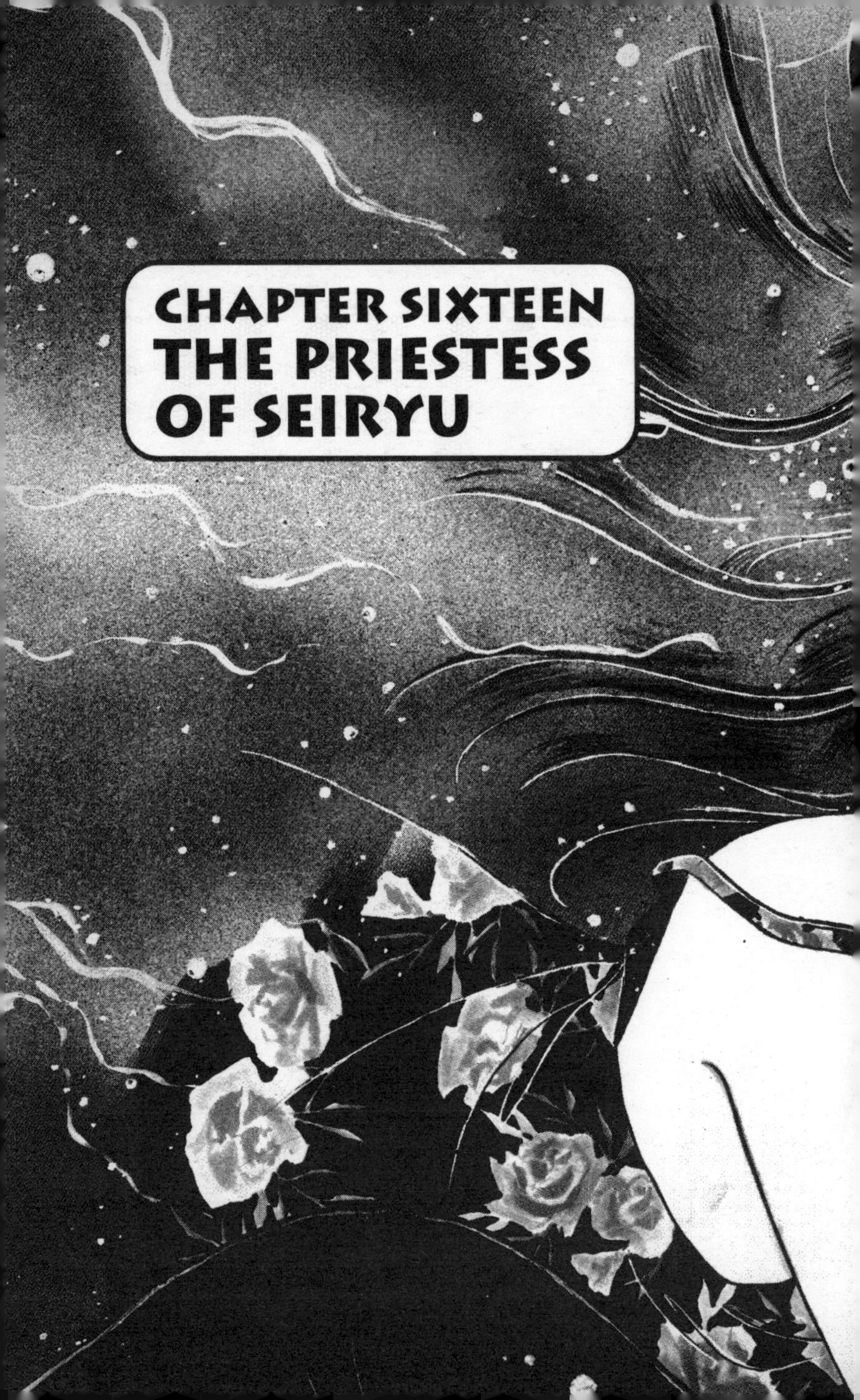
CHAPTER SIXTEEN
THE PRIESTESS
OF SEIRYU

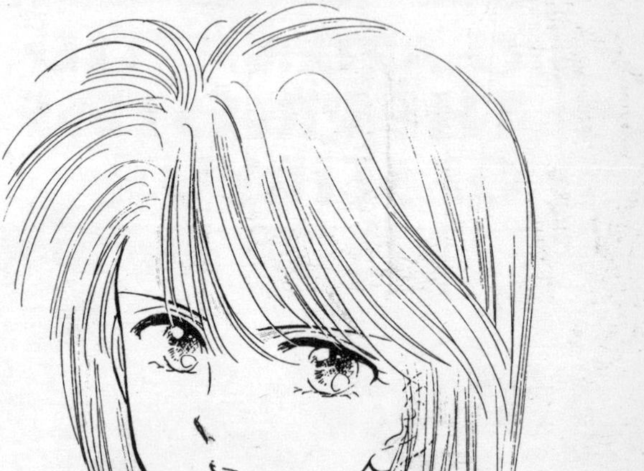

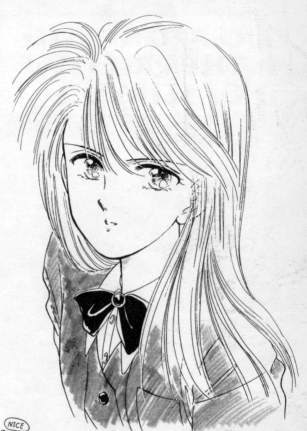

YUI WITH NICE LONG HAIR.

SHE HAD IT LONG UNTIL THE 8TH GRADE. SHE CUT IT SHORT TO AVOID ALL THE ATTENTION SHE WAS GETTING FROM THE BOYS.

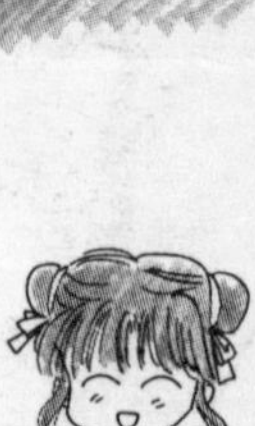
I'M SO PROUD SHE'S MY FRIEND!

100

YUI!

HOW'D YOU GET THIS SCAR!?

I WAS SUDDENLY SUCKED INTO THE BOOK, AND I HAD NO IDEA WHAT TO DO.

THAT MAN SAVED ME.

OH, THIS? IT'S NOTHING.

JUST A SCAR!

...I PROBABLY HURT MYSELF ENTERING THE BOOK.

THREE MONTHS AGO WHEN I WAS AT THE LIBRARY, A BRIGHT BLUE LIGHT BURST OUT OF *THE UNIVERSE OF THE FOUR GODS*...

HIS ARMOR MAY BE HOT, BUT IT LOOKS SO GOOD!

102

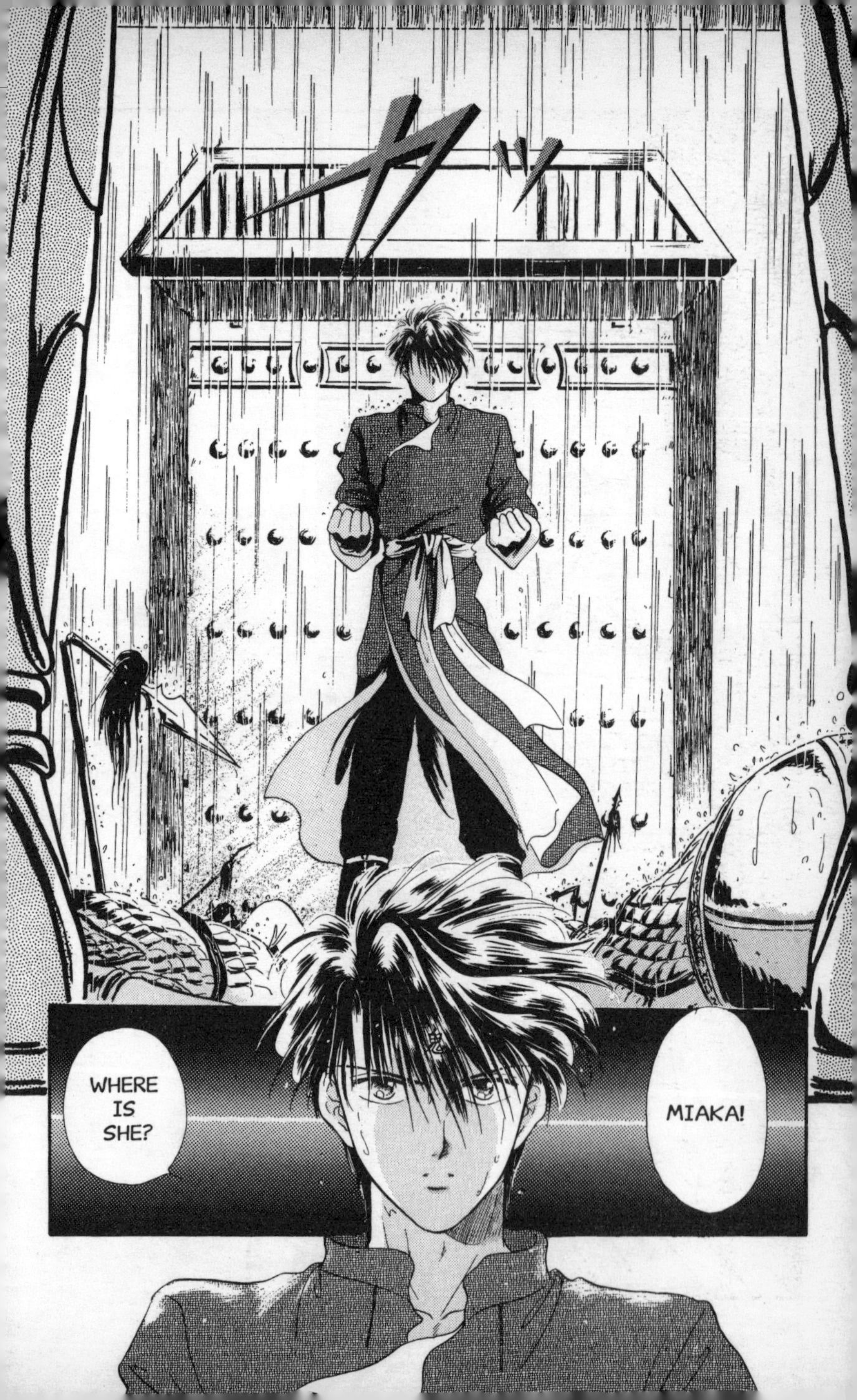
MIAKA!
WHERE IS SHE?

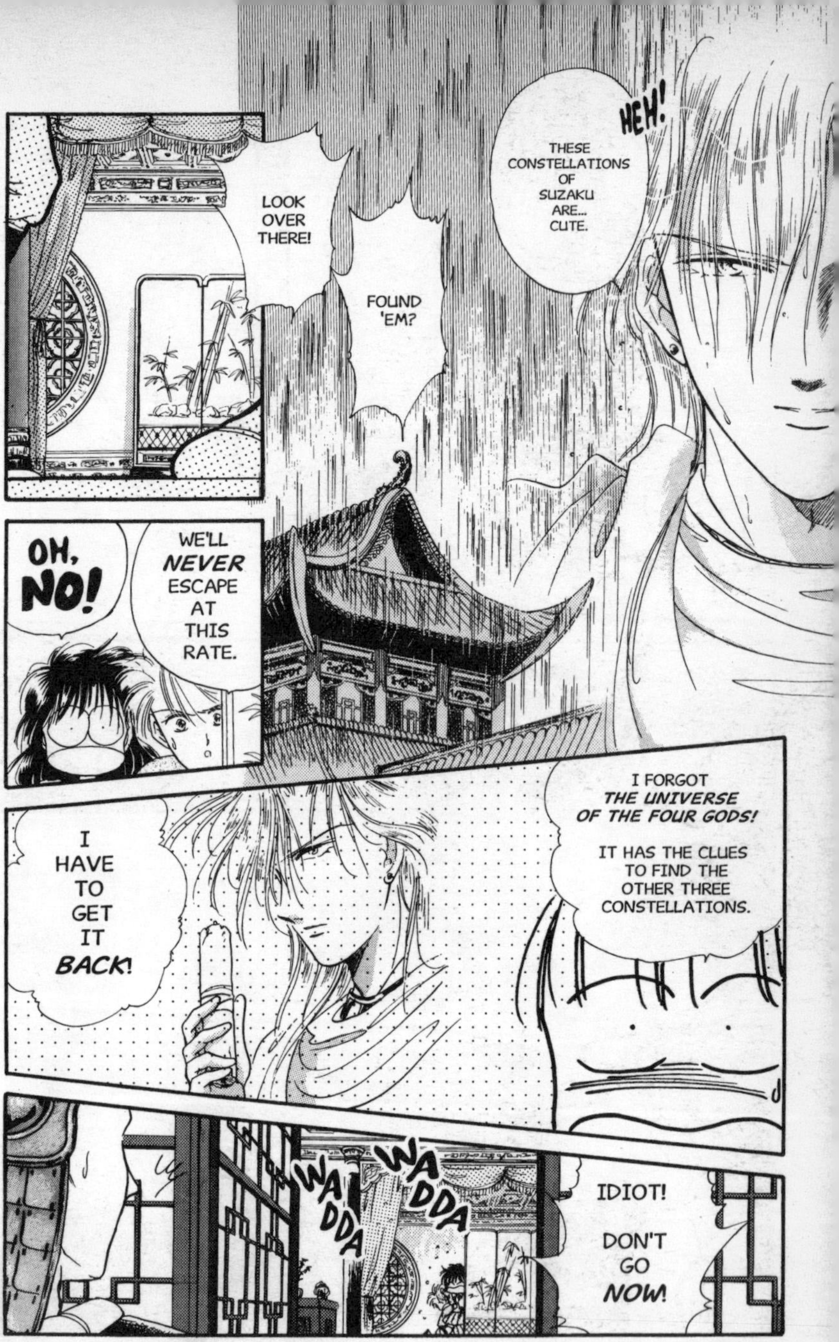
LOOK OVER THERE!
FOUND 'EM?
HEH!
THESE CONSTELLATIONS OF SUZAKU ARE... CUTE.
OH, NO!
WE'LL *NEVER* ESCAPE AT THIS RATE.
I HAVE TO GET IT *BACK*!
I FORGOT *THE UNIVERSE OF THE FOUR GODS!*
IT HAS THE CLUES TO FIND THE OTHER THREE CONSTELLATIONS.
WADDA WADDA
WADDA
IDIOT!
DON'T GO *NOW*!

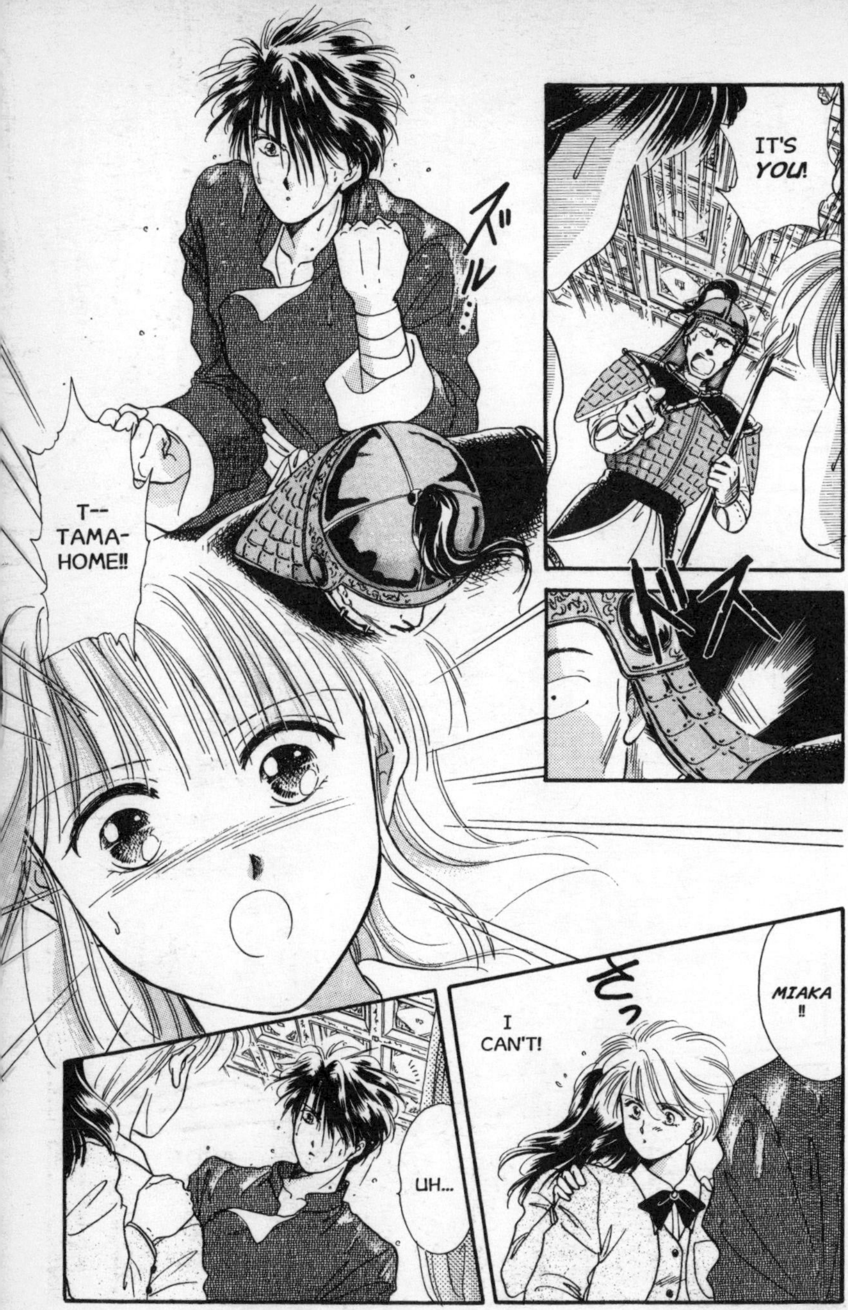
IT'S YOU!
ズル
T-- TAMA-HOME!!
MIAKA !!
I CAN'T!
UH...

UH... YUI... RIGHT?

IT'S BEEN A WHILE.

TAMA... HOME?

SO YOU... RE-MEMBER ME?

"Where did the title Fushigi Yûgi come from?" I usually don't have trouble coming up with titles, but this one gave me a hard time. I've been planning this story since I was eighteen, but its tentative title, "Suzaku," just didn't seem right, so I had to work really hard for a title that would fit the right image. I looked through a whole bunch of magazines to come up with a good rhyming title, and that's how I came up with "Fushigi Yûgi." I actually think it's a pretty nice title. The kanji for "Yûgi" show up a lot in Hong Kong films. There's Bruce Lee's "Shibô Yûgi" (The Game of Death), for example. I didn't intend it to mean "frolic," but a nuance more like "game." I guess it would mean "Mysterious Game."*

I was talking about computer games with my assistant M., who insisted that "Fushigi Yûgi" would be a great computer game. We talked about this endlessly. It's not just because we were talking about my story, but because it seemed really fun. Computer games usually begin by introducing the story with drawings, but this one would start with opening the book *The Universe of the Four Gods*. Then a map would come up and you'd see Qu-Dong, Hotohori's palace, Daichi-san, and Tamahome's village. You could follow the plot the same way as the manga, or you could start from any random location and try to find all seven celestial warriors. It'd be an RPG game, so you'd have random enemies appearing, and everybody has different powers and abilities so the way to fight would always change. When you start losing, you could call on Chichiri, who'd suddenly appear and cast a spell. If Tamahome dies (for example), he might be revived at a certain location if he has enough money stored away. Other ideas: If you go to Qu-Dong immediately without gaining enough experience points, you'd get yourself killed. If Miaka's a player-character, you'd have to have a gauge, not just for power, but for love too. Of course, she'd have to lose a lot of love points when she's away from Tamahome. When she returns to reality, that's the end of the game. Miaka could get advice from her brother. The ideas go on and on.

*But something like "Miracle Game" just sounds so corny!

...?

ONE OF OUR MEN IS DOWN!

WHAT HAPPENED!?

YOU! GO REPORT TO THE GENERAL!!

OH, SORRY ABOUT THAT!

WHOOPS

PHEW

U-UMM.

To be continued...!

111

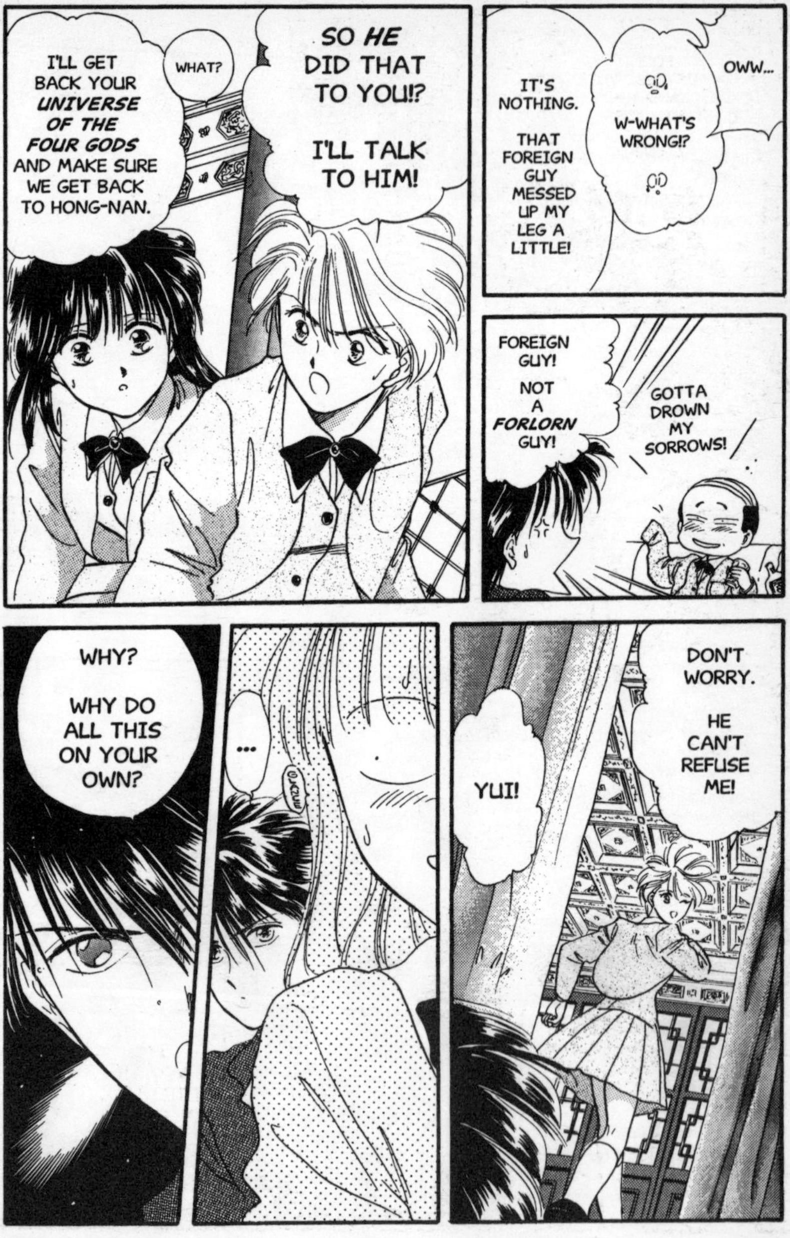

I'LL GET BACK YOUR *UNIVERSE OF THE FOUR GODS* AND MAKE SURE WE GET BACK TO HONG-NAN.
WHAT?
SO *HE* DID THAT TO YOU!?
I'LL TALK TO HIM!
OWW...
W-WHAT'S WRONG!?
IT'S NOTHING.
THAT FOREIGN GUY MESSED UP MY LEG A LITTLE!
FOREIGN GUY!
NOT A *FORLORN* GUY!
GOTTA DROWN MY SORROWS!
WHY?
WHY DO ALL THIS ON YOUR OWN?
...
DON'T WORRY.
HE CAN'T REFUSE ME!
YUI!

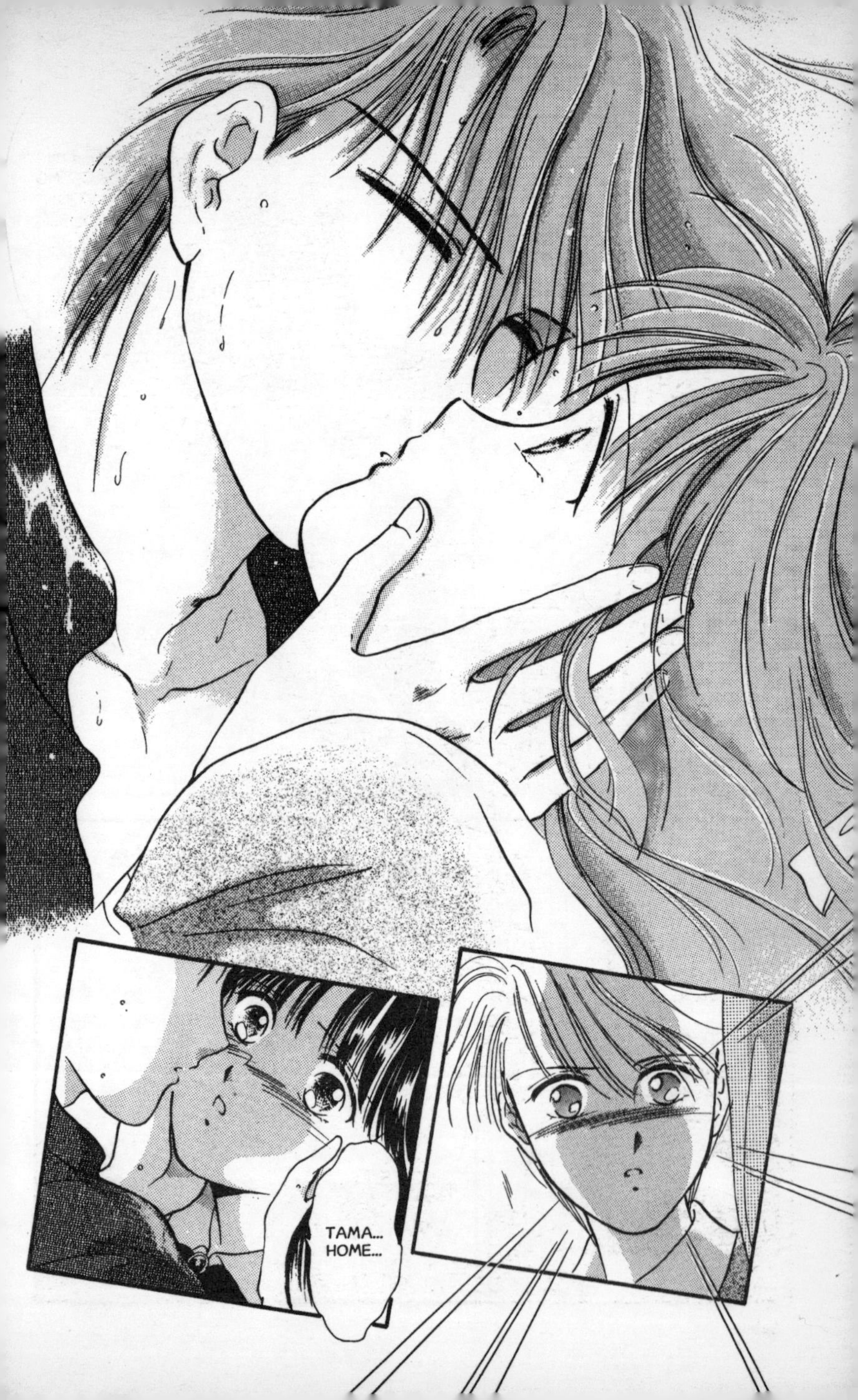
TAMA...
HOME...

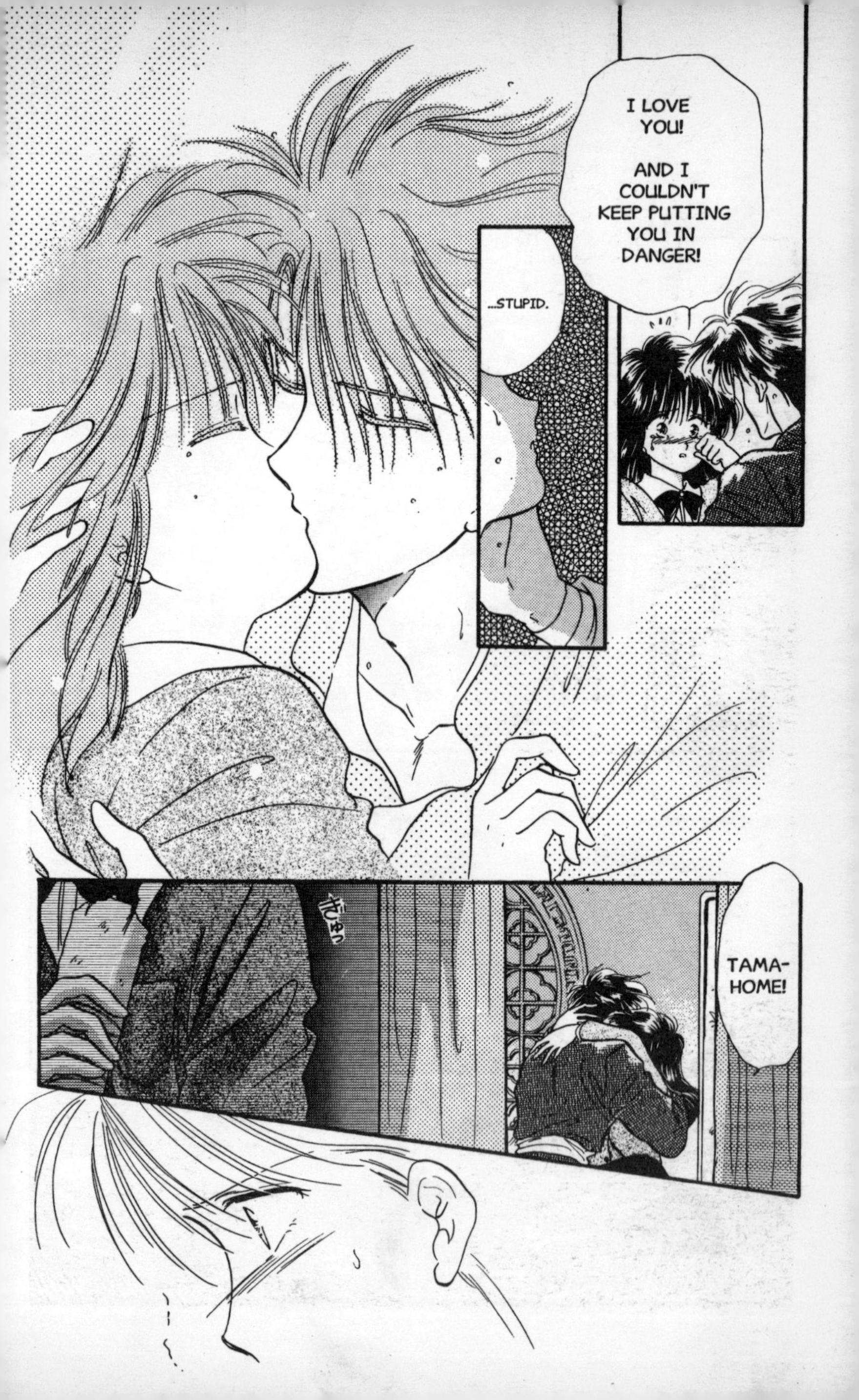
I LOVE YOU! AND I COULDN'T KEEP PUTTING YOU IN DANGER!
...STUPID.
TAMA-HOME!

"TRY TO RECALL THE SITUATION THREE MONTHS AGO WHEN I FOUND YOU"

MIAKA.

BWAH

TAMA-HOME...

I'M GOING BACK TO HONG-NAN WITH YOU.

HERE'S *THE UNIVERSE OF THE FOUR GODS.*

WE'RE DONE HERE, RIGHT?

LET'S GO.

125

ANOTHER
IDEA
←BY
MANGA
ARTIST
Y.M.

CHAPTER SEVENTEEN
SOULS DRIFTING APART

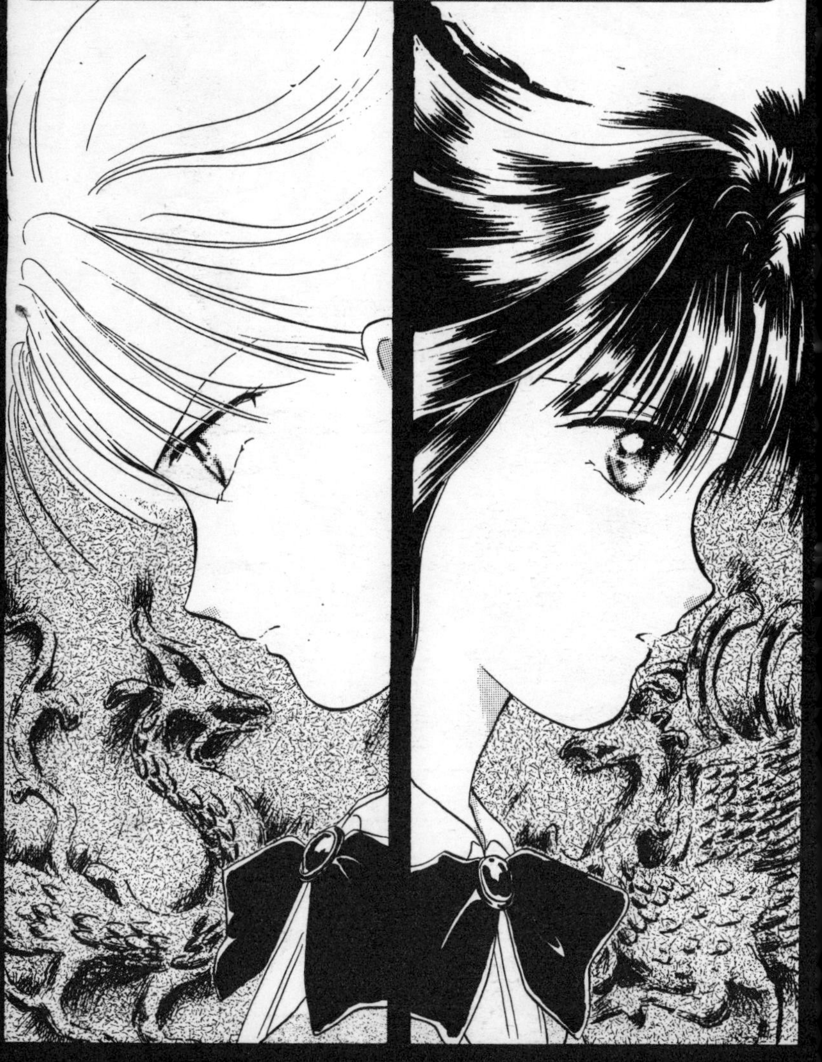

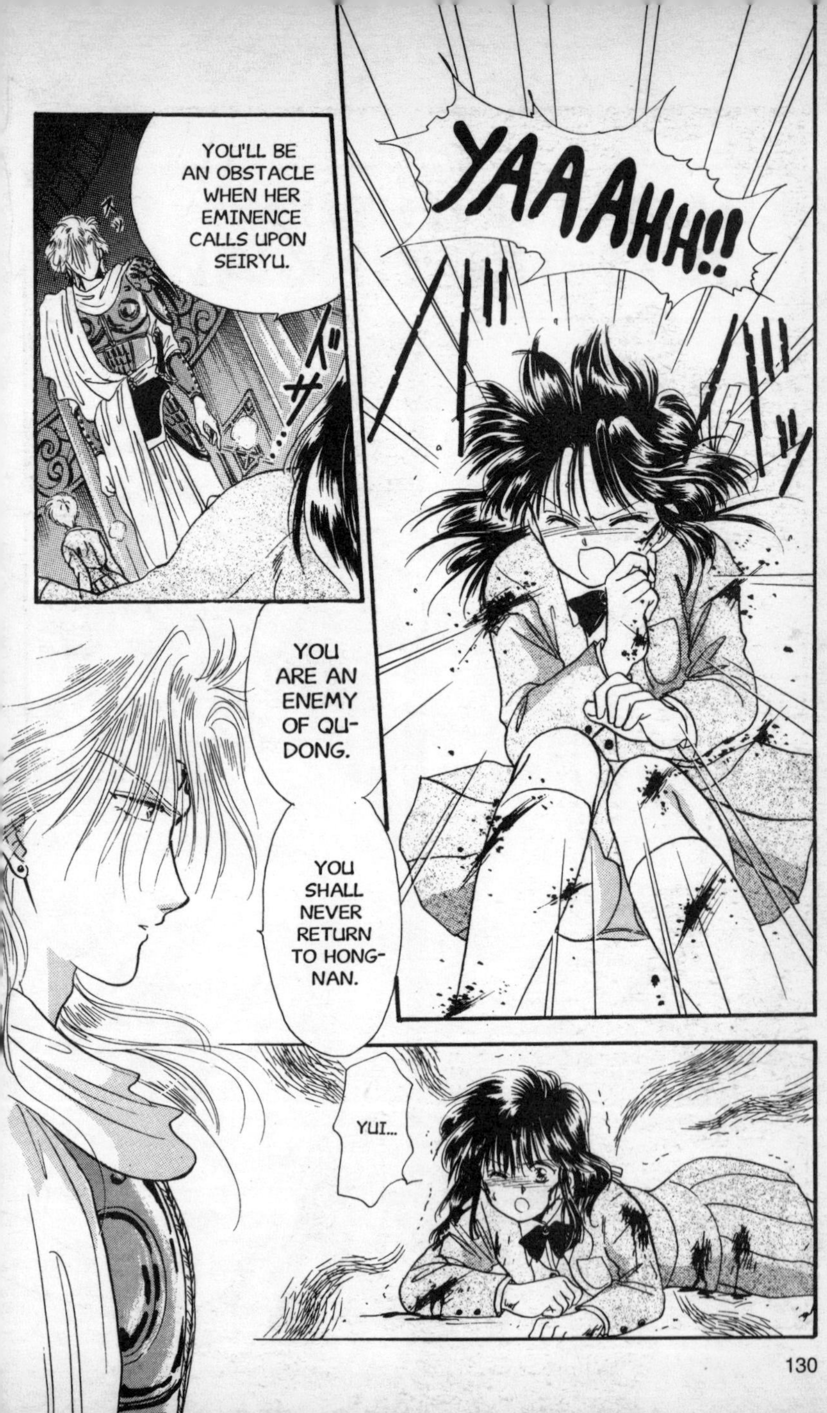
YOU'LL BE AN OBSTACLE WHEN HER EMINENCE CALLS UPON SEIRYU.
YAAAHH!!
YOU ARE AN ENEMY OF QU-DONG.
YOU SHALL NEVER RETURN TO HONG-NAN.
YUI...

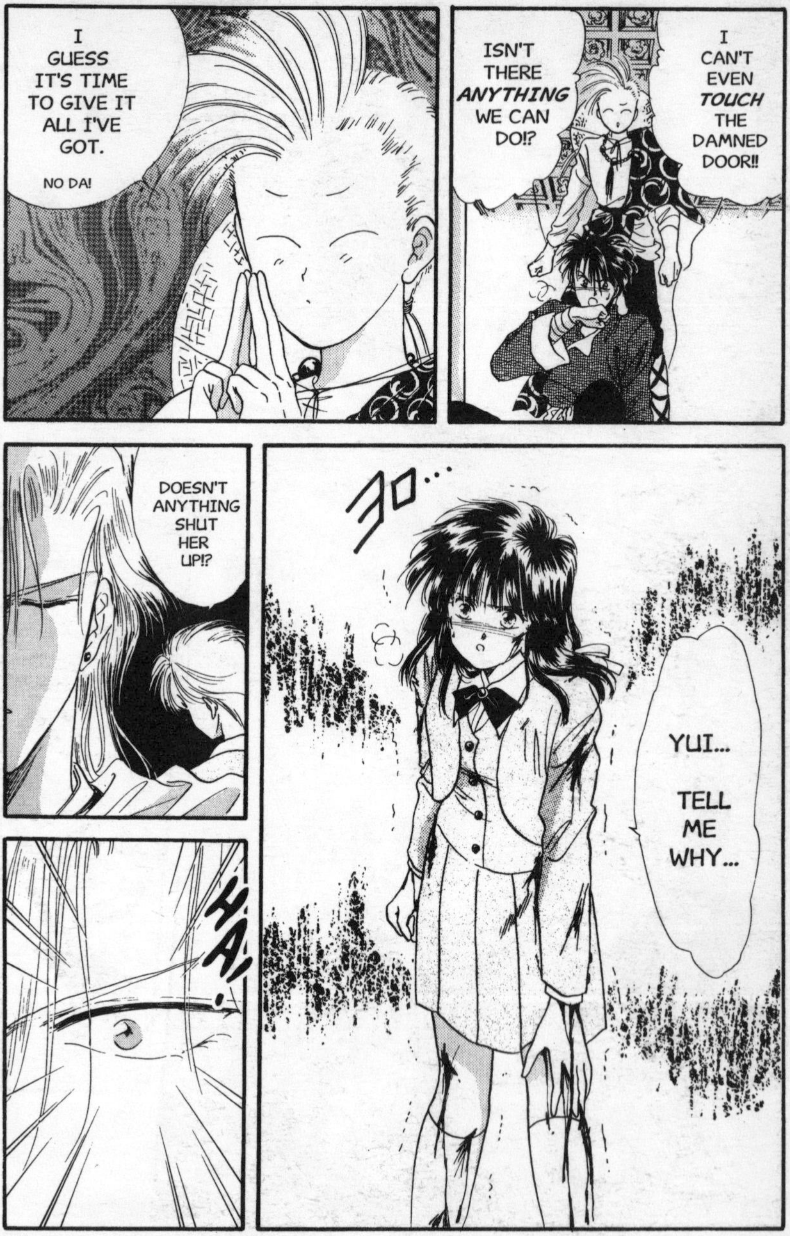
I CAN'T EVEN TOUCH THE DAMNED DOOR!!
ISN'T THERE ANYTHING WE CAN DO!?
I GUESS IT'S TIME TO GIVE IT ALL I'VE GOT.
NO DA!
ヨロ…
YUI...
TELL ME WHY...
DOESN'T ANYTHING SHUT HER UP!?
HA!

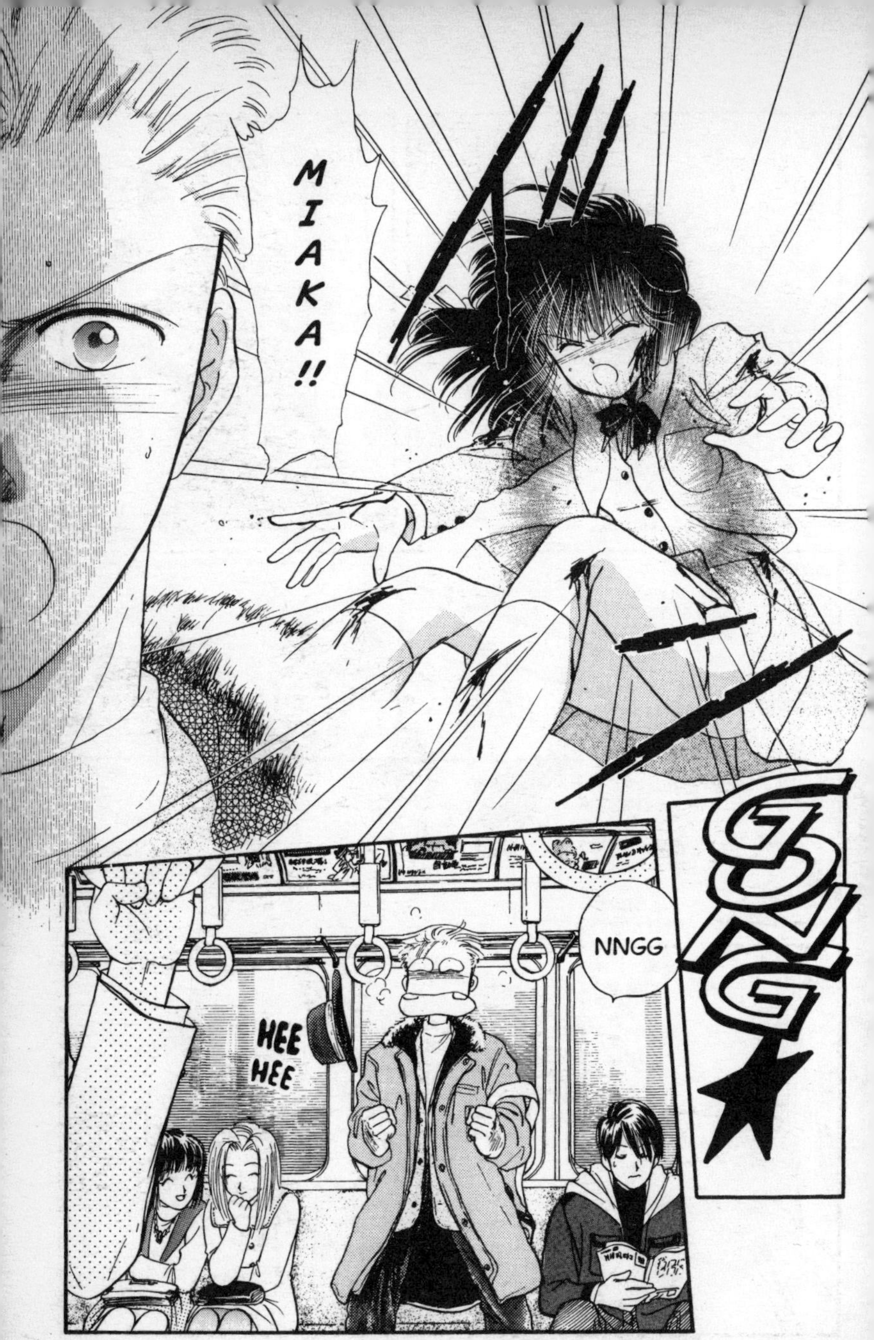
MIAKA!!
GONG
NNGG
HEE HEE

According to M, the best thing about computer games is the computer graphics. "I look forward to the sequences when you clear each stage." What's to look forward to? Your favorite character stripping! Okay, for women over age 20... If you stroked his ego, Hotohori might be willing to take it all off. But when we realized that most of the players would be guys, our ideas got really out of control.

"Fushigi Yūgi Uncensored!"

"What if Miaka and Yui were young boys and each of the constellations were different kinds of gorgeous girls!?"

"The boys wouldn't be able to resist that!" "Okay, if you finish the entire game the regular way, the special "For Boys" version will appear." Will someone make this game!?

The other thing we thought of was a SD Chichiri doll. When you squeeze it, it says "No da!" I'm sorry for getting so carried away. But these ideas do seem like fun, huh? I'm not serious, of course! So, now that you've finished chapter 16, it must have been something of a shock. BWA HA HA HA! This was part of my plan all along! I only had the stories through chapter 16 planned at the start, though. Who'da thought this series would have ever gone 15 chapters in the first place!? Now the readers become divided between supporting Miaka or Yui. One thing that made me go "Eh!?" were the letters from readers who wrote in claiming that, "after reading Chapter 16, I don't like Miaka because she's a liar!" Please read from Chapters 12 to 15 again, okay? Miaka lied to Tamahome in order to find Yui. Are you really reading this story closely? I don't mind it if you've always disliked Miaka. Sometimes, people change their minds, and that's interesting in itself. Anyway, I'm taking all your responses into consideration.

By the way, I just remembered, speaking of games, (Sorry, I'm changing the subject all the time) my game system was disconnected when I moved recently, and I forgot to have it reinstalled!! AARGH! I can't play Final Fantasy! Actually, I don't have any time to play!! Game Boy is more popular at my place anyway. When I'm stuck or need a break, Parodius is good to play. I wish I had time to play more games!!

135

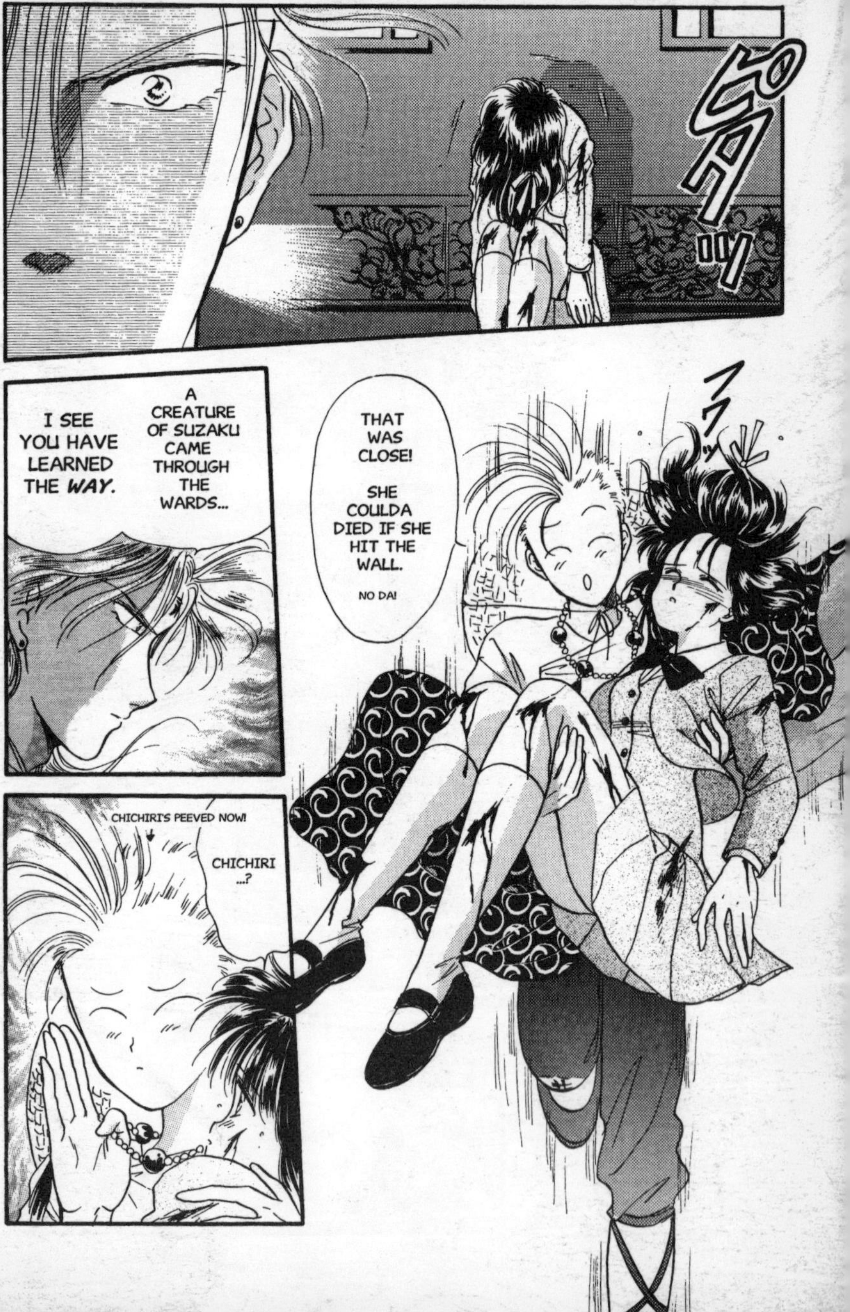
I SEE YOU HAVE LEARNED THE *WAY*.
A CREATURE OF SUZAKU CAME THROUGH THE WARDS...
THAT WAS CLOSE!
SHE COULDA DIED IF SHE HIT THE WALL.
NO DA!
CHICHIRI'S PEEVED NOW!
CHICHIRI ...?

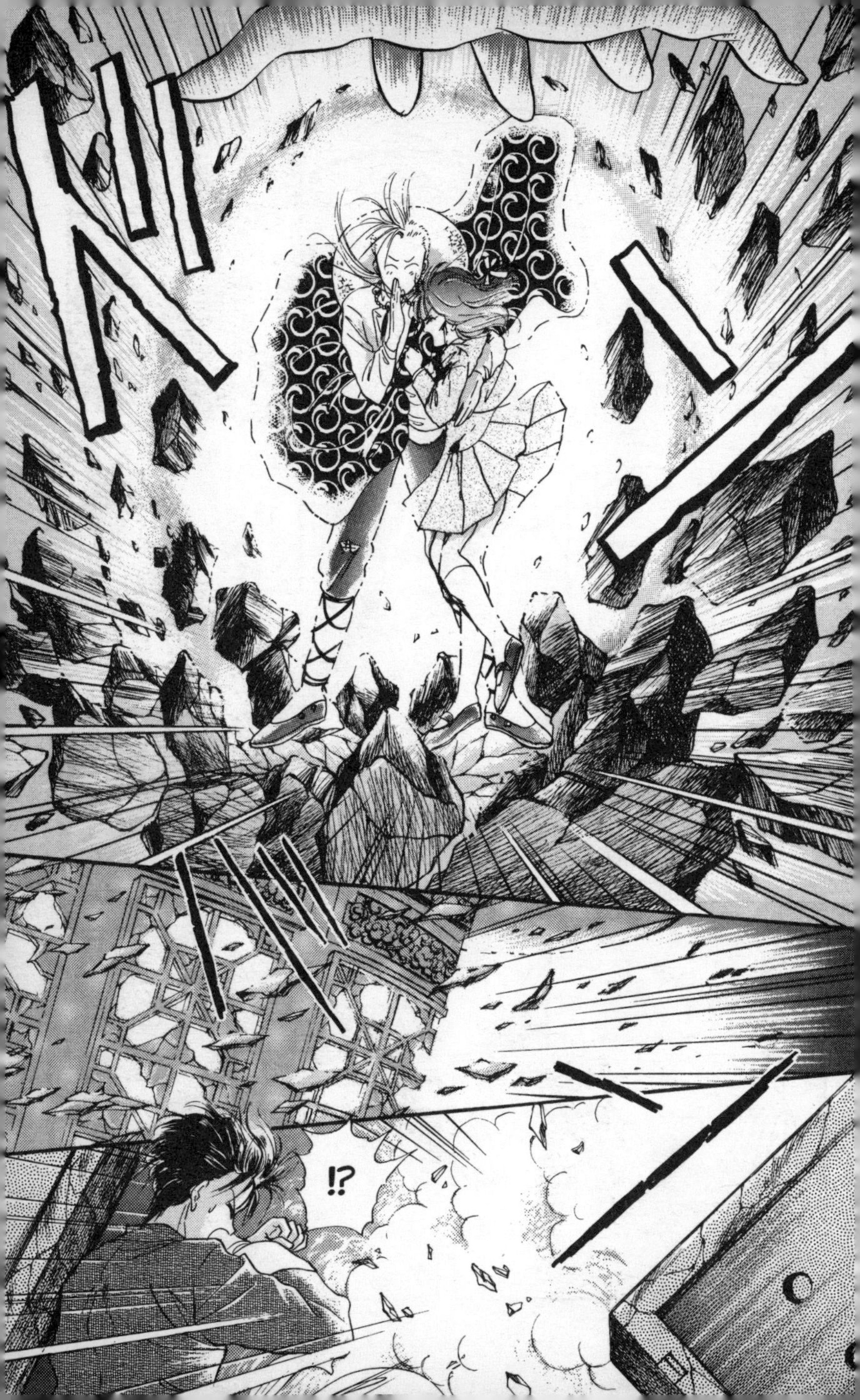
!?

138

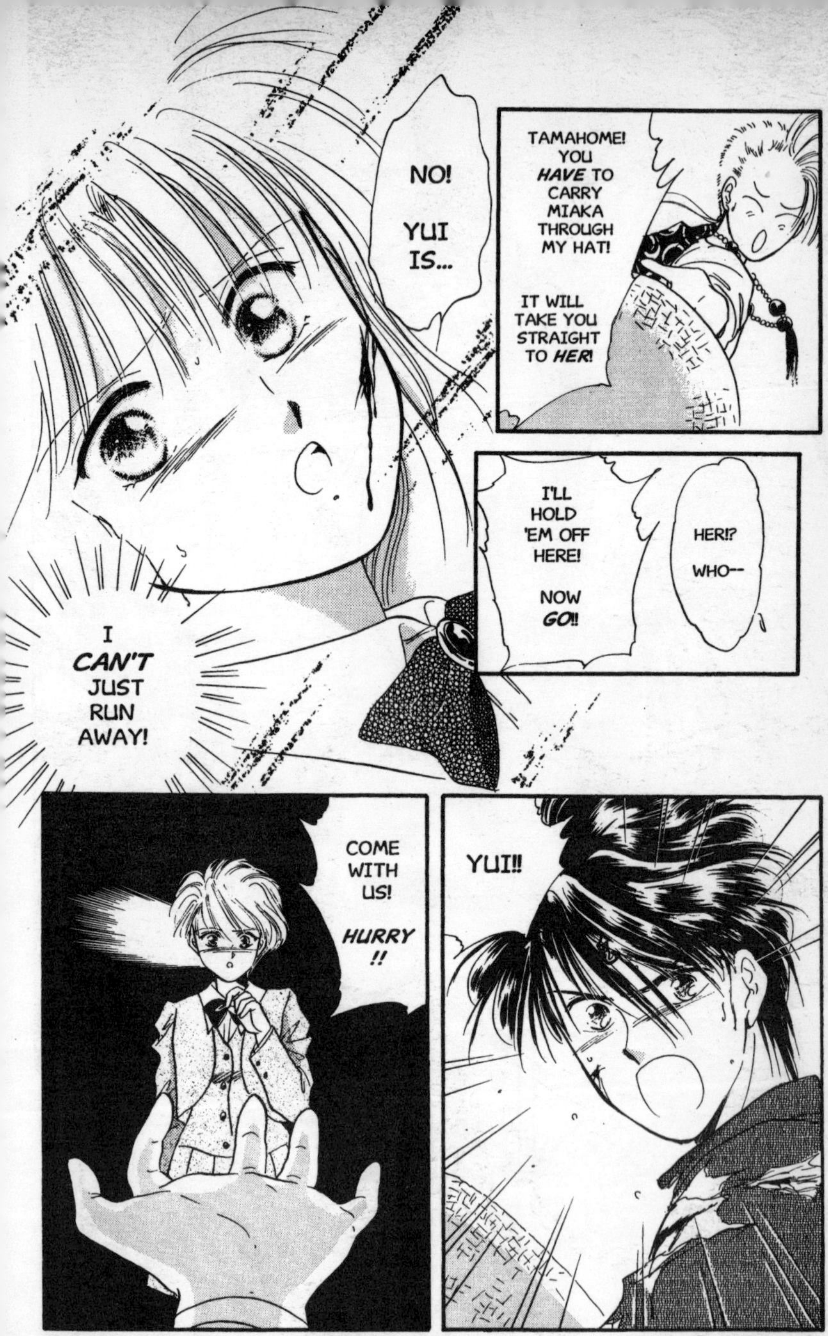
NO! YUI IS...
TAMAHOME! YOU HAVE TO CARRY MIAKA THROUGH MY HAT!
IT WILL TAKE YOU STRAIGHT TO HER!
HER!? WHO--
I'LL HOLD 'EM OFF HERE! NOW GO!!
I CAN'T JUST RUN AWAY!
COME WITH US! HURRY!!
YUI!!

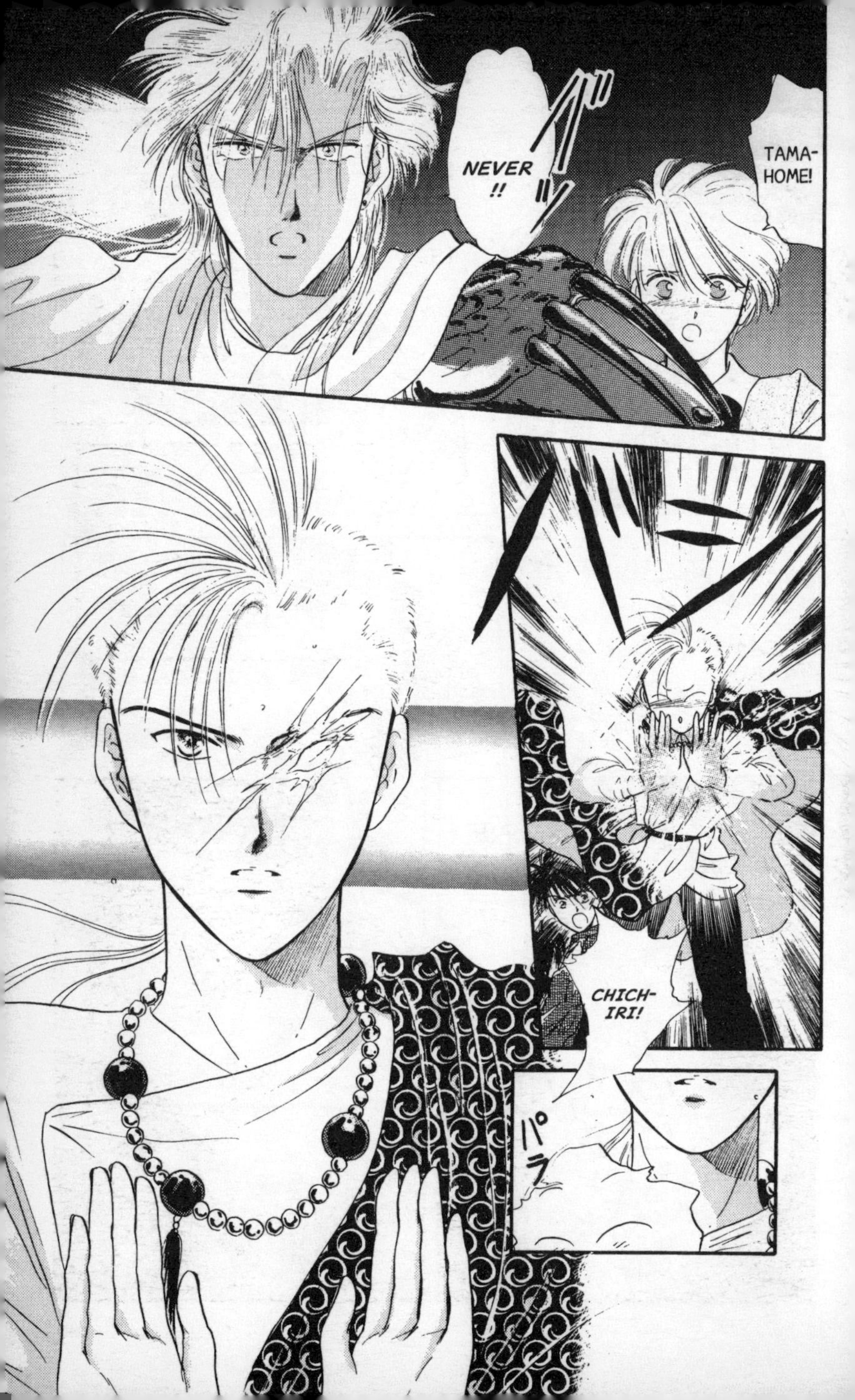
TAMA-HOME!
NEVER !!
CHICH-IRI!
パラ

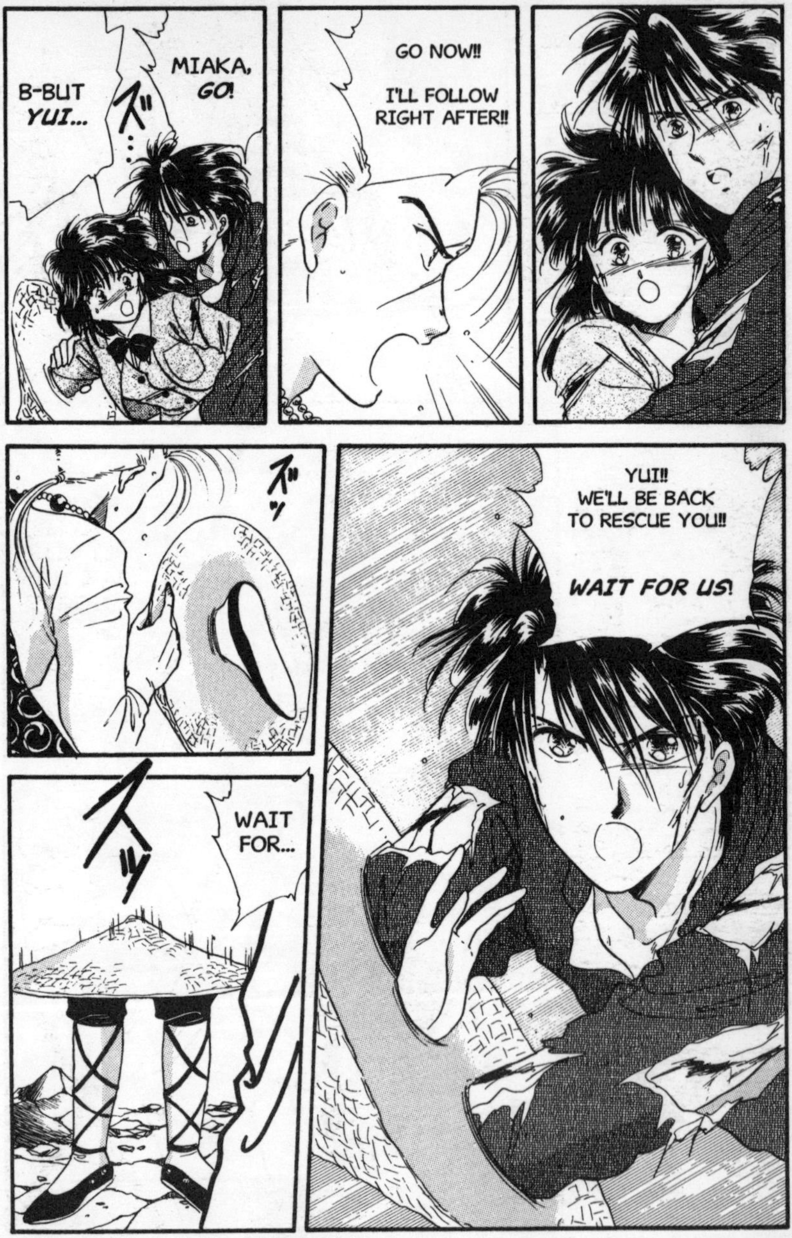

MIAKA, GO!
B-BUT YUI...
ズ
GO NOW!!
I'LL FOLLOW RIGHT AFTER!!
ズッ
スッ
WAIT FOR...
YUI!! WE'LL BE BACK TO RESCUE YOU!!
WAIT FOR US!

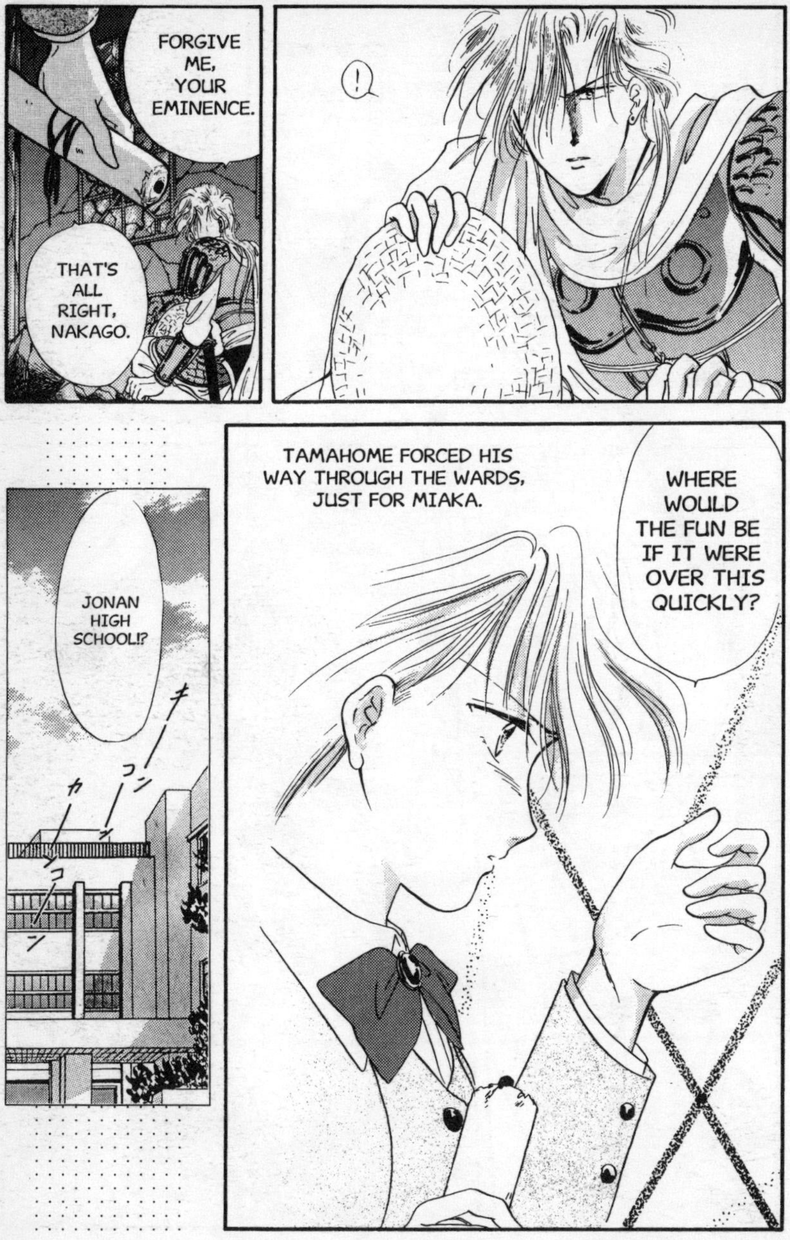
!
FORGIVE ME, YOUR EMINENCE.
THAT'S ALL RIGHT, NAKAGO.
TAMAHOME FORCED HIS WAY THROUGH THE WARDS, JUST FOR MIAKA.
WHERE WOULD THE FUN BE IF IT WERE OVER THIS QUICKLY?
JONAN HIGH SCHOOL!?
キーンコーン
カーンコーン

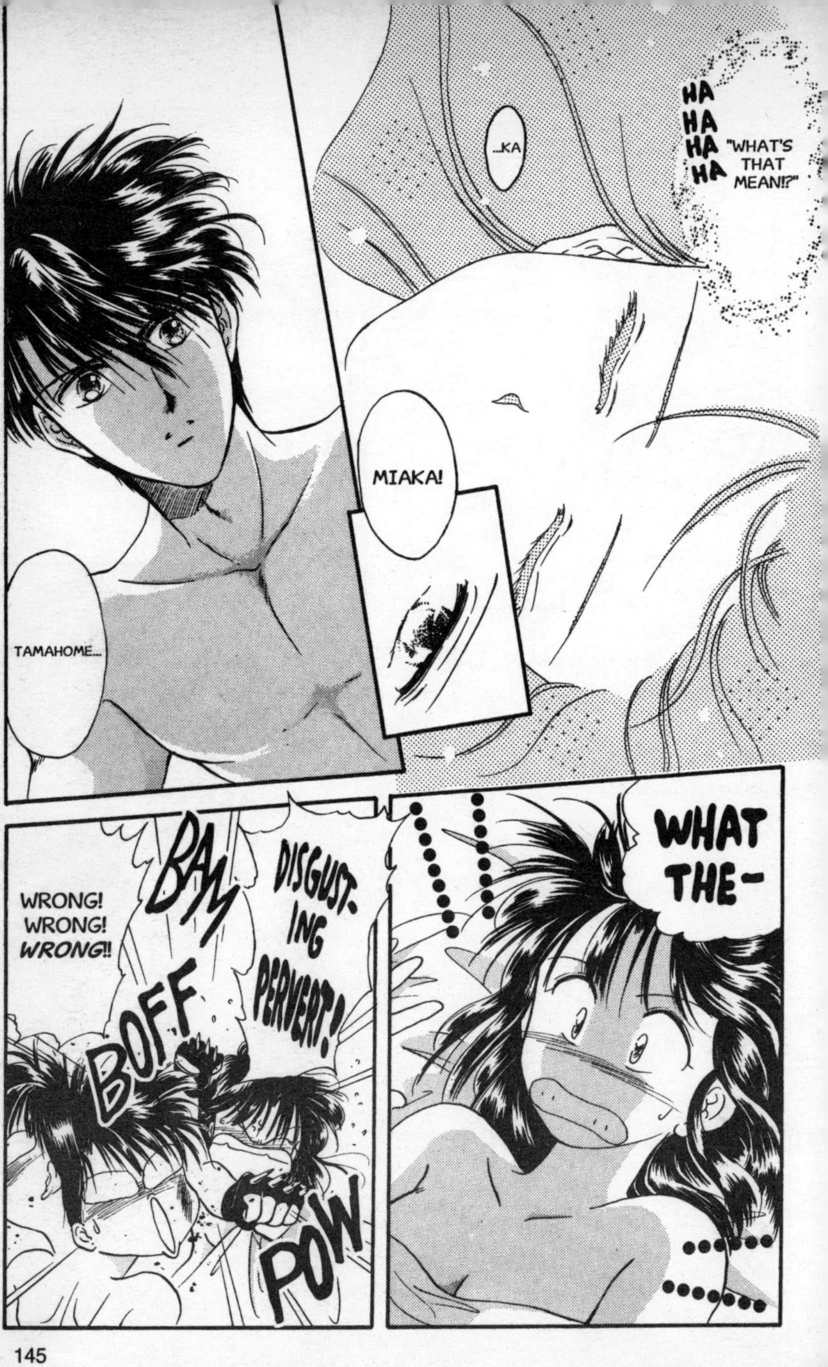

...KA
HA HA HA HA
"WHAT'S THAT MEAN!?"
MIAKA!
TAMAHOME...
WHAT THE-
......
......
DISGUST-ING PERVERT!
BAM
WRONG! WRONG! *WRONG*!!
BOFF
POW

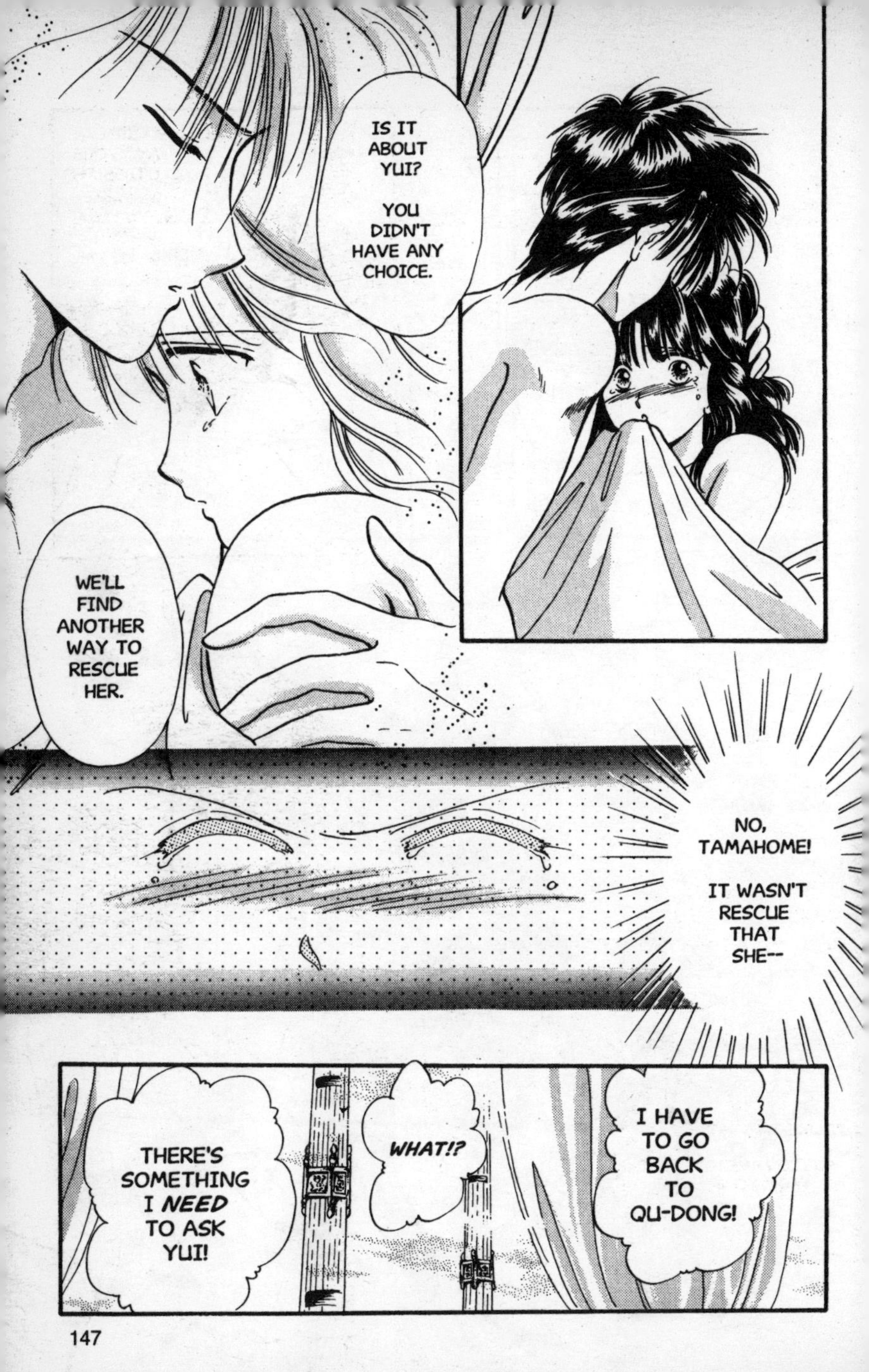
IS IT ABOUT YUI? YOU DIDN'T HAVE ANY CHOICE.
WE'LL FIND ANOTHER WAY TO RESCUE HER.
NO, TAMAHOME! IT WASN'T RESCUE THAT SHE--
I HAVE TO GO BACK TO QU-DONG!
WHAT!?
THERE'S SOMETHING I *NEED* TO ASK YUI!

FORTUNATELY, YOUR WOUNDS WERE LIGHT, SO I--

FIXED YOUR CLOTHES!

FIXED YOUR CLOTHES!

HEALED YOU!!

HEALED YOU!!

CHICHIRI SUDDENLY APPEARS CARRYING YOU TWO, AND YOU'RE COVERED IN BLOOD!

MIAKA! LONG TIME NO SEE!!

IT'S BEEN A WHILE, MIAKA, TAMAHOME.

THEN THIS IS DAICHI-SAN?

EVERY-BODY SAW!!

CHICHIRI, WHY WOULD YOU...

NO DA.

I CAN'T GET A WORD IN--

YEA! YEA!

...OF TRAINING HERE FOR THREE YEARS.

NO DA.

I HAD THE HONOR...

THERE'S SOMETHING I *NEED* TO FIND OUT FROM YUI!

WHAT HAPPENED TO HER THREE MONTHS AGO!!

SO YOU INSIST ON GOING BACK TO QU-DONG?

I CAN HEAR YOU FINE FROM A DISTANCE, TOO.

FOLLOW ME!

IF YOU INSIST...!

BUT THERE IS NO NEED FOR YOU TO RETURN TO QU-DONG.

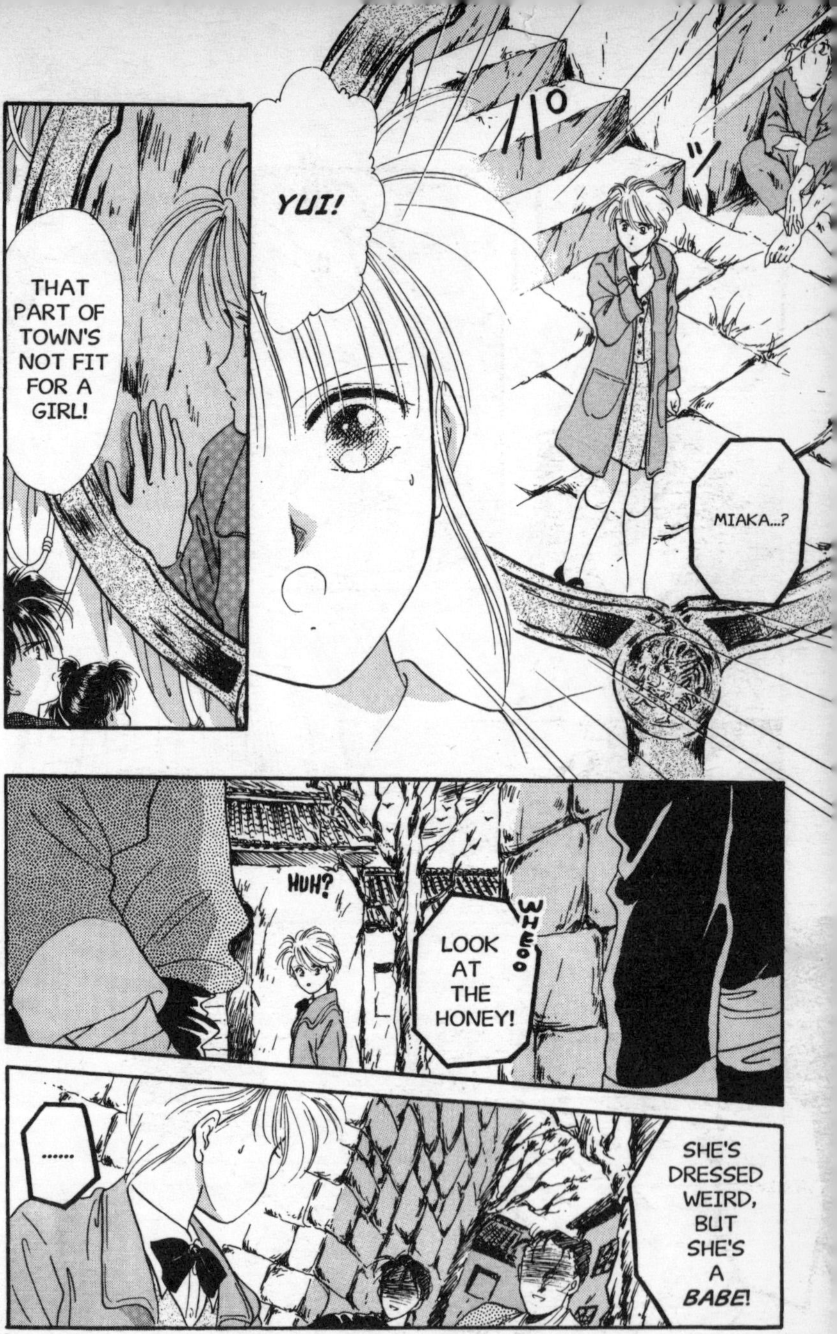

YUI!
THAT PART OF TOWN'S NOT FIT FOR A GIRL!
MIAKA...?
HUH?
WHEEOO
LOOK AT THE HONEY!
SHE'S DRESSED WEIRD, BUT SHE'S A *BABE*!
......

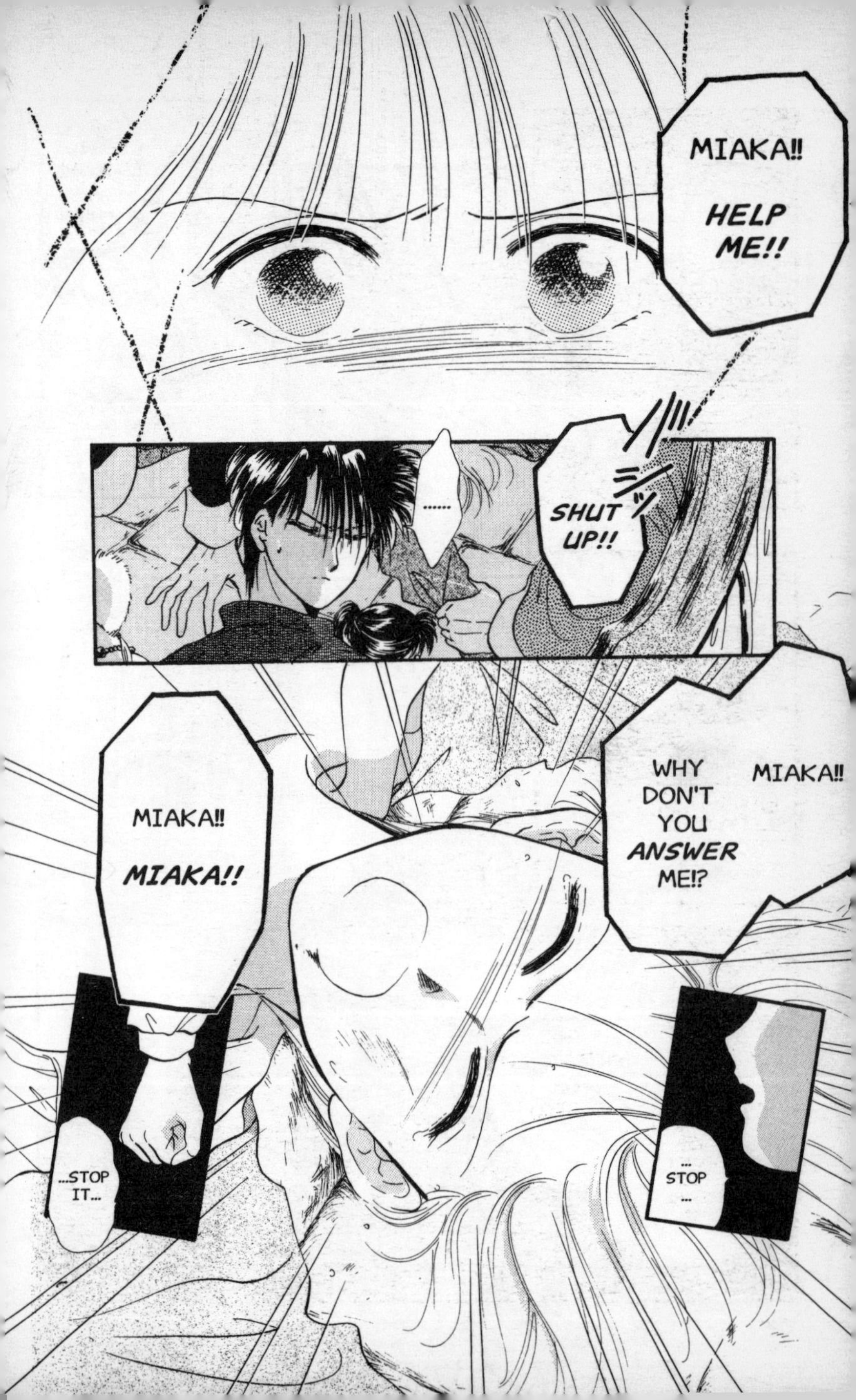
MIAKA!! HELP ME!!
SHUT UP!!
......
WHY DON'T YOU ANSWER ME!? MIAKA!!
MIAKA!! MIAKA!!
... STOP ...
...STOP IT...

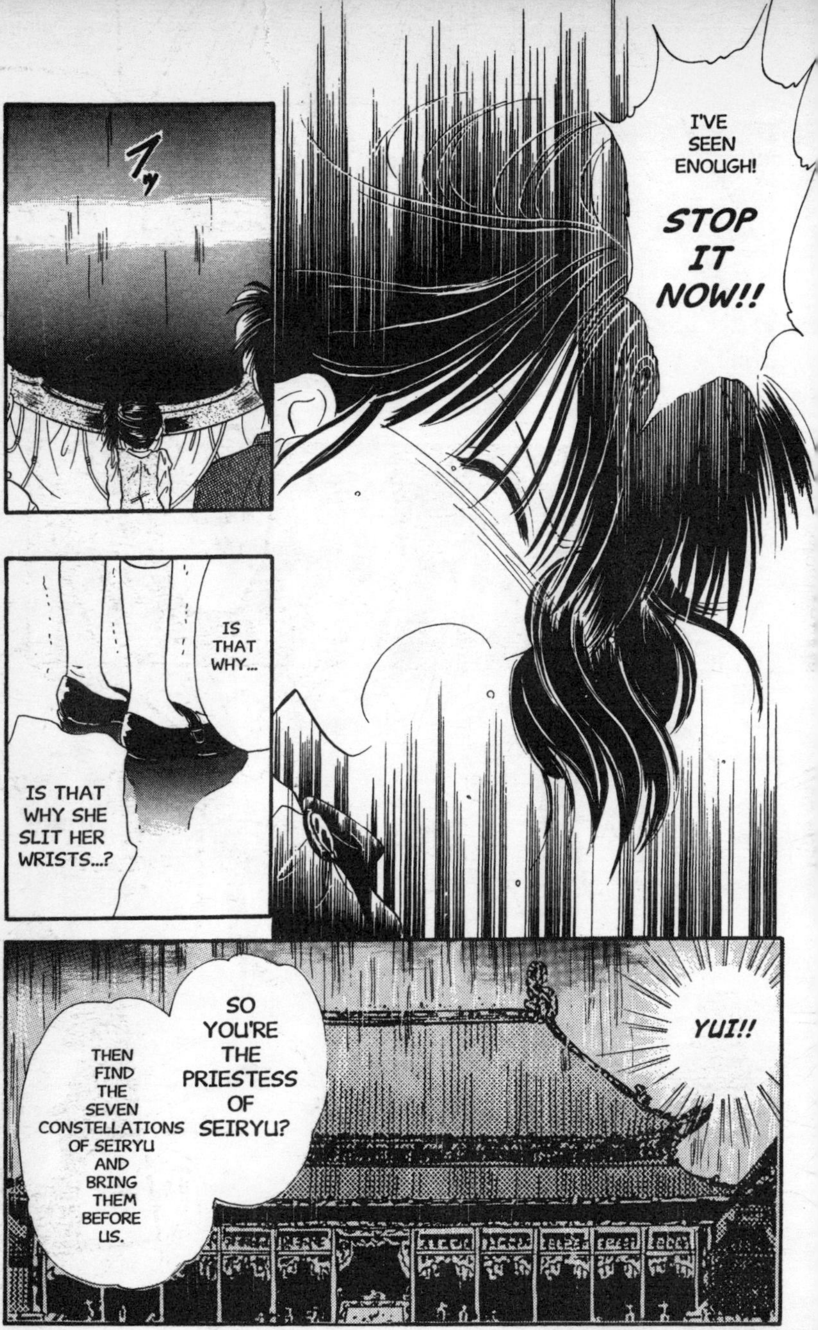
I'VE SEEN ENOUGH!
STOP IT NOW!!
IS THAT WHY...
IS THAT WHY SHE SLIT HER WRISTS...?
YUI!!
SO YOU'RE THE PRIESTESS OF SEIRYU?
THEN FIND THE SEVEN CONSTELLATIONS OF SEIRYU AND BRING THEM BEFORE US.

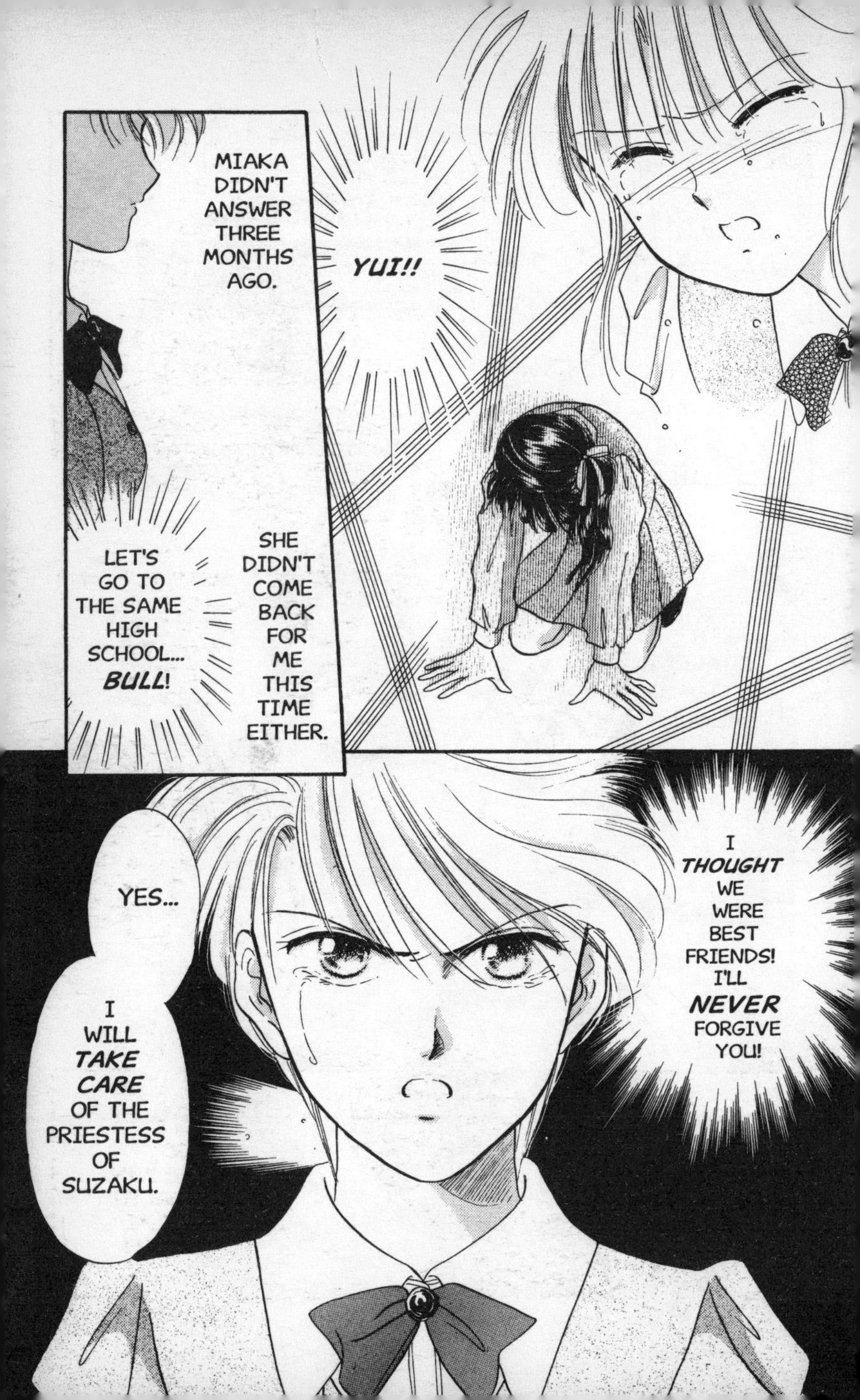
YUI!!
MIAKA DIDN'T ANSWER THREE MONTHS AGO.
SHE DIDN'T COME BACK FOR ME THIS TIME EITHER.
LET'S GO TO THE SAME HIGH SCHOOL... BULL!
I THOUGHT WE WERE BEST FRIENDS! I'LL NEVER FORGIVE YOU!
YES...
I WILL TAKE CARE OF THE PRIESTESS OF SUZAKU.

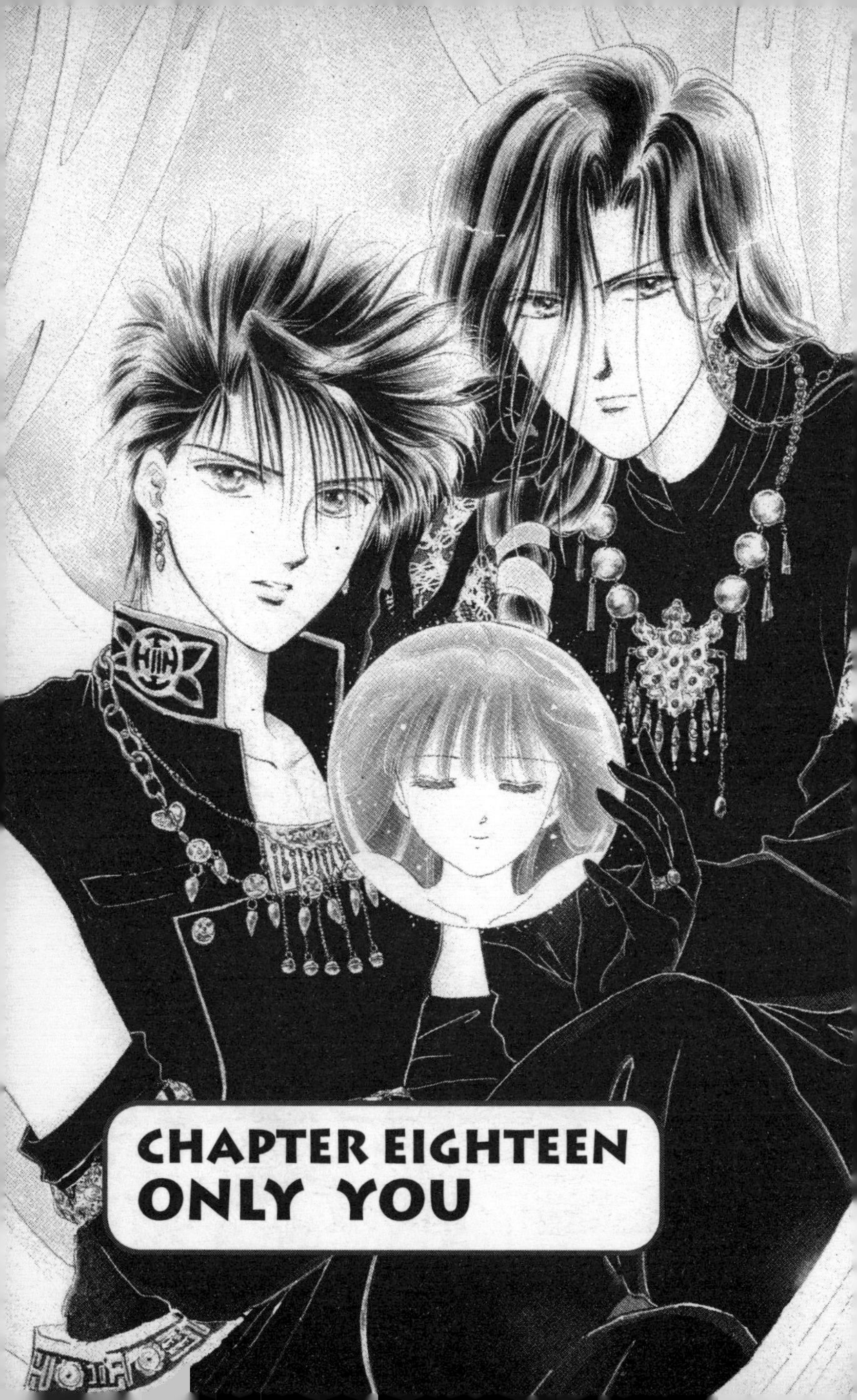
CHAPTER EIGHTEEN
ONLY YOU

YOU'LL NEVER FIND HAPPINESS WITH TAMAHOME!

I **WON'T** LET YOU HAVE YOUR WAY!

MIAKA, THERE'S NO TURNING BACK NOW.

I UNDERSTAND.

WAHHH!

FWOOP

NO GOOD.

SHE WON'T COME OUT OF HER ROOM.

AT THIS RATE, SHE'LL...

TAMAHOME, HOW'S MIAKA?

NO DA?

164

Well, I've been getting responses from you regarding this free chat section. One person wrote in to complain about how I wouldn't give official approval for a project. According to the letter, my failure to give official approval indicated that I was becoming more distant from my readers. But it was my editors' decision. I guess they had problems in the past. I'm not trying to distance myself from my readers! I'm glad to hear that you wouldn't want that, but there's no need to get hung up over getting "official" approval. So don't worry about it, okay? Just because there isn't an official approval doesn't mean that I don't like it. I keep on receiving a lot of fanzines, and I take the time to look through all of them. So go right ahead and make fanzines or dojinshi and send them my way. I thought I'd said that before already. I think it's fine to draw parodies of my work (as long as they're not gross or boring).

Once my story gets published in a magazine, then it becomes part of each reader's imagination, fueled by the way he or she feels about the characters. That's how a work finally becomes complete. I don't know what I'm saying! All I want to say is this book in your hands is your own unique "Fushigi Yûgi." If you see what I mean. Manga is for the reader so... Urgh, I'm getting confused. Those readers who were fans of my work before it merited any "official seal of approval" became the ones that I respect the most. I'm not getting distant! AARGH, I'm getting all jumbled up!

-after a rest-

So fanzines are fine, okay? Oh yeah, I forgot during my rant, I have to apologize for the "Prepubescence Special Edition" not coming out on time. It's not my fault this time! The good news is that a book of illustrations is scheduled to come out next year (I hope). If it doesn't, sorry again! It should be a book of colored illustrations for "Prepubescence" and "Fushigi Yûgi." You want a story, too? Yessir!! I'll do my best.

One last common question: "Do you do illustrations for novels?" I've never had any requests to do one. That's all. This time I answered a lot of questions. Lotta work for those who read through this section.

But who's working hardest here!?

165

AIEEEE WHAT-- THE HEEEE- EEECK!!

THIS IS SCARY!

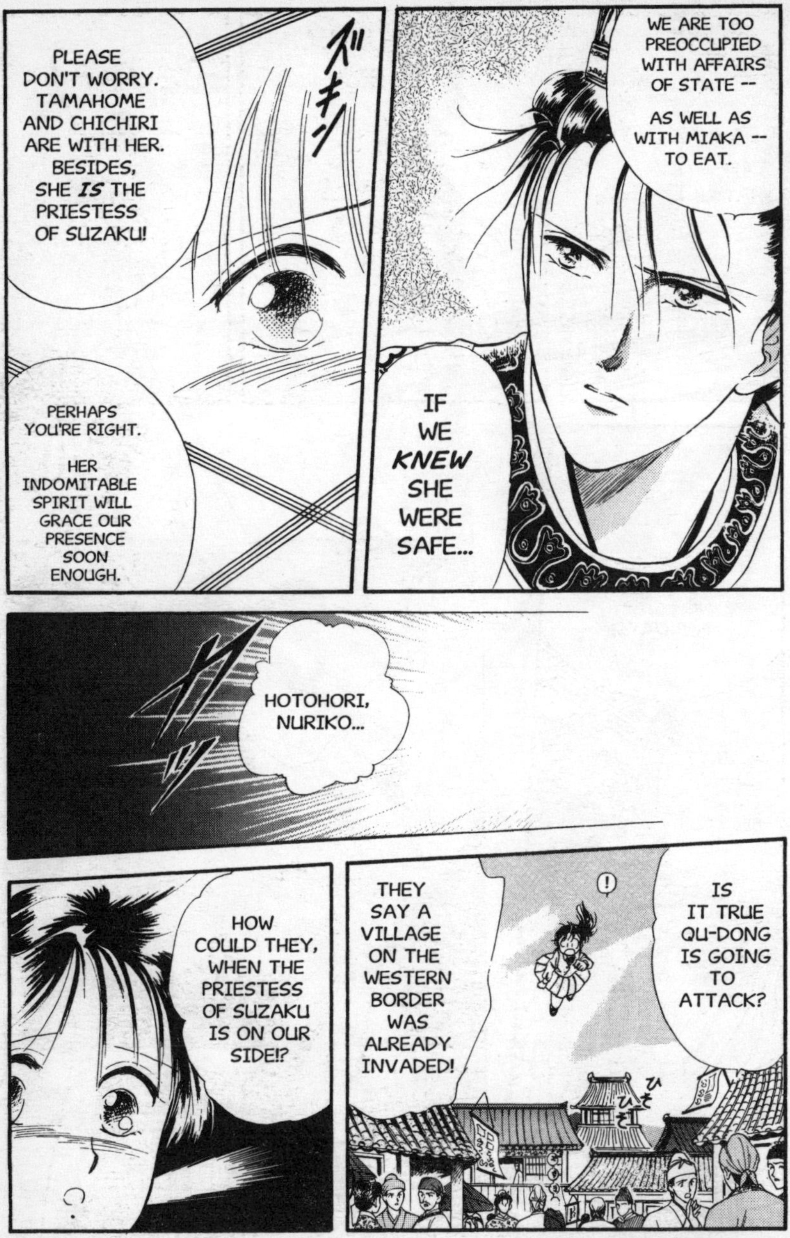
WE ARE TOO PREOCCUPIED WITH AFFAIRS OF STATE --
AS WELL AS WITH MIAKA -- TO EAT.
IF WE *KNEW* SHE WERE SAFE...
PLEASE DON'T WORRY. TAMAHOME AND CHICHIRI ARE WITH HER. BESIDES, SHE *IS* THE PRIESTESS OF SUZAKU!
ズキン
PERHAPS YOU'RE RIGHT.
HER INDOMITABLE SPIRIT WILL GRACE OUR PRESENCE SOON ENOUGH.
HOTOHORI, NURIKO...
!
IS IT TRUE QU-DONG IS GOING TO ATTACK?
THEY SAY A VILLAGE ON THE WESTERN BORDER WAS ALREADY INVADED!
ひそひそ
HOW COULD THEY, WHEN THE PRIESTESS OF SUZAKU IS ON OUR SIDE!?

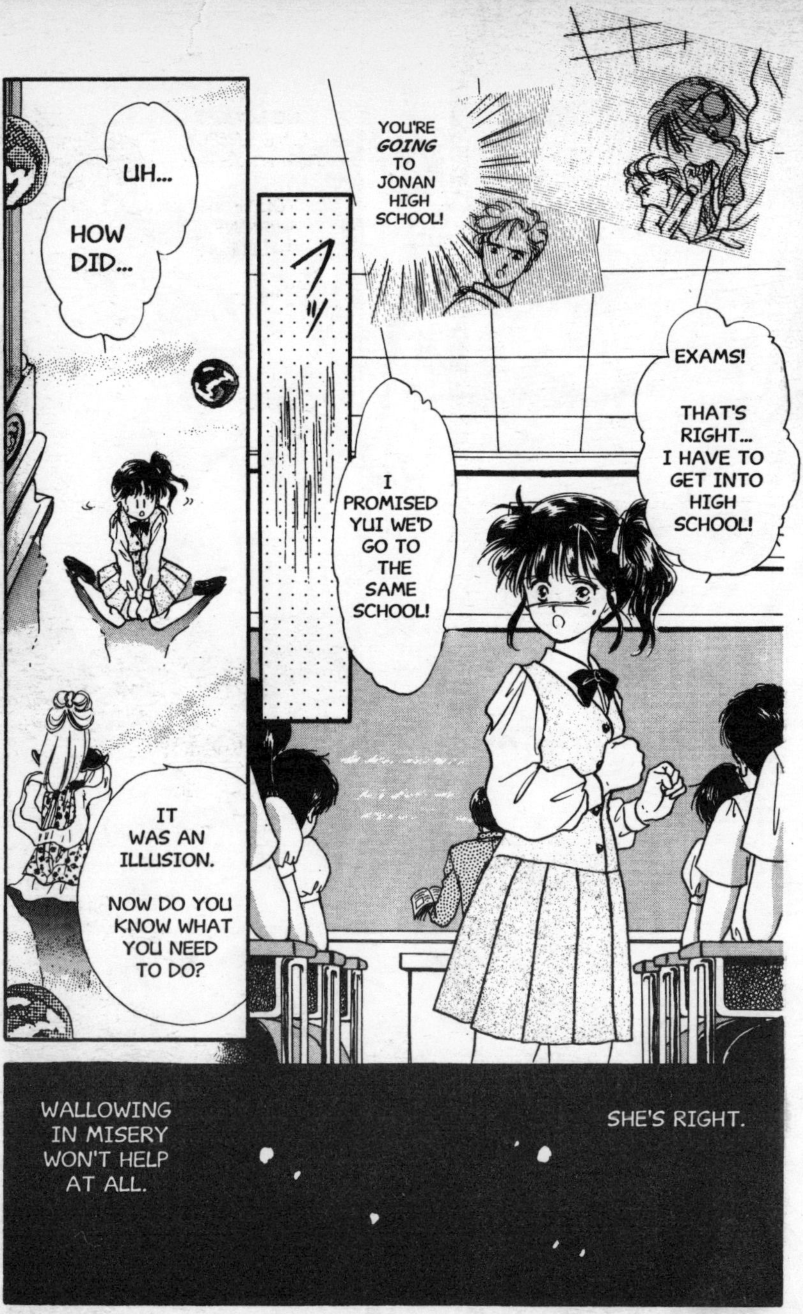
UH... HOW DID...
IT WAS AN ILLUSION.
NOW DO YOU KNOW WHAT YOU NEED TO DO?
YOU'RE *GOING* TO JONAN HIGH SCHOOL!
EXAMS!
THAT'S RIGHT... I HAVE TO GET INTO HIGH SCHOOL!
I PROMISED YUI WE'D GO TO THE SAME SCHOOL!
WALLOWING IN MISERY WON'T HELP AT ALL.
SHE'S RIGHT.

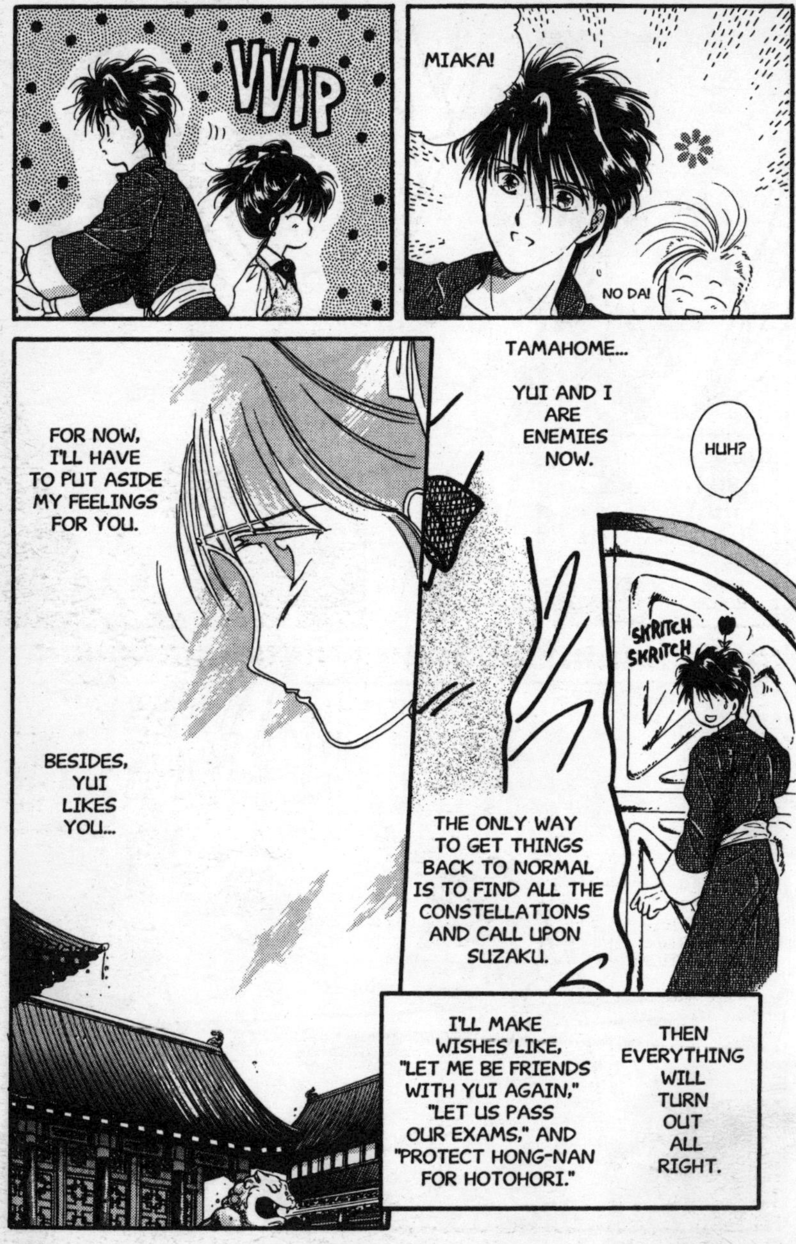
VVIP
MIAKA!
NO DA!
TAMAHOME...
YUI AND I ARE ENEMIES NOW.
HUH?
FOR NOW, I'LL HAVE TO PUT ASIDE MY FEELINGS FOR YOU.
BESIDES, YUI LIKES YOU...
SKRITCH SKRITCH
THE ONLY WAY TO GET THINGS BACK TO NORMAL IS TO FIND ALL THE CONSTELLATIONS AND CALL UPON SUZAKU.
I'LL MAKE WISHES LIKE, "LET ME BE FRIENDS WITH YUI AGAIN," "LET US PASS OUR EXAMS," AND "PROTECT HONG-NAN FOR HOTOHORI."
THEN EVERYTHING WILL TURN OUT ALL RIGHT.

NOTHING.

WHAT IS WRONG, YOUR EMINENCE?

WERE YOU THINKING ABOUT THAT SUZAKU BOY?

スッ

YUI!

WERE YOU?

THAT MAY BE FOR THE BEST.

YOU DESIRE THAT "TAMAHOME" BOY, NO?

EH... WHAT?

173

174

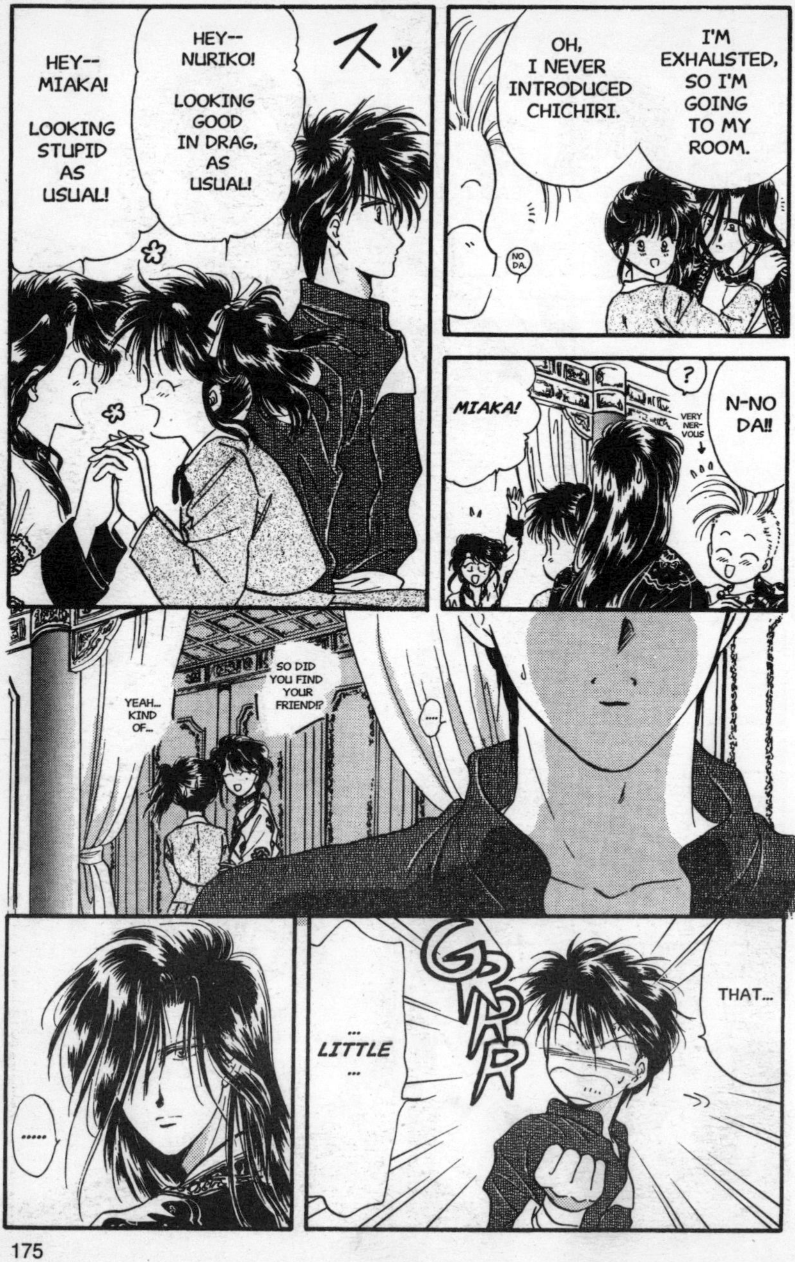

HEY-- MIAKA! LOOKING STUPID AS USUAL!
HEY-- NURIKO! LOOKING GOOD IN DRAG, AS USUAL!
スッ
OH, I NEVER INTRODUCED CHICHIRI.
I'M EXHAUSTED, SO I'M GOING TO MY ROOM.
NO DA.
MIAKA!
?
VERY NERVOUS
N-NO DA!!
YEAH... KIND OF...
SO DID YOU FIND YOUR FRIEND!?
....
......
THAT...
GRRR
...LITTLE...

STUFF I BROUGHT FROM MY WORLD!

WHAT THE HECK IS THIS?

YOU *PERVERT!!*

YOU WOULDN'T, WOULD YOU?

DON'T YOU KNOW *ANYTHING?!*

SHE'S WEARING A CAMISOLE.

WHY ARE YOU AVOIDING ME!?

TAMA-HOME!!

OH, YEAH!

THAT'S NOT WHAT I CAME HERE FOR!!

OLD HABITS TOOK OVER!

ZOOOOM

TAMAHOME.

FROM TOMORROW ON, I'LL BE DEVOTING MYSELF TO THE SEARCH FOR THE CONSTELLATIONS OF THE SUZAKU.

WHAT DOES THAT HAVE TO DO WITH ANYTHING?

...

I'M THE PRIESTESS OF SUZAKU.

YOU'RE A CELESTIAL WARRIOR.

WE HAVE TO BEHAVE OURSELVES.

SO YOU CAN'T JUST COME BARGING INTO MY ROOM LIKE THIS!

AND...

179

181

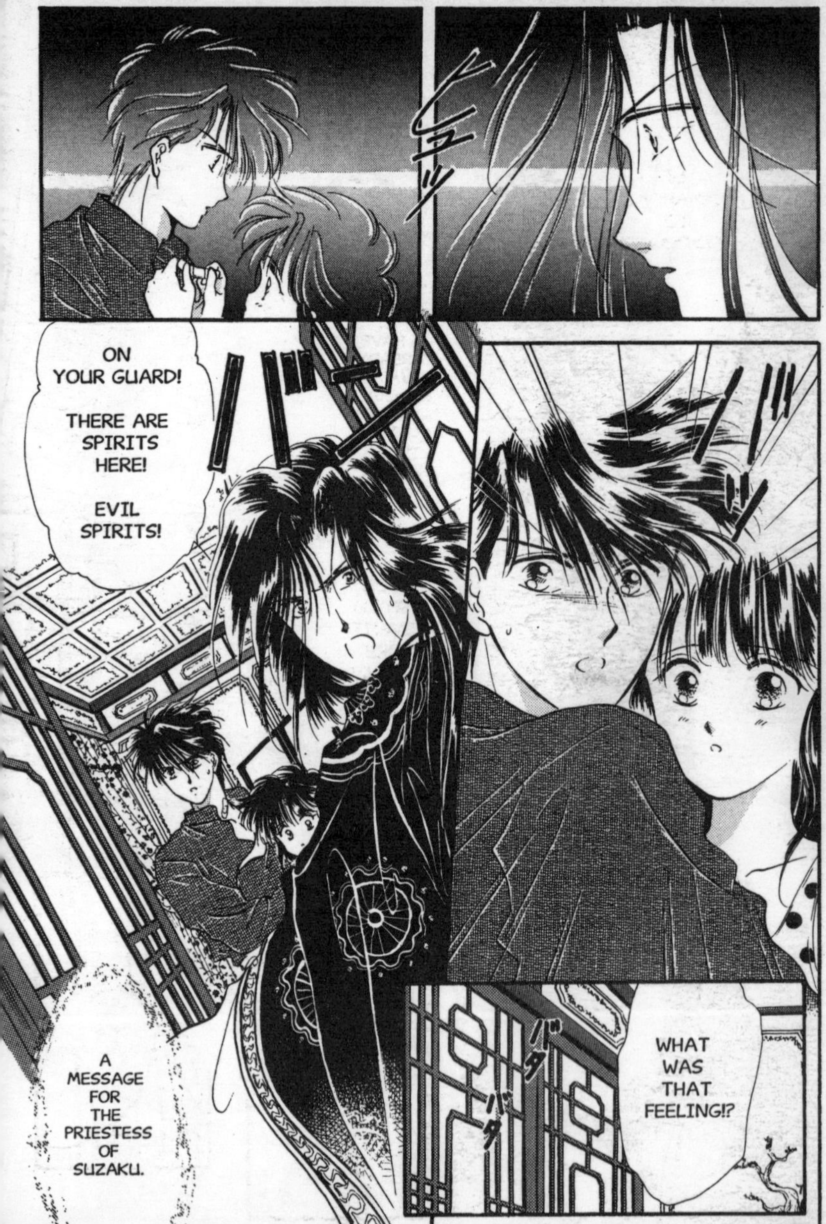

ON YOUR GUARD!
THERE ARE SPIRITS HERE!
EVIL SPIRITS!
WHAT WAS THAT FEELING!?
A MESSAGE FOR THE PRIESTESS OF SUZAKU.

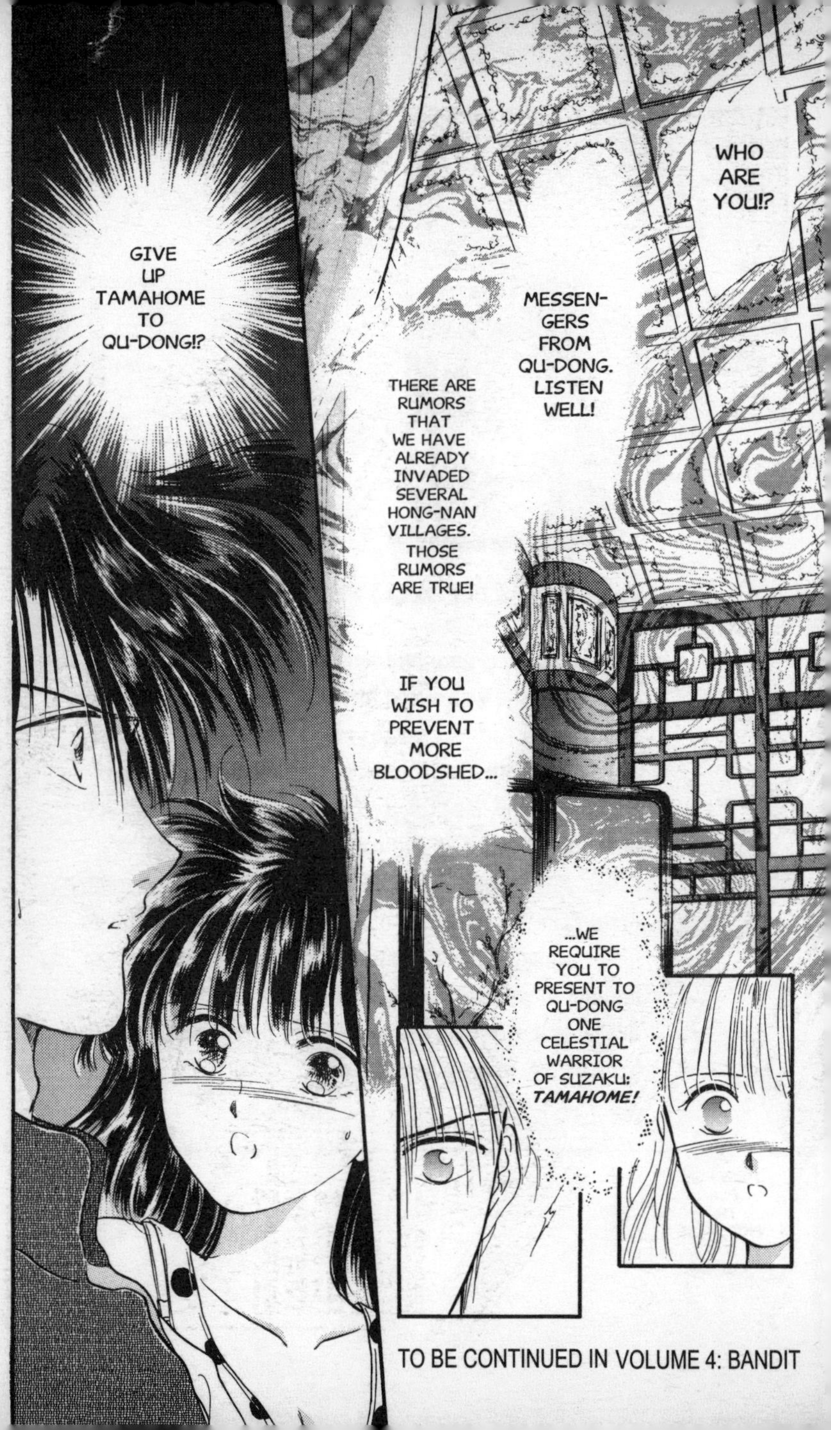
WHO ARE YOU!?
MESSEN-GERS FROM QU-DONG. LISTEN WELL!
THERE ARE RUMORS THAT WE HAVE ALREADY INVADED SEVERAL HONG-NAN VILLAGES. THOSE RUMORS ARE TRUE!
IF YOU WISH TO PREVENT MORE BLOODSHED...
...WE REQUIRE YOU TO PRESENT TO QU-DONG ONE CELESTIAL WARRIOR OF SUZAKU: *TAMAHOME!*
GIVE UP TAMAHOME TO QU-DONG!?

TO BE CONTINUED IN VOLUME 4: BANDIT

ABOUT THE AUTHOR

Yuu Watase was born on March 5 in a town near Osaka, Japan, and she was raised there before moving to Tokyo to follow her dream of creating manga. In the decade since her debut short story, *PAJAMA DE OJAMA* ("An Intrusion in Pajamas"), she has produced more than 50 compiled volumes of short stories and continuing series. Her latest series, *ZETTAI KARESHI* ("He'll Be My Boyfriend"), is currently running in the anthology magazine *SHŌJO COMIC*. Watase's long-running horror/romance story *CERES: CELESTIAL LEGEND* and her most recent completed series, *ALICE 19TH*, are now available in North America published by VIZ. She loves science fiction, fantasy and comedy.

COMPLETE OUR SURVEY AND
LET US KNOW WHAT YOU THINK!

❑ Please do NOT send me information about Gollancz Manga, or other Orion title, products, news and events, special offers or other information

Name: _____

Address: _____

Town: _____ County: _____ Postcode: _____

❑ Male ❑ Female   Date of Birth (dd/mm/yyyy): __ / __ / _____
                    (under 13? Parental consent required)

What race/ethnicity do you consider yourself? (please check one)

❑ Asian   ❑ Black   ❑ Hispanic

❑ White/Caucasian   ❑ Other: _____

Which Gollancz Manga title did you purchase?

Case Closed	Dragon Ball	Fushigi Yûgi	Yu-Gi-Oh!
❑ 1 ❑ 2	❑ 1 ❑ 2	❑ 1 ❑ 2	❑ 1 ❑ 2
❑ 3	❑ 3	❑ 3	❑ 3

What other Gollancz Manga do you own?

Case Closed	Dragon Ball	Fushigi Yûgi	Yu-Gi-Oh!
❑ 1 ❑ 2	❑ 1 ❑ 2	❑ 1 ❑ 2	❑ 1 ❑ 2
❑ 3	❑ 3	❑ 3	❑ 3

How many anime and/or manga titles have you purchased in the last year?
How many were Gollancz Manga titles?

Anime	Manga	GM
❑ None	❑ None	❑ None
❑ 1-4	❑ 1-4	❑ 1-4
❑ 5-10	❑ 5-10	❑ 5-10
❑ 11+	❑ 11+	❑ 11+

Reason for purchase: (check all that apply)
- ❏ Special Offer
- ❏ Favourite title
- ❏ Gift
- ❏ In store promotion If so please indicate which store: _____
- ❏ Recommendation
- ❏ Other _____

Where did you make your purchase?
- ❏ Bookshop
- ❏ Comic Shop
- ❏ Music Store
- ❏ Newsagent
- ❏ Video Game Store
- ❏ Supermarket
- ❏ Other: _____
- ❏ Online: _____

What kind of manga would you like to read?
- ❏ Adventure
- ❏ Comic Strip
- ❏ Fantasy
- ❏ Fighting
- ❏ Horror
- ❏ Mystery
- ❏ Romance
- ❏ Science Fiction
- ❏ Sports
- ❏ Other: _____

Which do you prefer?
- ❏ Sound effects in English
- ❏ Sound effects in Japanese with English captions
- ❏ Sound effects in Japanese only with a glossary at the back

Want to find out more about Manga?
Look us up at www.orionbooks.co.uk, or www.viz.com

THANK YOU!
Please send the completed form to:

Manga Survey
Orion Books
Orion House
5 Upper St Martin's Lane
London, WC2H 9EA